Decolonising Counselling and Psychotherapy

Decolonisation is a term which has become a modern-day buzzword as we look to understand the influences of the systemic structures of oppression which have moulded all of our identities. Yet in the worlds of counselling and psychotherapy, there has been a struggle to understand what this term means in regard to our profession. *Decolonising Counselling and Psychotherapy* considers the ways in which the systems of colonisation have taken over and are continually reconstituted within our profession.

This book challenges our profession by offering practical ways in which we might diversify our practices, proffering varying perspectives about how to create pathways for greater inclusion in training courses and examining the many opportunities to explore and expand the ways in which we undertake research. Most importantly, it will encourage the therapist to look at the internalised experiences of colonisation on themselves. The book shows that working creatively with techniques common to counselling and psychotherapy could lead the profession to not only broaden out what it knows and understands of human nature but, through a process of decolonisation, assist in meeting the needs of a wider range of clients.

This book will be invaluable to counsellors, psychotherapists and psychologists working in the helping professions and to those whose activism drives them to want to make our helping professions more inclusive and equitable.

Dwight Turner is an activist, writer and public speaker on issues of race, difference and intersectionality in counselling and psychotherapy. A psychotherapist, supervisor, workshop facilitator and conference presenter in Private Practice, he is also currently the course leader in Humanistic Counselling at the University of Brighton, UK.

Decolonising Counselling and Psychotherapy

Depoliticised Pathways Towards
Intersectional Practice

Dwight Turner

Routledge
Taylor & Francis Group
LONDON AND NEW YORK

Designed cover image: ilbusca, Getty

First published 2025
by Routledge
4 Park Square, Milton Park, Abingdon, Oxon OX14 4RN

and by Routledge
605 Third Avenue, New York, NY 10158

Routledge is an imprint of the Taylor & Francis Group, an informa business

British Library Cataloguing-in-Publication Data
A catalogue record for this book is available from the British Library

ISBN: 978-1-032-61431-1 (hbk)
ISBN: 978-1-032-61433-5 (pbk)
ISBN: 978-1-032-61434-2 (ebk)

DOI: 10.4324/9781032614342

Typeset in Times New Roman
by Newgen Publishing UK

Contents

Acknowledgements

A book as challenging and as far reaching of our profession as this one cannot really be dedicated to any singular person or organisation. So, this book, which seeks to outline just how we might decolonise counselling and psychotherapy, goes out to all the ChangeMakers. This book is dedicated to all the activists, the contemporary theorists and researchers, to the charities, training organisations and to those universities, who in their own ways are working hard to reinvent and rebirth our profession for these modern times. This book is dedicated to all those assisting in the growth of our understanding of mental health and human nature and our explorations of just how we have been, in fact, how we all still are, colonised.

Thank you!

#StrongerTogether

Chapter 1

Introduction

I completed my doctorate in counselling and psychotherapy in July 2017. This was the culmination of a five-and-a-half-year journey where I studied part-time. My work involved trying to understand the unconscious process contained within experiences as the other, utilising creative techniques common to transpersonal psychotherapy. I found this journey to be both challenging and enlightening in a variety of ways, but there was one story from my academic pathway, which stood out for me and which I would like to regale as part of this volume entitled *Decolonising Counselling and Psychotherapy: Depoliticised Pathways towards Intersectional Practice.*

On a doctoral journey, there is a mid-point, a Transfer Viva, as it was called at my university. This was the point where the researcher is encouraged to share their work with both a supervisor and an examiner to ascertain whether their work is of a high enough standard for it to progress from an MPhil onto the full doctoral circuit. My appointment for said examination was back in early 2014. As part of this examination, I had to submit two chapters of what would become my actual thesis, both of which were for the purpose of this examination around 8–9,000 words long. The first of these chapters was a literature review; a review of all the literature in the field, which explored issues of difference and otherness upon which I was basing the ideas of my doctoral research. The second chapter would explore the methodology and the methodological underpinnings of my work. Both chapters were submitted following many a revision where my supervisors understandably encouraged me to write and rewrite; to construct, deconstruct and reconstruct my ideas as a way of refining them so that they would come across in a coherent narrative and make total sense regarding what I was attempting to achieve in my doctorate.

The professor who examined my work was herself a psychologist and was incredibly understanding of what I was attempting to achieve in my explorations of difference and otherness. The examination, which took approximately 90 minutes, was thorough, interesting, amusing and enlightening, but there was one aspect of the examination, which stayed with me back then and which has formed the kernel of an idea around which this book has been borne. The question that she asked me when reading my chapters was to say:

DOI: 10.4324/9781032614342-1

Why is it Dwight, that of all the references you have provided in your review of the literature, that some 85% of those are old, white men?

For me at that moment, it felt like a bell had gone off. I remember sitting back in my chair, my eyes wide open, wondering how in the world I could have written something around difference and otherness and yet have allowed my work to have become so dominated by one particular culture, that even I had marginalised the many disparate, rich voices of the other in explorations of privilege and otherness. I left out the Crenshaws, the Hills-Collins and the Lordes. I left out the De Beauvoirs, the Benjamins and the Butlers. I left out the many other voices from the LGBTQ community. I left out disability theorists and those from a neurodivergent background. I had allowed my ideas, many of which had become so much better formed by the time that you read this book, on the backburner and had not recognised how internalised my own sense of colonisation had become. My writing did not represent me; it represented the face I was supposed to show myself as understanding white academia to fit in within a colonised framework.

This important story is my own; and yet in my practice, in my teaching, in my studies with other people, I come across similar narratives. Our courses in counselling and psychotherapy are more often than not taught from such a similar background, which privileges the voices of many a white, often older, male therapist or theorist so that we more often than not marginalise the many varied voices of the other who might have so much more to say about the psychological world around and within us. We privilege, even within our work around say dreams, the ideas of certain white men who, although they have done their research and researched distinct cultures and ways of understanding dreams, mean that we fail to recognise that those perspectives are filtered through one colonised lens.

We, in our adherence and belief in the superiority of whiteness in these instances, fail to go back to the source of these ideas. We unconsciously or wilfully ignore the colonised source which might enlighten us to as to why dreams are so important to say Afrocentric cultures, or Indigenous cultures. We deny our own selves the chance to develop a phenomenological understanding of said experience that then removes from, or challenges at least, the ideas when filtered through a white patriarchal lens.

There are some things, which are especially important to explore when it comes to decolonising our work. One of the first things to say, echoing Le Sueur's viewpoint about this subject, and underpinning some of the ideas taken further in this book, is that decolonisation is not just about the rewriting of lists of books that we can all read and review (Le Sueur, 2003). As Mbembe states in his excellent work on the experiences of those who are the colonised other, 'our ego has always been constituted through opposition to some Other … that, at bottom, we are made up of diverse borrowings from foreign subjects' (Mbembe, 2016, p. 30). The idea that we are colonised is therefore not just in a literal sense; it is in a psychological sense that this form of colonisation reconstitutes itself repeatedly. This therefore means that any form of decolonisation must include not just how we rewrite and restructure and challenge the building blocks of our profession, but also how we might also challenge, disempower, and therefore reconstruct a sense of self, which is less influenced by the systemic levels of colonisation we are all borne into.

This is a crucial point. When we talk about colonisation, when we talk about the world that we are born into and how we perform certain narratives to maintain this system, it is important to recognise that this, this system, is all of us. White men are colonised into being a certain type of man, be it in their dress sense, whereby to wear trousers is seen to not only represent a sense of maturity and civilisation, whereas conversely to wear a skirt is often seen to be more barbaric and less human (Rovine & Rovine, 2018); and in the same way certain behaviours as men are seen as being more desirable of a man of a certain standard and status than others (Haider, 2016; Stroud, 2012). Or the expression of aggression, which within a colonised framework is seen as a force to be harnessed and utilised to maintain this cultures sense of superiority, yet if one is seen as acting out one's aggression in some disparate way, then one is marked out as being barbaric and less than human, or in other words, more savage (Beauvoir, 2010; Memmi, 1974).

For those of other minorities who are reading this, there are many ways in which this book will look to explore, show you and understand just how colonised ones thinking and being actually is. This therefore means decolonisation is not just about challenging one's ability to cognitively understand the world around us but is also about recognising and exploring the underlying behaviours that reinforce said cognitive structures of supremacy.

The importance of decolonising counselling and psychotherapy

Counselling and psychotherapy since its inception over 100 years ago have struggled with the idea of growth. Whilst there have been certain notable exceptions to this more generalised rule, and whilst there have been certain theorists who have come along and challenged some of the more traditional aspects of counselling and psychotherapy, which were considered to be the norm or the standard bearers, what has often happened is that there has been a struggle for new voices within our world. At best we have, over this period, seen a central line drawn between Psychodynamic Psychotherapy, Jungian Analysis, to Person Centred work to Existentialism, with Cognitive Behavioural Therapy taking up a position as well. Whilst we see alongside some of these a number of other ways of working which step outside of those more centralised boundaries, such as the Transpersonal, Eco-Psychology, Equine Therapy and many others, what we often have within what is considered mainstream psychotherapy is the big five or six ways of working and their patriarchal patrons which sit central to these ideologies.

Ideas such as ecopsychology where the position in the world is considered, and in particular within nature, is one of these new ways of working, which is often marginalised and occasionally looked at with scorn (Cianconi et al., 2020; Eaton,

2012). Yet, it is also an incredibly rich and incredibly important way of understanding our relationship to another other, which this time seen as the planet itself, for us to understand and helps us to understand a relationship accordingly. Equine therapy, where the intuitive knowing of horses is used in a symbolic and metaphorical fashion to explore anything from the attachment issues of clients to how working with those deemed anti-social by society, to former soldiers suffering from PTSD, although garnering some strength and prevalence within our profession is seen as a bit of a fad and something not to be mainstreamed (Burgon et al., 2018; Earles et al., 2015; Rosing et al., 2022) .

I should add that the term I am using here, that of *Mainstreaming* here also holds another angle and this is where the ideas of capitalism come into play. Mainstreaming involves, for some types of psychotherapy, the ability to provide worth, often financially when it comes to how clients experience their mental health. The fact that mental health has become a commodity therefore means that mental health practice has become as colonised as any other profession. So that targets need to be hit, ways of working have to be cost efficient, and a client needs to hit the targets on a CBT student's chart for it to be seen as successful.

The ideas of success and failure when attached to an idea of worth within the mental health field change the whole framework of counselling and psychotherapy in ways that many of us really do not really understand or have never explored. It places an added onus onto the practitioner to get it right, but it does not place within that onus a responsibility for the therapist to create a strong enough relationship to get said recovery 'right' (Hawkins & McMahon, 2020). Psychotherapy, like any other profession, like any sporting occasion (the World Cup, the Olympic Games, etc.) has become commodified. This book is therefore not necessarily a clarion call to deconstruct capitalism and strip it out from counselling and psychotherapy (because I do not think that is possible). What this book aims to do is to raise from the depths to surface the levels and the range of capitalist co-option which counselling, and psychotherapy has undergone for it to maintain any sense of survival and therefore growth. Decolonising counselling and psychotherapy are therefore important as it allows us the chance to broaden the range not only of ways of working but also of ways of achieving growth, progress and mental health stabilisation for not only our clients but for ourselves and therefore for the greater world around us.

Another aspect of why it is important for us to be talking about decolonisation of counselling and psychotherapy is that the more we consider how colonised, how white middle class and female in a British sense, or how white middle class and male in a European or American sense, dominated our professions have become. When we begin to explore this aspect of our profession, then we start to see just how the colonisation aspect of counselling and psychotherapy involves the maintenance of said structures of patriarchal, white supremacist, capitalist counselling and psychotherapy. The aim here is to therefore begin a longer-term process in the redressing and challenging imbalances within the profession as we fight to give back something to our wider communities within which we all work.

Methodological underpinnings

For this book to work, this is not just going to be a book about tearing apart the structures of our profession as counsellors and psychotherapists. It is going to offer a considered, measured exploration of what may have happened for us to get to this point where we are right now.

One of the main ways of exploring much of this material is by approaching it through the lens of phenomenology. What this actually means is I will predominantly be utilising the ideas of Merleau-Ponty and one or two other phenomenological theorists who recognise that how we make meaning in the work is not through the singular perspective raised within one of these structures of oppression, it is through the collective understanding of our collective lived experience (Eriksson, 2015; Hegel, 1976; Merleau-Ponty, 1962). The reason I use the word *collective* in that last sentence was to help the reader understand a couple of things:

1 I am not authoring this book to say that I have all the answers to all the questions in this ongoing process of decolonisation as that places me at some kind of patriarchal pinnacle of understanding, which leaves us still embedded within the coloniser narrative.
2 Anything that I raise here through my experience, through my own sort of wisdom going through numerous hours of study, pain and trauma, although based on my own experience, is to help this book is to open a doorway. A doorway for practitioners, for students, for courses, for our profession to have a deeper, longer, ongoing consideration of just how we can make our courses more inclusive, how we can make our client work more inclusive and how we can make the work that we do individually on ourselves, more inclusive of the shadow parts of ourselves, which we have marginalised and which lead us to marginalise others.
3 Decolonisation means the movement from the singular approach to understanding human nature, removing us from that colonised need for certainty, that capitalist, individual way of observing humanity. It returns us back towards a more collective, relational exploration of our journey(s) of human existence.

The idea that any one theorist should therefore hold all the answers is one of the biggest traps and biggest obstacles against decolonisation. It sets up a massive power dynamic whereby if said theorist is in vogue and one has enough of a following, then one is accepted and incorporated accordingly. Conversely, to question the ideas, which are raised and posited means the other is then often seen as problematic, as angry or as not quite getting it. This book is therefore designed to open the playing field of just what it is to be a human being, thereby allowing several voices to come through to play their game and explore their meanings accordingly. This does not mean that every voice is as valid as another one; what it does mean is that in the ploughing of a field of potentiality, those voices, which hold the most weight and are most relevant will rise to the surface and take their positions alongside those early theorists whose ideas we still revere today. It means that there will be an ebb and flow of vocality, of understanding and of relevance, and that the sought-after rigidity of knowing is replaced with the discomfort of the complexity of the journey towards continued understanding.

The second part to presenting the methodology behind some of these ideas is to recognise that this book is not about the stripping out of what is already there. Sometimes, and I will explore this later on, some of the work that has been presented through the lens of some of the early forefathers and mothers of our profession has been adapted within said structures of courses and writers and so on, and filtered to such an extent that their original meanings or their original breadth have become lost. This refinement is nothing new; it is a common facet of the meaning-making that we all go through when we encounter ideas and theories, which are alien to us.

For example, any student on a course who hears the words of a lecturer as they talk about early life presentations of say Bowlby, Winnicott or Klein will often filter it through what they understand of their family and of their upbringing to make sense and understanding of such (Bowlby, 1988; Mitchell, 1986; Winnicott, 1961). That filtering process of a lecture, of a book, which may have taken hours, days or weeks to write, then shows how reductionist we all are in creating understanding. It is exceedingly difficult to understand a topic and still maintain and hold the breadth of knowledge, experience and history that may have gone into creating said theory or theoretical understanding at the same time. We reduce things down to make it easier for us to absorb, and simultaneously, we filter any said new knowledge through our own colonised and adapted intersectional identities. Any approach to said works and writings will therefore always be reductionist. So, to decolonise, we must return to broadening out and sitting with the complexities of who we are, what we do and why we do it. This is before we can even begin to sit with the complexities of those we are learning about.

This book will therefore look to explore several areas along the way as we look to understand decolonisation. Firstly, we will be:

- Thinking about what we do: why are we psychotherapists; what does it mean to be a counsellor and psychotherapist; what does our profession look like as a counsellor and psychotherapist in the current era?
- How do we do it? How do we do our work? How do we conduct our research? What does it mean when we do what we do?
- Why do we do what we do? We are starting to think here in a lot more depth about the nature of our profession and not just take it as rote that what we do works because it has always been done in such a fashion.
- What is excluded from our profession altogether, and why? From the first days of its inception, counselling and psychotherapy have undergone numerous refinements and reformations, which have included and excluded the ideas and theories of not just marginalised communities but also of some of the greatest thinkers in our game.

- How can we do this work more inclusively, which, as it says in its subheading, is about actually recognising what we have lost or put down and marginalised, why we may have done that but also developing the means and ways in which we could better include these forms and ways of working, not just to the benefit of ourselves as practitioners but also to the benefit of our clients in our profession.

Understanding the layers, therefore, of prejudice, which, as I have already stated, will be a part of who we are and also a part of our profession, and recognising how deeply embedded these will be, is the first step therefore in helping us to understand, to write to study and to consider how we practice in a more inclusive and decolonised way.

Figure 1.1 Structures of decolonisation.

Figure 1.1 looks at the therapist as a phenomenological construct, defined through the varying aspects of its career to come to some sort of coherent hole. To explore what it actually means, the idea here is that the therapist sits at the centre, and it is moulded by its training, its experience of psychotherapy; personal therapy and the books that it reads; the research around psychotherapy that it itself has done; and its clinical practice, be it within placements during training or external to this once qualified. These four aspects help construct the fifth phenomenological part, which sits centre, this being the psychotherapist.

The psychotherapist is therefore not built in isolation. It does not mean that we become a psychotherapist or a counsellor instantly. We are formed, we are moulded and we are enticed into ways of being. We learn skills and qualities; we listen to our dreams; we work creatively in sand play work or with creative imagination; and we do sculpts. We use a few creative and cognitive techniques to help us understand who we are in order that we may become a psychotherapist and work in an environment where we are looking to assist in the growth of the other. This identity formation of a psychotherapist will be very much influenced by the colonised nature of all these parts, which sit in the external ring. For example, our trainings are often influenced by the voices of white, older men so that, much like my initial example where I spoke about what it was like for me during my doctoral transfer examination, our ideas and ways of being as a psychotherapist will be moulded so much by what we are told are the internal structures, which form counselling and psychotherapy.

The world of psychotherapy itself will also play a massive role in this identity formation. Given that psychotherapy is by its own admission a reflection of the society within which it works, the experiences of trainees, for example, during their trainings will be very much tainted and moulded, not only by the external world they inhabit but by their own therapists' visions of how that world may have played a part. For example, the struggles of working-class trainees to get on to courses and to survive them is often minimised by practitioners from more middle-class backgrounds who see the struggles that these trainees undergo as being part of their psychological development, ignoring the social economic reality that these trainees may well inhabit.

Another facet of psychotherapy trainings and psychotherapy environments could also be seen to involve the role of privilege and the confidence that privilege gives certain trainees when it comes to either obtaining a placement area for them to do their work whilst training or for how well developed their ability is to construct a career as a counsellor and psychotherapist post qualifying. I have encountered several instances where some very professionally qualified psychotherapists have really struggled with the next stage of their career, which is to establish and build a practice. Whereas others who have perhaps struggled with the experiential elements of their courses, yet because of their business acumen gained through working in corporate environments or attending Russell Group universities, are therefore able to use these skills to give themselves a lift upwards in obtaining clients and establishing themselves within a client base, which may pay far more money.

This is not to judge one perspective as better than the other, but it is to explore the social economic realities of psychotherapy and psychotherapists experiences of such. Recognising that there is a huge disparity not just at the beginnings of trainings where students struggle in some ways to obtain funding for courses versus those who are returning to work or who have moved out of the corporate field with sums of money large enough to pay the tens of thousands of pounds required to train as a counsellor and psychotherapist.

These two parts discussed here within Figure 1.1 therefore speak to the role of capitalism as a structure of inequality. So, for us to even consider decolonising our profession, we need to recognise these inner qualities are as much embedded within our profession as they are within the cultural framework within which counselling and psychotherapy resides.

Returning to Figure 1.1, research and how research is conducted is another aspect of decolonisation that will be discussed in this volume. The fact that in my own research I have had to develop means, methods and methodologies, which objectify less that which is being studied. This thereby allows for a more relational understanding of the world being explored. A move away from say the methodologies of Grounded Theory which, although birthed in a qualitative environment, took as its starting point the language and verbosity of the quantitative standard bearers (Charmaz, 2006).

Research can be encountered and performed in many ways, and this book will look to consider not just the ways that we do it but the other types of research and the other types of knowledge-making, which exist and reside within the world. These will include areas such as storytelling, such as some of the other more transpersonal ways of conducting research, structures and ideas, which may be considered to not have the scientific basis for some of the more mainstream qualitative research methods but which still hold their own worth within the communities wherein they were devised nonetheless (Braud & Anderson, 1998; Messner, 2011).

Clinical practice is an interesting area that is already being reconstructed and decolonised as I write this volume. The global pandemic, which occurred in 2019 and took over the ways of the world, meant that many of us as human beings resided at home for many months at a time. For those of us who are counsellors and psychotherapists, this therefore meant that we were overnight challenged regarding how we were going to keep on supporting our clients. Instantly, psychotherapists and counsellors signed up for accounts with Zoom, Skype, Microsoft Teams and other forms of software, which would allow us to still relate to our clients and maintain our practices. The world of counselling and psychotherapy in the West was therefore changed instantly forever. Governing bodies such as the BACP and the UKCP were challenged into constructing narratives and rules for how we were going to work in this new environment whilst psychotherapists, psychologists and researchers explored the prevalence and the success of working within an online framework (BACP, 2023).

Anecdotally, for example, one of the more interesting perspectives I have come across, which I would enjoy seeing researched, is the uptake of counselling and psychotherapy by students on university courses around the country. This uptake has increased given their generations already usage of Internet technology and software, combined with counselling and psychotherapy's sudden willingness to engage in a new way with an often challenging and hard-to-reach client group. This is not to say that the ways of working online are the only way and the best way that we should work. What it is to say is that psychotherapy in its evolution has the chance to step out of the straightjacketed environments of purely face-to-face, chairs-opposite relationships between one and another.

Decolonisation for clinical practice therefore becomes, in this instance, a way of stretching and learning about how we can do the work we do in a more effective and inclusive way. Especially as, using the example of working online once more, other potential clients, like those who identify as having a disability, are suddenly easier to reach for those of us who are working online.

This book is structured in such a fashion that there will be five sections to consider. The first one is obviously about decolonising psychotherapy; how has psychotherapy become adapted, what has it lost along the way and what are the stories of adaptation, which have allowed psychotherapy to function, let alone flourish? And what do we need to do to restructure psychotherapy in such a fashion that it regains some of its originality and returns to its origins, as well as opens the doors to future developments and richness in a changing time?

The second part will consider decolonising our psychotherapy trainings. In this section, we will look at some statistics and figures about the levels of marginalisation within our trainings, be they in the student cohorts or in the teaching structures, and how and why these may have come into being. In conjunction with this, we will also look to consider what our courses within a capitalist structure may need to do to make their environments safer and more inclusive for minority groups.

For the third section, we will look at decolonising practice, the logical next stage. Practice here is not just when one leaves the confines of a training institution; this will also involve clinical practice in clinical placement areas where students, for example from middle-class backgrounds, may often find themselves working in and amongst minority groups they have had little to no connection with previously.

The later sections will look at decolonising the psychotherapist and at decolonising psychotherapy research. To start with with research, as per my initial story, one of the things about those initial chapters that I submitted was that they had come from within the colonised part of my own psyche. If this was something that I had been taught, or I had imbibed, then it made perfect sense that this would display itself in my research. Often our research, our research methods and those who write about our research do so from a very white, Eurocentric perspective.

The reason for this incident was the failure to decolonising the myself the therapist. None of these matters if we ourselves have not done the work to consider, explore and contain the aspects of ourselves, which have become adapted within a colonised structure. So, it is therefore imperative for us as practitioners to weigh up and consider just what it means to be a colonised psychotherapist.

Intersectionality and decolonisation

For us to understand what decolonisation will entail, it is important to take, in my view, an intersectional approach to the topic area. What this actually means, therefore, is that I will be exploring decolonisation by using the work of Patricia Hill-Collins, Kimberley Crenshaw, Audre Lorde and a number of other theorists who have raised ideas for intersectional theory (Carastathis, 2014; Collins & Bilge, 2016; Lorde, 1984). By exploring the themes presented here, this then allows space for me to continue exploring how these might be incorporated into counselling and psychotherapy courses and trainings and practice in order for us to better understand the range and diversity of identities of our clients, students and courses (Turner, 2021).

We need though to say a bit more here about intersectionality and its theoretical meaning. The theory explored the varying structures of oppression and came from the start point that we all live within a capitalist, white supremacist, patriarchal system, which moulds, defines and constructs our identities. Alongside this, any failure to recognise these social constructions also invisibilises the experiences of minorities accordingly. Although all three theorists spend far less time exploring this next example of systemic structure, which creates the other, I would also like to add in that of the systemic oppression tied to religion. This is not to say that to be religious is to be an oppressor, but it is to say that when these structures are combined, when three then become four, that religion is therefore used to oppress, marginalise and reduce the other accordingly.

Intersectional approaches recognise that we are a few different iden-tities, which interact and jostle for position at varying moments in time in our lives, careers, work, home life and other avenues within which we exist. Intersectionality is an approach and understanding, which has become increas-ingly prevalent over the past 30 or 40 years and grew out of a critique of fem-inism by non-white and white feminists who saw that their approach to issues of gender difference often marginalised the voices of minorities contained within the feminist movement.

In my book, *The Psychology of Supremacy* (Turner, 2023), I make the point of exploring these systems to a deep level to show that we are all born into said sys-tems, and it is very difficult to find a voice and a narrative beyond them. In fact, much of the work that we do when we look to shed the adaptive cloak of a fake sense of self and become more individuated and real also involves the stripping back of these systemic structures, which dominate us. This does not mean that we ever become free from said structures, because I do not believe it is possible to live in this environment at this point in our cycles on earth and do that. What it does mean, though, is that we find a way to live a more authentic life whilst still paying our bills and taxes, whilst still existing within a structure, which oppresses minor-ities, and whilst still living in an environment where these structures reinforce inequality. We do so hopefully with a greater sense of morality as found and dis-covered from within, not as defined and imposed from without.

Conversely, psychotherapy has become no less adept at marginalising differ-ent voices. So many of our courses, as I have previously stated, preach a white, middles-class, male theoretical perspective on the issues of the psyche, the soul and the self, for example. This thereby leaves out perspectives from say indigenous communities who also have an awful lot to say about working with dreams to prof-fer one particular example, thereby contrasting with the more westernised angles of work presented by say the likes of Carl Jung around this same topic (Johnson, 2015). This one example thereby raises the idea that psychotherapy, quite under-standably, has become as adept at the marginalisation of other voices as the wider society within which it is embedded. That there are a sizeable number of LGBTQ+ theorists writing about issues of identity from a different and no less important perspective also needs to be noted in this tome. The likes of Meg-John Barker, Dominic Davis and many others and their work around anything from issues pertaining to the trans community to how to work with Kink in the world of counselling and psychotherapy (Barker, 2019; Davies & Neal, 2000). These important voices then contrast with some of the original views around identity, which marginalised and pathologised many of the identities they have sought to explore and normalise within our profession.

The wonderful work of Jessica Benjamin, Judith Butler and numerous other feminist theorists has also done a great deal to explore and expand our understanding of anything from gender difference to early life attachment (Benjamin, 1998; Butler, 1990). All these brilliant feminist theorists have sought out ways and means with which to deconstruct the pathologisation of women within the patriarchal structure, which has infected the work of counselling and psychotherapy. From my own community, the ideas of Eugene Ellis, Guilaine Kinouani and numerous other correspondents from the African diaspora have had a wide-ranging impact on our understanding of just how race and racism impact the identities of those from said communities and also from those who identify as white (Ellis, 2021; Kinouani, 2021).

I could list many, many more theorists who have explored issues like neurodivergence, disability theory, ageism, eco-psychotherapy and so on, as it is important to recognise the immense names and perspectives who have written around our phenomenological experiences as human beings who have been marginalised (Blytheway, 1995; Cianconi et al., 2020; Goodley et al., 2018). The idea therefore of an intersectional approach to understanding who we are and why we exist in our diverse range of complex identities should also therefore be allowed space to exist within our profession in its mainstream, not as a marginalised add-on on our training courses, in our practices and in our lives. It means a greater engagement with the difficulties and the complexities of privilege and otherness. It means the recognition that we as a species hold many ways of being whilst we are all one at the same time. It also recognises that our experiences across the board are equally as valid as those of the others, thereby recognising, as a hint for future chapters, the embedded hierarchical nature of patriarchy and how, when we talk about our own struggles, we often compare as being less worthy of attention than somebody else accordingly.

Yet, the aim of this part is to show that from psychotherapy's humble beginnings, where it was very much embedded within a structure of white patriarchal masculinity, it has evolved in its attempts to broaden out the previously blinkered narratives. There have been attempts to pluralise our perspectives, and these are ongoing. *The Philosophical Decolonisation of Counselling and Psychotherapy* is therefore already happening, but what is also taking place is the steady resistance towards change, against said restructuring, and the deeper recognition of how said structures of oppression impact upon us all.

Summary

As we have seen here in this introductory chapter for this volume, the systemisation of our world is a constant. We all reside within systems of oppression; we are all moulded by them, we function within them as much as we can and we are colonised very much by them. This book, though, is an exploration of how these forces, patriarchy, white supremacy and capitalism, in their colonisation of our profession and our professionalism, actually hinder the rights and abilities of both practitioners to do some of their best work and therefore provide our clients with a route towards functioning within said systems without the psychological fear and distress that so many of them endue.

The next stage of this exploration will therefore be quite simply one of a consideration of just how and why psychotherapy has become colonised over the years. It will also look at just what it might mean to decolonise psychotherapy, what forms that might take and what structures might need to be put in place for this to happen. Given that colonisation is an enormous area within counselling and psychotherapy, as it is within the wider world, any ideas presented in this volume are not definitive but are here presented to open the flood gates in any restructuring. This though should not just impact our profession, but it should allow our profession to also offer varied means and ways to therefore influence the wider cultural, political, religious and other frameworks.

The next chapter will then segway succinctly into Chapter 3, which explores how this might work on deeper levels in our trainings as counsellors and psychotherapists. In our practice areas, be they whilst training or also how we work beyond our trainings. They will also look at the ways we perform our research within the psychological disciplines before circling back around and into just what it means as psychotherapists to decolonise the work that we do.

The next chapter is therefore simply entitled *The Decolonisation of Psychotherapy*.

References

BACP. (2023). *Working online in the counselling professions: Good practice in action 047*. BACP.

Barker, M.-J. (2019). *Life isn't binary: On being both, beyond, and in-between*. Jessica Kingsley Publishers.

Beauvoir, S. de. (2010). *The second sex*. Alfred A. Knopf.

Benjamin, J. (1998). *Shadow of the other*. Routledge.

Blytheway, B. (1995). *Ageism*. Open University Press.

Bowlby, J. (1988). *A secure base: Parent-child attachment and healthy human development*. Basic Books. https://doi.org/10.1097/00005053-199001000-00017

Braud, W., & Anderson, R. (1998). *Transpersonal research methods for the social sciences*. Sage Publications Inc.

Burgon, H., Gammage, D., & Hebden, J. (2018). Hoofbeats and heartbeats: Equine-assisted therapy and learning with young people with psychosocial issues–Theory and practice. *Journal of Social Work Practice*, *32*(1), 3–16. https://doi.org/10.1080/02650 533.2017.1300878

Butler, J. (1990). *Gender trouble*. Routledge.

Carastathis, A. (2014). The concept of intersectionality in feminist theory: The concept of intersectionality in feminist theory. *Philosophy Compass*, *9*(5), 304–314. https://doi.org/10.1111/phc3.12129

Charmaz, K. (2006). *Constructing grounded theory: A practical guide through qualitative analysis*. Sage Publications.

Cianconi, P., Betrò, S., & Janiri, L. (2020). The impact of climate change on mental health: A systematic descriptive review. *Frontiers in Psychiatry*, *11*(March), 1–15. https://doi.org/10.3389/fpsyt.2020.00074

Collins, P. H., & Bilge, S. (2016). *Intersectionality: Key concepts*. Polity Press.

Davies, D., & Neal, C. (2000). *Therapeutic perspectives on working with lesbian, gay and bisexual clients*. Open University Press.

Earles, J., Vernon, L., & Yetz, J. (2015). Equine-assisted therapy for anxiety and post-traumatic stress symptoms. *Journal of Traumatic Stress*, *28*, 149–152. https://doi.org/10.1002/jts

Eaton, H. (2012). Mapping ecotheologies: Deliberations on difference. *Theology*, *116*(1), 23–27. https://doi.org/10.1177/0040571X12461224

Ellis, E. (2021). *The race conversation: An essential guide to creating life-changing dialogue*. Confer Books.

Eriksson, K. (2015). *Understanding you: A phenomenological study about experiences of empathy among social workers working with forced migrants*. Lund University.

Goodley, D., Liddiard, K., & Runswick-Cole, K. (2018). Feeling disability: Theories of affect and critical disability studies. *Disability & Society*, *33*(2), 197–217. https://doi.org/10.1080/09687599.2017.1402752

Haider, S. (2016). The shooting in Orlando, terrorism or toxic masculinity (or both?). *Men and Masculinities*, *19*(5), 555–565. https://doi.org/10.1177/1097184X16664952

Hawkins, P., & McMahon, A. (2020). *Supervision in the helping professions*. Open University Press.

Hegel, G. (1976). *Phenomenology of spirit*. Oxford University Press.

Johnson, M. P. (2015). African dreamers and healers. *Psychological Perspectives*, *58*(3), 265–308. https://doi.org/10.1080/00332925.2015.1063333

Kinouani, G. (2021). *Living While Black: The essential guide to overcoming racial trauma*. Ebury Press.

Le Sueur, J. (2003). *The decolonization reader (Routledge readers in history)*. Routledge.

Lorde, A. (1984). *Sister outsider*. Crossing Press Limited.

Mbembe, A. (2016). *Necropolitics*. Duke University Press.

Memmi, A. (1974). *The colonizer and the colonized*. Souvenir Press.

Merleau-Ponty, M. (1962). *The phenomenology of perception*. Routledge.

Messner, M. A. (2011). The privilege of teaching about privilege. *Sociological Perspectives*, *54*(1), 3–13. https://doi.org/10.1525/sop.2011.54.1.3

Mitchell, J. (1986). *The selected Melanie Klein*. Penguin Limited.

Rosing, T., Malka, M., Brafman, D., & Fisher, P. W. (2022). A qualitative study of equine-assisted therapy for Israeli military and police veterans with PTSD—Impact on self-regulation, bonding and hope. *Health and Social Care in the Community*, *30*(6), e5074–e5082. https://doi.org/10.1111/hsc.13922

Rovine, V. L., & Rovine, V. L. (2018). Colonialism's clothing: Africa, France, and the deployment of fashion. *Design Issues*, *25*(3), 44–61.

Stroud, A. (2012). Good guys with guns: Hegemonic masculinity and concealed handguns. *Gender & Society*, *26*(2), 216–238. https://doi.org/10.1177/0891243211434612

Turner, D. D. L. (2021). *Intersections of privilege and otherness in counselling and psychotherapy* (1st ed.). Routledge.

Turner, D. D. L. (2023). *The psychology of supremacy*. Routledge.

Winnicott, D. W. (1961). The theory of the parent-infant relationship. *The International Journal of Psycho-Analysis*, *1960*, 585–595.

Chapter 2

Decolonisation of psychotherapy

Introduction

Between the years 2000 and 2005, I trained to become a psychotherapist. My training took place at a centre in West London and began at the end of a period of introspection, where I had undertaken my own therapy post the end of a difficult end of a relationship. My very first year, as it would be for many of those reading this book, was one of undertaking an introductory course, equivalent to a Level 2 or Level 3 certificate in counselling.

On my course, we were taught some of the basics of Freud, Jung and Klein, our reading and lectures being very much based around the picture books on these theorists, books which explored in the most basic of fashions their ideas. At this point, what I should also emphasise here is that the fact that within psychotherapy colonisation involves the reductionist approach to the ideas of certain theorists. This is not just something which happened to Sigmund Freud, this is something which happens to a sizeable number of theorists from several modalities and backgrounds. When we try and make sense and create understanding, what we often do is fail to see not only the complexity of the ideas presented, but also the ground from which they were raised, born and birthed. For example, the fact that Dr Freud's ideas came out political landscape where he was an outsider is a hugely important facet in understanding some of the background to these perspectives (Freud, 1930). Our failure to do so has often led to a number of other theorists from different modalities and backgrounds critiquing Freud as being anything from sexist to homophobic to anything else in particular (Beardsworth, 2005; Kernberg, 2002; Said, 2003).

Sometimes, though what needs to be understood is that in the colonisation of the ideas of Dr Freud within the existing systemic frameworks, it is the frameworks themselves which hold these aspects of prejudice, sexism, homophobia, ableism, etc. It is then when these ideas are commodified (and I have chosen this word for a particular reason), that marginalisation of certain groups is seen, expressed and continues to this day. Therefore, the more recent contemporary attempts to decolonise curriculums and bring in diverse voices, whilst being incredibly important and something which needs to continue, must also include a deeper understanding

DOI: 10.4324/9781032614342-2

of the original theorists themselves and therefore their ideas. This is not to say that the persons presenting said ideas are all perfect, it would be naïve for me to believe that, but it is to say that actually to free them up from the shackles of systemic colonisation, then offers us a whole new narrative around just what is being taught and expressed around human nature and our psychology.

It is also about recognising that many of these theories and ideas are taught within a systemic framework and as such will always marginalise voices of the other. For example, Kakar (2012) in his psychoanalytic book looking at childhood and society in India offered a very unique perspective on the psychology of a very different and diverse group, from a psychoanalytic perspective. That this book was written in 1978, means it runs very much counter to some of those theorists expressed within westernised perspective. Yet, it is a text which, although interesting enough widely enough read within minority groups, is not taught anywhere near the courses or expressed in any format within our profession. The richness of ideas looked at from without the world of westernised psychotherapy offers a broader perspective, for those theorists and practitioners working within diverse communities. It is therefore hugely important that within psychotherapy we are open to decolonising our profession to a degree whereby it becomes normalised to explore our psychologies, our diverse intersectional psychologies from a range of different perspectives.

Another reason for this attempt at decolonisation is that it challenges some of the hierarchies that sit within our environs. To emphasise this point, I would like to proffer an experience I had at a governing body meeting some years ago. In sitting in the meeting as a transpersonal integrative psychotherapist, it soon became apparent just how hierarchical psychotherapy had become to the extent that it was strange and yet interesting to see those of a psychodynamic persuasion looking strangely out of the side of their eye at those who were perhaps more person centred, existential or transpersonal. This is not to give one modality a challenging time over another. What it is to say is that this behaviour is 'normal.' The number of times I have sat within supervision groups and watched conversations whereby transpersonal theorists complain and moan that nobody is as spiritual as them or heard how existentialists do something similar towards those who are more person centred. It is astonishing that these issues are not explored for what they are, which is that within any system of supremacy there will always be a need to place one's own position higher than that of the other.

So, therefore even within the worlds of psychotherapy, that drive for one modality to place itself as more superior to the other or to another or others, means that there is always a conflictual nature to what is seen and represented within our profession. This also has an impact upon how we use psychotherapy and the practitioners within it. The fact that the Nazis termed psychotherapy as a Jewish science (Frosh, 2005; Havsteen-Franklin, 2007) says quite readily that even in the early days of its inception, that it was going to have to travel a difficult road in order for it to be accepted within mainstream, western, white supremacist societies. The fact that Kakar's work sits outside of western grouping, even though there are a sizeable number of practitioners working with Asian families and clients, says an awful lot again about the unconscious nature of systemic supremacy and where it sits within counselling and psychotherapy. Sitting alongside this is the path followed by the BAATN Network, which was only established in 2003, giving a platform to a respectable number of theorists and practitioners of colour who have written and produced work accordingly. These stories, although separate, all have at their core a central idea; that the work of minorities, the ideas of those who are racially different within counselling and psychotherapy, has always been marginalised. And that this ongoing separation of ways, ideas and visions, speaks to the centralisation of power within our profession, not only within our courses but also within our practitioners themselves.

This is the other part to understanding what colonisation is within psychotherapy and it touches on aspects I will speak about in Chapter 5. It is that the colonised system within psychotherapy is made up of all of us. We are all a part of any system, it does not exist separate to us, it does not exist out in the ether, what it does is it exists through us. We more often than we like to realise, play an active part in maintaining its social structures so that they do not fall, falter or dissolve in any way (even if it is only unconsciously). It is therefore incredibly difficult to challenge the self-replicating nature of these systems, given that we are said systems, and because we act so unconsciously in maintaining said systems. Yet, it is also imperative that the more aware that we become of our positioning and of how co-opted we have become in maintaining the systemic supremacy of certain modalities and ways of working. So, that only then are we able to challenge and change and alter, even incrementally, the power systems have upon all of us, our profession and therefore the wider environment of which we are a mirror for.

At no time in the first six months of that first year of my training did I assume and decide I wanted to be a psychotherapist. That came later, during a series of lectures where I was introduced to these works of Sigmund Freud, Carl Jung and Melanie Klein. The professor who undertook those lectures inspiring me to read that bit deeper about the theories and ideas presented about our psychology. My interest by this point was piqued. The second part of this story actually involves the fact that I did not go to university, although having attended a fairly prestigious school in West London I left at 16 with three O Levels, few career prospects and feeling disillusioned with the schooling system, given its ability to marginalise and denigrate those seen as the racialised other.

To return to education in my late 20s and early 30s therefore felt right for me, although I had no idea at the time just how far I would be able to go. Staying to train on said course for the next four years of a post-graduate diploma then led for me to start to become the psychotherapist that I am today. I studied more Freud, more Jung and more Klein. I was introduced to Winnicott, Bowlby, Rogers, Heidegger, Husserl, and the transpersonal words of Wilbur, Washburn and Almass.

On my course in those four years though, we spent two hours doing anything around difference and diversity, this process only starting in the fourth year of the course. There was nothing on LGBTQ issues on the course and truly little from a feminist perspective. In fact, as a side note, I remember a colleague of mine calling this out in the very first term of the very first year, asking why we were reading about white men in psychotherapy. She did not receive an answer. This book is not to criticise any one training, because these types of stories, mine included, are stories that I have heard on numerous occasions over the years from students up and down the country. Yet, although there are some very good courses that look at difference and diversity, such as the Cara Counselling training in Worthing, East Sussex, and the CPCAB who run courses nationwide, both of whom spend a good amount of time on issues of diversity and difference and looking at how we are moulded by our environment, these are very much few and far between.

Since 2020, when George Floyd was murdered, I have presented at 30 or 40 different organisations, within the counselling and psychotherapy field, be they trainings or practice organisations, all of whom have been looking for ways to understand better what it is to work with diversity. That there is a movement here, in my view is undeniable. That this movement should ever have needed to come into place in the first place is a question for another day and another book. What is most important is that this process of decolonisation, this process of looking at just how our socially constructed identities have left us adapted, is ongoing, has begun and will continue.

So, whilst we watch as in the United States of America certain States have rejected any view that the teaching of LGBTQ issues, that issues around race should be banned from schools, and whilst in the United Kingdom there have been moves within the British Government to ban the teaching of critical race theory on our courses, what also needs to be noted is that these are very much rooted in structures of supremacy and have been called as such by organisations such as the United Nations (Litvinova, 2018; Lynn & Adrienne, 2013; Merrick & White, 2021).

The systems themselves work to maintain their position of superiority. So, anything that comes along which might even subtly disrupt said system from its position of superiority, will be resisted against much like the ego resists the shadow it has pushed to one side for a millennium. This chapter therefore recognises that psychotherapy is as much a part of the wider world, including the political world, as any other structure or organisation accordingly. Psychotherapy is as much embedded within the white, patriarchal system of superiority that defined so many of our training courses based upon the ideas of so many of our theorists. It also recognises that in doing so, it pushes to one side and has subtly in its own way forced into creation the likes of the BAATN Network, Pink Therapy in the United Kingdom, Queer Therapy in the United States, feminist writers such as Jessica Benjamin and others who sit outside of the cultural norm and yet write brilliantly about the work that we do, yet do so from an entirely different angle and one that needs to be recognised within our fields (Benjamin, 1990, 1998; Davies & Neal, 2000; Ellis, 2021; Morland & Willox, 2005).

This chapter, although written from my own perspective as a black man, also recognises though that many of the ideas that we use on our courses are bastardisations of the original perspectives presented by those original thinkers and that what the system actually often does is reduce said ideas down into manageable chunks which will fit neatly within the rules of said system. This is important to recognise. We all play a part in incidents of oppression, were born into them, were moulded by them, were then told how to perform so as not to disrupt them. Psychotherapy, therefore, is no different and many of our theories when we consider the original theorists, their ideas, their ways and their lives were often borne from outside of the system.

Edward Said (1993a) talked about this in the role of the intellectual where he saw that role as being implicit, not explicit, in helping to define the structure of a culture, of a creed, of a religion and of which it was observing. The intellectual as the other, the psychotherapy theorist as another, therefore is there to see the psychology of a group or of an individual, be they children, be they adults, be they men, women, trans individuals and recognise and see them in their fullest. The problem with this perspective thought is when those ideas are then absorbed back into subjective centre, that these ideas are often manipulated, reconstructed, denigrated, moulded, although some might say refined. What gets kept is often that which will more simplistically keep and maintain the structure alive, but what gets lost is that which may contrast and contradict the system's role of superiority.

For us to better explore decolonisation, it is important to understand what colonisation is and then how we might philosophically decolonise our profession from the internalisation of these systemic structures. To do this, the next section will therefore cover what colonisation is, how I view colonisation and the layers of colonisation that we all endure. Following on from this, there will then be a section on how colonisation has impacted the world of psychotherapy. This will therefore create a framework within which colonisation and decolonisation of our profession can sit and reside.

Understanding colonisation

On 7 January 2023, Tyre Nichols was murdered in America by five police officers who conducted a traffic stop whilst he was on his way home. The beating that Mr Nichols received actually led him to remain in hospital for several weeks before he finally died on 20 January 2023 (Plett Usher & Tawfik, 2023). Whilst this incident is no different to many others that have occurred in the United States, and in other parts of the Global North including the United Kingdom, what was most staggering about this was the fact that the people who killed Mr Nichols were five Black police officers. In discussions held on social media forums and in the press, although the idea of white supremacy was raised as being central to this, a respectable number of correspondents were struggling to understand how, given the fact that these were Black police officers, that white supremacy was still a principal factor in this murder investigation.

In a blog that I wrote around that time, what I emphasised was the fact that white supremacy is nothing to do with colour, it has nothing to do with culture or even gender. White supremacy, much like patriarchy and capitalism, are systemic systems of oppression (Turner, 2018). Therefore, it matters not the type or colour, or race, or gender, or sexuality or ableism of the person that resides within said system. What matters most of all is that the person upholds and enacts the rules of the system to their fullest, the reason being that that is what they are being paid to, asked to, encouraged to actually do (Turner, 2023). This is a form of colonisation, although presented on a smaller scale, meaning that colonisation is therefore the sense that we give up our identity, our rules and structures, or moral fortitude. We give up the parts that make us who we are to fit in with a structure that is not our own and we do so either willingly or less so, dependent on the power of the structure to define us or control us.

Although this example is a more contemporary example, ideas of colonisation have filtered through cultures for thousands of years. Empires have formed and risen and fallen on the back of their ability to incorporate, colonise, mould and then control other huge groups, populations and genders accordingly (Cesaire, 2000; Pereira, 2016). The movement of patriarchy from a more sustenance driven societal norm to one which is more based around the ideas and structure and needs for control of women is another form of colonisation. And such, even the ideas of capitalism and communism in their own individual ways have a colonistic way about them, whereby they inveigle and encourage or even beat and destroy the other, in order that they may maintain structures of power within their systemic auspices.

Colonisation is something which sits around us all the time. We are told that we must pay our taxes, we are told that we must be at the office for a certain time of the day or leave at a certain time at night, hence the idea of rush hour. We are told what we should wear through the narratives presented in fashion magazines and in commercials. We are told how to be as men, as women, as children and as the elderly. We perform all the time to fit within this colonised way of being. Our very identities, our psyches and as much as that our souls are adapted within this framework.

Another important facet of colonisation is that it automatically sets up a hierarchy; a hierarchy of being, a hierarchy of thinking, a hierarchy of acting and so on, where one group is therefore positioned as better than, or more central to, or more complete than the other. Offering an example from his wonderful book *Discourses in Colonialism* by Aime Cesare (2000). Although this book was written over a century ago, the fact that Cesare recognised quite clearly the idea that the other is colonised into a way of being through a racialised framework was very intuitive and imaginative for its time. He even saw that colonisation through a racialised lens involved the expression of one race as being superior and therefore more powerfully dominant than the other and saw that this is an experience which did not just resonate within the racialised factors in America, but also sat within the colonising powers within Europe, such as France, Belgium and the United Kingdom.

Ideas of colonisation and what they meant also sat within the work of Albert Memmi (1974), who in his book explored the symbiotic connection between the coloniser and the colonised and how the colonised often performs in a way that uplifts the position of the coloniser to one of superiority and supremacy. In this wonderful book, Memmi's attempt to actually breakdown the layers that sit between coloniser and colonised, although presented through a collective colonial lens, would have echoes both within the individual and in their ability to separate out who they are and who they are not, both here as well as within other forms of colonisation such as patriarchy and capitalism. The importance of recognising this also extends to critiques of say female genital mutilation which, although often seen in some instances as being culturally important, is often I will add here, argued to be a facet of the patriarchal colonising of women's identities which is upheld not just by men but also strangely, and interestingly, by women within said cultures (Jefferson, 2015; Wade, 2012).

The cost upon the colonised other can therefore be anything from a physical cost, where one loses an aspect of themselves in service to an idea or ideal presented before them, to a psychological cost, whereby one's ideas and sense of their identity is sabotaged to an extent that they no longer understand who they are, or that they believe the stereotypical ideas presented about their mirrored selves.

A brilliant example of this comes from the life of Muhammad Ali who, in his journeying to Zaire for the now famous and fabled Rumble in the Jungle, where he fought George Foreman to a standstill, beating him with now infamous rope-a-dope style of boxing (Hauser, 2021). Ali talked a lot about his experience and understanding of Africa pre-visiting there as being one very much built upon the ideas and images presented in old films such as Tarzan starring Johnny Weissmuller, or books and serials presented on television. These visions were often quite stereotyped, showing the African as being savage, immature and in needing of westernised coercion and control. Yet, when he visited Zaire (now the Democratic Republic of Congo) and was greeted by the thousands of people, men, women and children, he realised quite quickly that actually what he had been told was a lie, and that his thinking had been colonised to believe that they were less than anyone else in the world.

These ideas even filter through to the world of counselling and psychotherapy. One of my own stories involves a conversation post one of my own visits to Africa, whereby I was talking to a colleague about her travels all over the world. This was a colleague who had visited India on numerous occasions, China on numerous occasions, Europe, America and South America on numerous occasions, all in the hope of learning that bit more about her spiritual beliefs and understandings. Yet, when challenged by myself on why she had never visited Africa, she expressed that she was afraid of visiting the 'Dark Continent because she felt threatened and did not know what she would find there.' On hearing this myself, I was not only shocked but also saddened that this narrative, this idea, sat so readily within a fellow colleague of mine and that it had never been challenged or brought to the surface to be looked at in a deeper way by said colleague. It also contrasted greatly with my own experience, especially as I had just recently returned from Zanzibar and Tanzania myself.

The colonisation of thinking through these lenses is therefore something which we all endure. I have offered you there two examples, one from a white perspective and one from a black perspective, which highlight just how deeply embedded this type of thinking can go. What is important to recognise here is that this type of colonisation is common; we make sense of our world through projections and stereotypes because we have not got the time, more often than not, especially in the Global North, to actually be in the moment and get to know every single person, child, woman, ability, age, that we encounter on a day-to-day, week-to-week and month-to-month basis. We therefore reduce people down in order to make sense of our world, or we live in a world of constant othering (Kirschner, 2012). Yet, as counsellors and psychotherapists, we are challenged to stretch that out from these centralised forms of meaning making which are incredibly reductionist.

To offer you some other examples of how colonisation plays a role even within certain organisations and set ups: Bhabha (1985, 2004) wrote extensively about the need for cultures to consider how their systemic environments have been colonised not just externally, but also internally, during the period of colonialism and also capitalism. His ideas proffering up a mirror on the difficult engagement necessary with internalised cultural colonialism, his writing from an Indian perspective being particularly important to the post-colonial movement. Whereas, Francoise Verges (2021) in an incredible book on decolonising feminism from a French perspective looked at how white feminism in France was often very much rooted within a colonial paradigm. This therefore meant that the voices of non-white women in France, or more specifically non-white feminists in France, were often limited and marginalised accordingly. The whitening of French feminism therefore meant that it remained within a colonial framework and set of ideas.

To follow on from a point that Verges makes in their chapter on decolonial feminism, Mignolo and Walsh (2018) explore the role that intersectional feminism takes in recognising the plurality and possible inter-relationship of feminist ideas and perspectives from a number of varying angles. This broader exploration of feminist ideas is one that helps to decolonise and root out that which has become unconsciously embedded within a movement. This is no different to the struggles inhabited within civil rights movements and other fights for equality. The recognition within the LGBTQ community for example, that their ideas and ideologies needed to be more diverse and stretched wider and broader and therefore allowing them to become more inclusive was a master stroke of thinking and excellence. That there are a whole range of identities and perspectives which now sit on Pink Therapy and Queer Therapy websites books and blogs, enhances not only our understanding of ourselves but also, as psychotherapists, allows us to reach out and delve into the diverse world of groups and persons who we would never have approached some 30 or 40 years ago (Davies & Neal, 1996; McCann, 2019; Morland & Willox, 2005). This is what I mean about the work of decolonisation being an ongoing project which has already started to occur. But it is also what I mean when I say that there is still an exceptionally long way to go.

In varying ways, what I have explored here thus far is the idea that decolonisation is not just an external structural thing involving the fall of say the British Empire post World War II and the freedom of movement of those who were colonised and kept under its red, white and blue yolk. It is also the decolonisation of thinking and ideas and the recognition that any innovative ideas will already be colonised or potentially colonised for them to fit in and be incorporated within the wider cultural or political structures. Colonisation is therefore a massive topic; it has always involved more than just a toppling of several statues into singular Bristol canal (Otele, 2012). It has always involved more than just rooting out or talking about white supremacy as being that which is enacted only (Diangelo, 2011) by white people. It has always involved more than just allowing certain feminists the right to achieve financial parity with their white male, heterosexual, middle class colleagues (Abd Elaziz, 2021; Moon & Holling, 2020).

When we fail to actually decolonise, when we fail to root out and do the collective shadow work around these structures which have endured for hundreds, if not thousands, of years, then what we end up doing is actually placing ourselves within said structure and reinforcing the coloniser narratives for those who are still sat outside waiting for their chance to live and to shine. What this chapter and therefore what this book was also going to do is look at just how deep some of these structures run within the world of counselling and psychotherapy and as we do this, as we work with this material, hopefully we will start to become able, better able even, to actually consider the colonised psyches of not only ourselves and our profession, but also our clients, our environments and the wider worlds we live within. This is what decolonisation means in this book, how it impacts our profession and ultimately why this process is such a large, difficult and yet incredibly important one to attempt ad to achieve.

The colonisation of psychotherapy

Sigmund Freud was born on 6 May 1956 in Austria (Jacobs, 2003). A neurologist, whose work involved the creation of talking therapist and in particular psychoanalysis, Sigmund Freud is often seen as having been at the forefront of a movement to develop a means of understanding that which ails both the neurotic and the psychotic. His work, generated over 100 years ago now, was groundbreaking for its time. His ideas being revolutionary and leading to the formation not only of a group of therapists around himself who also took their own ideas forward to broaden the scope of the work that we do today, but also led to the realisation that much of what we know about mental health was very limited and flawed and basic.

Emerging out of a time where much of what we understood of mental illness involved the incarceration and the lack of treatment for those who were deemed as mad. Freud's ideas also offered a level of hope for those who could be talked through their malaises for them to seek out some type of potential cure. Alongside this, theorists such as Albert Adler, Jean Piaget, Melanie Kline, Carl Jung and others developed their own means and ways of understanding the psychological, therefore broadening out this base area and widening the scope of how we might see and treat the psychologically challenged other.

There were problems from the beginning though. For these ideas to flourish, Freud's early hope hinged upon making his ideas palatable to the mainstream medical establishment. This driver very much built out of a need for professional acceptance is quite a reasonable one. Yet, it led to a number of conflicts, most famously including that with his contemporary Carl Jung, whose own ideas of the occult and of the more spiritual or transpersonal ways of understanding the illnesses of the other sat uncomfortably with those of Sigmund Freud himself (Stevens, 1990). This pull between remaining closely aligned to one's own ethics, or allowing one's own ideas to be co-opted and coerced into conformity by a medical establishment was one of the reasons for their subsequent split and. Yet, whilst Jung is not blameless in any sort of issues that they had, the fact that there needed to be a split is one of the reasons why so much of our work as counsellors and psychotherapists exists in the world today.

Subsequently, whilst many of Freud's ideas have been accepted within the mainstream world of psychiatry, psychology and psychotherapy, some of his more challenging and rich ideas and perspectives say about the wider world have been left on the shelf, to gather some kinds of historical psychological dust. For example, in his work *Civilisation and Its Discontent*, Freud (1930) clearly posits an idea where the death drive, which was at the time seen as a huge part of his psychological framework, could be activated by the external cultural framework the client resides within. This shows a direct link some 100 years later to ideas of the political, the fact that for example the structures that we all inhabit, the political structures, the cultural structures and such, are those which are often seen to create discomfort and malaise within the individual or the collective.

Such groups as Sidewalk Talk and Counsellors and Therapists UK (CTUK) are currently exploring this link between psychology and the wider contextual environment, building ways of working which meet our clients within these environs. This sort of material, when we bring in the influence of culture, and particularly the political, offers a vastly different angle to that which has been co-opted and therefore colonised, suggesting that, especially around ideas of where the political resides within psychotherapy. The numerous arguments that even I have endured about whether the political should be anywhere near the psychological, suggests that there is a colonisation of thinking and thought to maintain the political and therefore the psychological status quo.

It is no different to when footballers, music or other artists, or others, speak up about their working class environments, the deprivation, the poverty, the suffering, and are then told that they should know their place and stay out of the political (Various, 2021). Especially, given their ideas are built out of the social pain and distress that they are witnessing. Colonisation in these instances is the sucking out of the marrow of an idea, whilst leaving the husk of potentiality to rot outside. Yet, what often happens is these externalised parts of the idea, the parts which motivated this whole ideological structure in the first place, grow their own legs and find their own way. A perfect example of this being Carl Jung's continued growth and his substantial, by any means, contribution to the whole discussions and debates around mental health.

Offering another example of the colonisation of thought, an idea from a more existential perspective, Friedrich Nietzsche is a perfect example. Born in 1844, Nietzsche was a German philosopher and writer who, in his early professional years, was a professor at the University of Basel where he worked in classical philosophy (Prideaux, 2018). At the time, he authored several books around philosophy, many of which have become classics and have formed the basis for much of the existential philosophical thinking that we all are aware of today. The sadness in Nietzsche's story came in his later years, where he had a subsequent breakdown. Unable to support his ideas any further, it appears that much of his work was left in the open to be picked up by his own sister and by many others including the Nazi party. These ideas were then distorted, with much of his expansive visions on humanity cruelly distilled to take out their purest meanings and being adapted to incorporate the systems of hate and destruction subsequently wrought out upon the world in World War II. Ideas which even appear in Neo-Nazi propaganda to this day (Rutledge, 2018).

Homo (1992) who was one of a good number of theorists to reclaim Nietzsche's ideas. This movement being a testament to the subsequent author's vision and honesty in realigning all of us to just how strong and powerful Nietzsche's perspectives on the psychological and the existential were. Again here, we see how in this instance the system, or in other words the political system of Hitler's Nazi Germany, used, utilised, distorted, and manipulated huge swathes of work to meet its own needs and ends. Colonisation here perhaps has a more malevolent feel to that which Freud endured but is no less a problem and an issue subsequently.

These two angles are simple examples of just how easy it is for systems to adopt, adapt, manipulate, coerce, mould and control that which is seen as unique, strange, different and therefore a threat, to the psychological status quo of its own systemic being. Some of the reasons for this are that the system, whilst willing to expand and to grow, is not necessarily as willing to lose its own position of prominence and power. Said system will therefore do only so much as it can do to alleviate the tension built into the appearance of that which it does not know or understand.

It could be argued that the works of Martin Luther King and in some other ways have also undergone a similar process. Dr King is very much seen as being at the forefront in the ideas of civil rights in the United States, and therefore in the United Kingdom as well, so much so that he is currently taught in many schools and universities around the Global North. Although he is held up as some kind of paragon of civil rights and civil virtues, what is often lost and forgotten in any reading about his ideas and perspectives, is that this was a man who also held some very challenging views around government, and especially the political left (Harvey, 2022). These views influenced his ideas on non-violent protest, a perspective so challenging at the time, that numerous members of his own entourage, those who followed him and believed in said positionality and in said means of protesting, were locked in prison and sent to jail for a number of years because they were just seen as being too challenging for the State (Butler, 2003; Karatzas & Каратзас, 2015).

Any reading therefore of Dr King, Friedrich Nietzsche, and Sigmund Freud is often simplistic, whereby just the simplest ideas, speeches, quotes are used and utilised and seen in a means of trying to understand them. The fact that the world that we live in, a world of means, gifts and emojis, simplifies so much of these persons, these individuals, these behemoths and their words, ideas and structures, is another form of psychological and intellectual colonisation, I can argue. So much so that anything more real with more depth, often gets left well, well behind.

Conversely, there are a good number of examples of theorists whose ideas were not adapted, were not colonised in the same way and whose ideas, or who themselves, the personalities, the persons, the intellectuals, were left on the outside to be destroyed, murdered, killed or left without any care when they fell seriously ill. These persons will include Malcolm X, James Baldwin, Angela Davis, who is very much seen as being on the outside in many means amongst many other feminist theorists. Ideologs who in their own way were seen as too controversial, too extreme, too outside of what the system was able to tolerate, that they needed to be either marginalised, locked up or positioned as a threat to society. This is no different to the early life of the feminist movement, where the Pankhurst's and many others endured incarcerations across the United Kingdom, or Edward Said and Franz Fanon, both of whom were unable to gain the treatment that they deserved and needed in their later years of life for the illnesses they both suffered.

Structures like these inhabit psychotherapy as well and often what we teach and what we know is just a couple of grains of sand on the clearest, most exotic, theoretical beach on the west coast of Zanzibar. We miss the existential rolling surf, our authentic relationship with the clear blue sky, the beach hut nearby because we are told to focus in on those few grains of sand presented as a form of reality so often on our courses. It soon becomes apparent for those who already identify as the other, that for them to be met they will need to step outside of the cultural, colonised framework of said course to obtain the information and the wider knowledge held within that wider psychological world.

Offering you an example, I recall studying with a colleague some 25 years ago, an interesting woman from the LGBTQ community, she was often extremely critical of the lack of diversity in thinking presented on our courses. Although she stayed for the full four years of the course and we became good friends and worked alongside each other, she recognised quite soon that for her to feel safe and met within this other part of her identity which was very much excluded within the course framework, that she would need to engage with the work of Queer and Pink Therapists. That she had to do that at all shows just how colonised the ideas on her course had become and how in this colonisation anything seen as the other was left on the outside.

Another perspective of colonisation, it is possible that we allow ourselves as practitioners to be colonised within the structure of psychotherapy. So, much so that when something re-invigorates or reignites our internalised other, that when this wakes up we realise just how adapted we have become and how much more we need to step outside of this adaptation in order for us to either serve our communities or in order for us to realise just how unsafe we have always felt, even within said adaptation.

To present another example of what I mean here, when collaborating with a colleague of mine who practised at an organisation in the north of England, we talked a lot around the time of George Floyd's murder. We looked at just how difficult it was to remain unseen when something so major had taken place. In their efforts to encourage the service that they were working in to take on more of the struggle to understand race and difference, one of the things that soon became apparent was that this was an organisation that was not willing to do so because, to use a quote from the service manager, *They did not believe in or want to get involved in the so-called culture wars.* This left the practitioner feeling, understandably, quite upset. Her own identity, that she had put to one side in order to feel adapted, allowing herself to be colonised within said adaptation, had been razed to the surface like a titanic from the depths by the death of one man; but this still was not enough for her to be taken seriously within said service, so much so that she found herself remembering how unsafe she felt and experiencing different levels of racism within said service. So, after further discussions she left. The safest thing for that individual was to separate themselves out and not allow themselves to be colonised once more. These are the struggles that occur within psychotherapy.

To understand and explore the colonisation of psychotherapy, we also need to see it through the lens of capitalism. It is important to recognise that within a capitalist framework, the commodification of any sort of entity, person, way of working, way of being or anything else, is an essential aspect of the capitalist structure and system. Psychotherapy is no less immune to this commodification of its ideas and ways of being. In fact, it is this which has led to the splitting up of varying ways of working and the honing down into saleable parts of ideas and structures defined by theorists who have been around for the past 100 years.

What I mean by this is simply that psychotherapy has become a financial venture. From its grass roots, whereby courses are set up around a certain modality and spread out over several years, these courses have therefore become so expensive that they exclude numerous others who might be better positioned to do the work of counsellors and psychotherapists. The ideas of our forefathers, the Freuds, the Jungs, the Adlers, the Kleins and others, have become commodified to such an extent that there are numerous schools of thought and, what I mean by saying schools is, institutions where their ideas are cobbled together in a saleable form over a number of years with an accreditation attached to the end of it.

This is the colonisation of our profession in this respect and often leads to the sense that certain modalities believe they are more superior than others because those courses either cost more or are longer or have managed to attract better teachers. Yet, what they all are is still maps of the human psyche, ways of understanding the work that we do when we recognise, and we watch and observe and mirror back to our clients who they are. They in no one way define the nature and the quality of the relationship. Where there are some positives in this approach, is that there is a possibility that a lot of them do meet the needs of a wide range of clients and client ways of working. But where there is a difficulty with that is in this commodification the best-selling types of psychotherapy are often those ones which become most available to our diverse client base. Meaning that the wide range of clients often find themselves shoehorned into singular ways of working, say through CBT models in the NHS or other ways of working in patient setting and charities.

There is a danger here for psychotherapy should it continue down this capitalist route; and that is that it will become even more splintered, even more diffuse and even more specialist, as training centres try and attract those students who could afford the fees for them to sustainably keep going. This increased level of commodification, this increased individualising of psychotherapy, is a huge factor in the reasons why so many of our clients feel unseen and unmet.

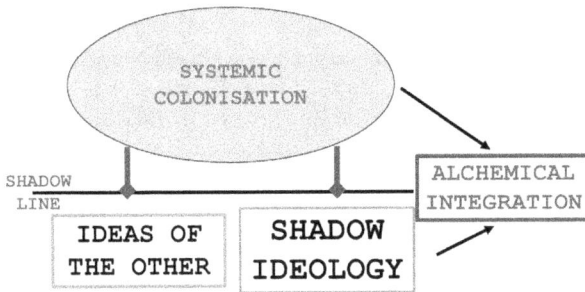

Figure 2.1 The colonisation of psychotherapy.

Figure 2.1 explores just how colonisation works. From the outside, we have the ideas of said theorists. For example, the ideas that Sigmund Freud originally talked about were not just the ego and the superego, they were very much about the political landscape at the time; his fears as a Jewish man living in Nazi Germany and how psychologically this fear might appear and need to be considered (Freud, 1924, 1930). These ideas, though, were often left at the door of medical establishment because they were not wanted within said system accordingly and therefore anything like these rich politicised ideas which very much change our vision of Sigmund Freud were then pushed into the shadow ideology. That his ideas were systemically colonised is without doubt because often on our training courses what we are taught is the very basics.

As a general point, when we study anything new what we do is we mould it around our own ability to understand. We do not grow into the ideas until much later. We take whatever we can, whatever snapshots or snippets or crumbs that we can ingest, and we take this down into our body, we internalise it. The challenge, though, is to remember that when we form an opinion about a Freud, a Jung, a Nietzsche, a Klein or whoever, that our opinion is based around a snapshot at the very best of who they are and what their ideas represented. What often happens, though is in that internalised colonisation of said ideas, we then author numerous papers and critiques about theorists and so on from that colonised othering nature, blaming them for the othering the system itself has performed. We tend not to go back to the shadow ideology. We do not return to that which was originally presented by the theorist, because to do so, not only challenges the internalisation of systemic colonisation as we become counsellors and psychotherapists, but it also means that any diversity of ideas is ruined as well. Our ability to critically think is stunted at source.

To therefore work towards any form of decolonisation of ideas, our trainings need to be able to encourage trainees, practitioners, the public even to think and look beyond those snippets. It is not that we are supposed to know everything about a theorist and their ideas, but it is about recognising that there is way, way more and that we are constantly left not knowing. Another way of seeing this is that the systemic colonisation of a type of idea becomes a need to know definitively and the more that we can stay with the fact that actually we do not know, that there is an open gap there in our knowledge and our wisdom about a theorist or a theory, means we then remain curious to what is beyond. This is the point at which our chemical reintegration through research, through reading, through podcasts, through whatever means we are most drawn to, then takes us on longer path towards changing our ideas and ideologies.

Returning to Figure 2.1, what is meant by indigenous ways of thinking is not just that these are culturally constructed. It could be any way and form of thinking which (a) sits outside of the centralised norm and (b) comes from a community or identity which has been marginalised in some fashion. Often, the knowledge held within psychotherapy is created from a pivotal point of heteronormative, patriarchal, white supremacist, upper class, ableist, ageist perspectives (or in other words anything which centres itself as all-knowing and leaves the other in the shadow). Indigenous knowledge in these instances then brings in the wealth of material which sits outside of these centralised perspectives. Material and knowledge which has already been left on the outside, which has already been marginalised. For example, the theorists of colour around psychodynamic theory who exist in our spheres and yet are often not seen, or experienced, or taught on our courses in order to proffer perspectives which may entice and encourage students of difference and colour in their understanding and reading of psychotherapeutic theory (Spivak, 1988, 1993, 2015).

Existentially, it could be that our propensity to just consider western theorists in the ideas of philosophy then marginalise such artists as Kitaro (1989) and Nishitani (1981) who have a fair amount to say about philosophy from an eastern perspective, thereby providing philosophy with a broader range of ideas and angles and making philosophy that bit much more phenomenological. Even the ideas out of the Kyoto School, which were very much influenced by the Frankfurt Schools of Philosophy, deserve their spaces on the theoretical and existential plains of consciousness (Carter, 2013; Tanaka, 2010).

Within the transpersonal, the ideas of Ken Wilbur, Michael Washburn and others are often taught on courses around the country with anything more esoteric and perhaps more indigenous having been co-opted and colonised into a form which is easily adaptable within transpersonal psychotherapy's world of whiteness (Washburn, 1995; Wilber, 1989). The fear that I have personally witnessed in the eyes of theorists when it came to even talking about Afrocentric ways of understanding spirituality, for example. The work of Asante and Somé and their ideas about spirituality and religiosity meant that these were areas that I often did not speak about on my own course when I trained and chose to then embed further on and later in my own writings, such as here today (Asante, 1998, 2008).

Offering a personal example of how this might work, during a trip some years ago across Central Africa, I remember walking through Lusaka, Capital of Zambia, and sitting at the roadside just watching the world go by in this busy, African capital. At some point, I remember watching a mother playing with her child. The child was held on the mother's back and both mother and child were smiling, laughing and sharing some kind of joke. The mother noticed myself and I looked back at said mother and smiled at them, happy to witness such a joyous scene. This image stayed with me of the bond between mother and child and the cultural experience of witnessing a child being carried by its mother, consistently. I contrasted this with a more westernised perspective on childcare and attachment, whereby often I experienced clients who were raised within a Victorian framework of being left to cry and emote on their own at the back end of a garden, or were pushed around in a buggy crying and emotional, sometimes maybe wishing to be carried and held (Moore, 2010; Ogden, 2004).

When we explore ideas like attachment, and I am using this as just one example, what we do as we see them through a very western lens of how parents and children should interact, is ignore any sort of knowledge, understanding or exploration from a non-western perspective, as this would offer a unique experience of childhood. Given the propensity for western theorists to valorise and centre their own angle, often what happens is that these varying other perspectives get lost in the narrative accordingly. That much of this is down to a level of intellectual prejudice and/or intellectual supremacy is without doubt as colonised cultures may have had knowledge which the coloniser could have learned from, which would have meant that the coloniser was not supreme, and this could not have been allowed.

Psychotherapy of the other

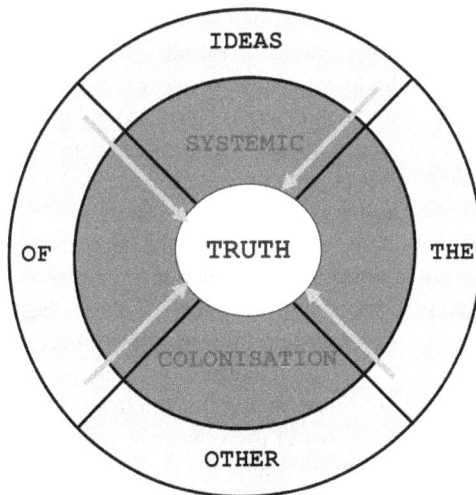

Figure 2.2 Colonisation of the truth.

Figure 2.2 considers how supremacy has always marginalised and rewritten history to maintain a centralised white patriarchal, capitalist narrative around itself. The rewriting of history, for example the failure in understanding the numerous non-white combatants who took up arms during World Wars I and II is a major factor in recognising just how powerful the centralised formation of history and therefore identity actually is (Turner, 2023). The marginalisation of the other, be it psychologically, literally, physically and in this case around knowledge and knowing was of course always going to be a factor in the creation of structures of supremacy whereby only one or two sets and types of knowledge can be acknowledged and seen.

Figure 2.2 therefore explores how this works and ties itself back to what happened to the works of Freud, Marks and Nietzsche earlier in this section. Borrowing from an idea posited by Haug (2008) and her ideas around power, power is not a hierarchical thing. For Haug, power involves the centralising of an archetype, I could suggest, around which we all circle accordingly. In understanding the systemic colonisation of ideas from without the cultural norm, what often happens though is that these ideas are filtered through an outer layer of systemisation. So, removing the idea of power an incorporating the idea of truth here, what I am trying to show in Figure 2.2 is that the system becomes the gateway for the considered truth, and therefore given power over, anything said outside of itself.

In some ways, there is a positive to this. For example, in Edward Said's (1993b) work around the intellectual as the other, his view that actually the intellectual as an outsider has a massive role to play in informing culture of its pros and its cons, etc., offered a perspective on truth which culture needed to hear and absorb. Where this become a negative, though is when truth becomes something which is inflexible. Truth as prescribed by the system is something which never changes, does not evolve, does not grow, does not mould itself to any sort of new time, and which by its very nature therefore becomes rooted in the past. Truth as an archetype though is something which is more flexible, which is constantly evolving, which has no start point and no end point, and which changes based around the information given to it, both within the system and without. Where the system though becomes more hardened therefore creates ideas which cannot be changed, whereby truth is solid and immovable. And psychotherapy has, at times in its history, fallen into a quick sand's trap, whereby truth drags one down into the depths, where one's own inner sense of truth or identity is never to be seen again.

Alternative viewpoints, and there are many of these, be they based around research, around psychology or around how we view ourselves and our relationship to the other, have often been marginalised by scientific communities as being unscientific and therefore not representative of the truth. The issue here, in these instances, is that in the Global North there has always been a craving for truth. Truth in the past was upheld by religious institutions, and in more recent times by the scientific community. Today though it has been co-opted and misused by the political realm. Therefore, any ability to stay with what is not known is lost or distanced from, and the incompleteness of our understanding of human existence is a massive factor in recognising that other voices, other perspectives need to be incorporated, included and to have their space and place.

In the United States, there have already been efforts to marginalise theorists' theories such as critical race theory from schools and to erase reference to LGBTQ+ theories in school and public environments (Matias et al., 2014). These efforts, the patriarchising and the whitening of knowledge, suggest an attempt to dominate what we see and what we know to control who we are and what we do. This erasing of the knowledge of the other is no different to things that have happened since time immemorial.

A brilliant example appeared on my Twitter feed one time, where H. G. Wells was promoted as being the originator and creator of the science fiction genre. This strange tweet received numerous responses and replies until it was pointed out by somebody that actually Mary Shelley at age 17 had written Frankenstein years before H. G. Wells himself created his first sci-fi tome (Shotwell, 2021). The fact that it was so easy to erase Shelley's ideas, power, intelligence and depth of understanding of a new genre, shows how easy it is for the patriarchal need for supremacy to take over and dominate.

Offering other examples, the numbers of Black or non-white inventors of items that we use every day, persons of colour who, for whatever reason may have created and constructed something to which we have all become accustomed and yet who are never given their due, is an ongoing discussion and debate held within said communities. In many ways, these are the reasons why we have things like Black History Month and why we have things like The International Day of Women in March, because they attempt in some small way to redress this historical erasure that creates a sense of otherness in how we view knowledge. Knowledge is not always that which comes out of the mouths of white middle class men. Knowledge is also that which has emerged from the other, be they women, be they from the LGBTQ communities, be they from diverse cultures, abilities, races, be they from colonised countries. So, any understanding of our place in the world should also come from these communities. This call for a restructure of how we view what we know is not impossible to achieve but it does mean that we must step outside of our colonised sense of who we are to achieve it.

What Figure 2.2 therefore does is it clearly recognises that there is already a body of work which sits outside of our colonisation of knowledge and from this position it takes a rare person to then delve outside of that principal place and dig that bit deeper for what it needs to know. Most people, most ideologists are more than happy to remain ensconced within that centralised position. Most researchers, most psychotherapists, most trainings are also perfectly comfortable staying centrally located because there is no need or requirement for them to push beyond the socially constructed boundaries.

I remember once teaching on a course and, after delivering an idea about Carl Jung's idea about projection, being told that they did not want that form of psychotherapy. When challenged it became apparent that they wanted something they termed 'real psychotherapy' and when being challenged on what real psychotherapy was, the idea was they wanted a white man to deliver white, male, patriarchal psychotherapy ideas. The strange thing about the colonisation of ideas is that it can even lead to forms of science and meaning making which are later then debunked as being unscientific or just plain wrong. The idea within, for example, race science and one which has been echoed in the understandings of women that persons of colour and women were inferior because they had smaller brains, was a theory which ran for a good length of time in the Global North (Saini, 2019). It was a theory that led to several perspectives which even have their ties through to eugenics. A time of meaning making built out of a sense of superiority and not grounded in any scientific reality which then led to the distress and destruction of hundreds if not thousands of people accordingly. It was built out of a sense that the knowledge of the time could only be gained from within that principal place and that anything which sat outside of that patriarchal white supremacist colonial angle, would therefore be flawed, unscientific and wrong.

This is not to say though that all science is wrong; because I am not here to deal in absolutes, but what it is to say is that there is always a flaw in what we know, there will always be gaps, we are always sitting with the not knowing and our inability to stay within that space of not knowing and our drive, or craving for certainty is often also underpinned by our own implicit, nay explicit, prejudices, racism, homophobia and sexism and such as like. These aspects of ourselves drive us to want to know definitively.

Client example

A was a man of 40 who had been raised in Central Africa. During his childhood, a war broke out in his homeland. A served on the front lines, but because his side lost the war, he had been forced to flee his home country, and had eventually ended up coming to the United Kingdom as a refugee. Within five years of his arrival in the United Kingdom though he had had a psychotic breakdown and been diagnosed as schizophrenic.

Whilst in a London psychiatric hospital, he was visited on his ward rounds by his psychiatrist. On this occasion, alongside this psychiatrist was an anthropologist, who was part of a team working at the hospital who were looking at alternative means of diagnosing clients. The psychiatrist asked him about his experiences during the war in his homeland, and A told him about the lives he had taken to survive. And told him that he heard the voices of those slain repeatedly, and feared he would never be free of them.

In their subsequent team meeting, the psychiatrist felt ready to continue to prescribe the medication already recommended to assist A with his 'schizophrenia.' Yet, when asked about his experience by an anthropologist he told him of the cultural ritual of taking or holding the spirit of those he had slain. On hearing about this cultural normality, the psychiatrist changed his prescription, and A was subsequently allowed to leave the hospital and return to the community.

The importance of this example here is that it shows us just what can potentially happen when we decentralise any sense of psychological knowing and are willing to engage with a wider narrative of meaning making, but for our clients and for ourselves. The client A presented here was not being seen in his fullest because of a systemic belief in knowing which linked the hearing of voices to psychosis. Yet, it was the intervention of the psychiatrist, offering the knowledge of the other, who was able to broaden out that sense of knowing, thereby casting an important light upon the client and their reality.

The colonisation of concepts therefore, as I have already stated, involves the reduction of ideas and concepts and therefore the loss of any potential ideas and meanings but within them to serve the said political and systemic structures which are built around them. Therefore, any sort of movement away from that means the systemic evolution or individuation of the systemisation of psychotherapy's egoic sense of self into which something more fluid and more authentic can find its place. This is where the decolonisation of ideas then becomes important, and this is also where the decolonisation of how we research and achieve those ideas becomes of equal relevance and importance as well.

Psychotherapy therefore needs its practitioners to step outside of the narrow confines of what they believe they know and research and therefore understand, areas of interest that they are drawn to that may inform their practices so they can access their clients accordingly.

The path to decolonisation in psychotherapy

Psychotherapy, as I have shown in this chapter, is an evolving beast. It is important throughout this book to offer some creative and inspirational examples of ways in which we can, as a profession, develop, grow and keep moving forward. This section here will offer some ideas as to how this might be achieved. It should be stated from the off that these are my own ideas, which although I have researched and considered and explored with my peers and colleagues, they are not the only ones that should be out there.

One of the first ideas, or a pre-idea if you will, is that any attempt at decolonisation must be modality specific. I am not here to offer a one route solution to all these theoretical perspectives, because that in its own way fits into a patriarchal narrative around what is right versus what is wrong. What I am here to do is to offer a more phenomenological exploration of what I believe decolonisation might look like. In doing so I aim to therefore open a few paths for practitioners and, in later chapters, for trainers and others, to explore their own routes to broadening out who they are as practitioners within counselling and psychotherapy. Thereby changing the landscape of how counselling and psychotherapy might look going forward years from now. We do not have to keep walking along one narrow yellow brick road, what we can do is walk several paths allowing ourselves to go in different directions.

The statement about following different modalities and specific paths is incredibly important. One of the reasons for this is that it starts to counter the human propensity for knowing, or for trying to define an absolute truth as posited in Figure 2.1 and Figure 2.2 earlier on within this book. This systemic habit is as much a human need for absolutism as it is one based within the modalities and the systems themselves, thereby meaning that the human and the system as cojoined at the psychological hip and inform each other. In an interesting way, this desire for absolute truth sits very much outside of the existential framework for example that I teach within. The ability to encourage students to think continually and to critically analyse what they believe they know and do not know is a core facet of the work of being a psychotherapist and is one which runs counter to the cultural norm of absolutism.

The second aspect to consider here is that this drive to a way of knowing which we all adhere to is quite reductionist. Reductionism here, as we have already discussed, involves the stripping away of diverse and complex narratives about a topic area to one or two key areas which we can use and pin our ideas upon (Sayer, 2010). In an interesting way, it is like a form of psychological othering, whereby instead of remembering that truth is a constantly evolving, constantly fluid beast of an archetype, that what we tend do is to narrow it down and form our own sense of identity around truth, thereby believing that we own it. This is the importance of Figure 2.3.

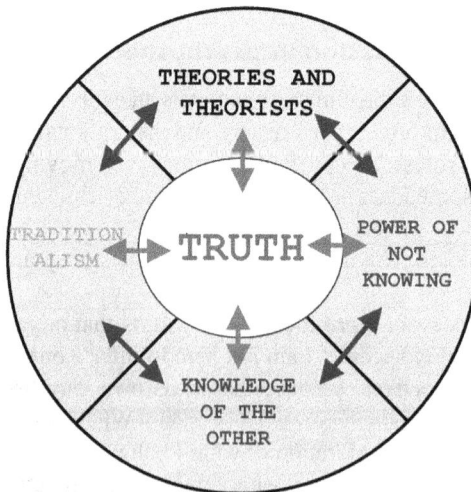

Figure 2.3 Decolonising psychotherapy.

The first thing to say about decolonising psychotherapy is that truth then becomes something which is constantly fed by the different narratives always rotating around it. This ability to constantly evolve is also a very human way of being. We are evolutionary beings so this need to cling on to a truth is a bit like a child hanging on to railing as it goes around the roundabout. Whilst it might feel safe for moments of time and less nauseous, the roundabout keeps rotating. Truth is like this. Truth evolves. The truth of St Thomas Aquinas and his belief in religion was a vastly different thing to that proposed by the current Pope in this era and in many ways, when St Thomas Aquinas using his example a little bit further, expressed his version of truth, it led to him being incarcerated for a number of years prior to his death (Tomarchio, 2002; Toner, 2010).

Truth is not just owned by the centre. This is the brilliance of the idea of truth and is something that as psychotherapists we then must start to challenge, not only within ourselves as practitioners, but also within our trainings, our practice and, and this is the most important part, within our profession. This is the importance of Figure 2.3 and looks at some of the ways of which this truth can be made up, this constantly evolving, rotating beast of a roundabout.

As we see on the diagram, the theories and the theorists need to be closer connected for it to inform our sense of truth. We need to be able to talk about Freud's flight from Austrian German during the rise of Nazism. We should be able to talk in more detail about the schism between himself and Carl Jung, one's attempts to find their own way into the space in the middle being countered by the other's need for a more existential, nay transpersonal understanding of human nature. We should be able to talk about Carl Rogers and his belief in the spiritual and how this informed much of his later ideas, many of which were not incorporated within traditional Rogerian therapy. Can we talk about the works and lives of feminist theorists within our modalities, whose voices were often overshadowed by those of older, white men? We must be able to stay with a constant sense of not knowing. The anxiety provoked within this and how actually in many ways this existential anxiety about not knowing, and how it brings us closer to some type of death, has been discussed within our modalities for several years. It is something that Freud discussed and that a number of existential psychotherapists have explored to their heart's content for a number of years (Laub & Lee, 2003).

There has to be more of a space for other ideas, other ways of making knowledge, other ways of understanding who we are as human beings, ways and means that perhaps challenge some of the traditional westernised scientific quantitative ideas of identity and behaviour, and bring in more qualitative explorations of what these ways and means might be. A perfect example is that this comes from Afrocentric perspective, whereby actually stories, narratives and archetypal meanings are often expressed through verbal means, meaning that any sort of knowledge base is not necessarily scientifically driven, it is driven by the use of metaphor and symbolism (Messner, 2011; Monteiro-Ferreira, 2005). Understanding this, and seeing its importance to unfamiliar cultural groups, brings a more nuanced recognition of just what human psychology is. Not to replace the traditional, if one wants to use this word, but to sit alongside and enhance it.

Any sort of decolonisation is not about throwing out the central tenets of all our modalities. It is about keeping those but recognising that they are not the only ways of understanding who we are, that much of the work that we need to do is about broadening the framework, bringing in other voices, bringing in other's perspectives. It involves grabbing back the theorists themselves in ways that we have not been able to do, or been willing to do, to make sense of the work about which we are talking. These traditional ideas though, together with their originators, together with a sense of not know, their drive to continually explore, recognises that these ideas are incomplete. Together they recognise that there are other ways of exploring some of this material, therefore broadens out the ideas and structures within psychotherapy to a way which moves beyond the colonised norm which sits central to all our experiences.

These attempts to decolonise psychotherapy therefore will also challenge the exclusivity of the work that we do. If I have students, for example, who I then send out to work in placements and clinical practice areas which are based within inner city areas or are funded to serve working class groups, often what happens is I end up with a good number of white, middle-class, often female students working with groups for whom psychotherapy is anathema; or in other words it makes no sense to them as it does not meet their needs and requirements. A decentred and decolonised psychotherapy, were we able to achieve it, therefore allows more space for the areas for psychotherapists who are practising in areas of diversity to see their clients through a less centralised, white, middleclass and patriarchal lens. One whereby the knowledge that they need to obtain to understand those groups is closer to hand or/and, there is a greater encouragement for them to remember that they do not know it all. Therefore, to gain greater knowledge, there is something about the engagement within those groupings, be it through the narratives of those groups or through the writings that might sit outside of the psychotherapeutic framework.

Another thing about knowledge is where we obtain it from. I remember between 2003 and 2005 undertaking a Masters project in understanding music as a life process. The general theme, and I will keep this brief, was to explore how music as a universal construct resonated with each of my clients; not that they necessarily had to play music but that they had a connection to music, music artists, certain songs and such. When undertaking my literature review for this project, one of the things I quickly realised was I needed to bring in perspectives to my research which sat outside of the psychotherapeutic norm. I therefore explored the writings and understandings of artists such as Daniel Barenboim (2009), remembering that he had explored this in his own stories for a number of years. Conversely, I also looked up and explored the words of Eminem, the rap artist, who talked from a different angle about what music meant to him (Eminem, 2009). Just using these two vastly different perspectives broadened my understanding of what music meant and therefore offered my research, and therefore my client base, something which they would never have obtained had I just stayed within the simple structures of psychotherapy.

This is not to say that I did not read Schopenhauer's writings round music (Schopenhauer, 2020). This is not to say that I did not look at the spiritual and in particular the Sufi writings around music but it is to say that by staying with my sense of not knowing, that I was able to intuitively recognise the path I needed to follow in order to explore and express what music meant to myself (Inayat Khan, 1996). Truth in this instance was formed from both within and without the field, the same way that truth for who we are and what it means to be a psychotherapist has to be informed not the interests we had before the course had even begun, that form a sense of who we are as individuals as we walk along this journey.

Knowledge, therefore, and truth in a decolonised context, as I have tried to show in this chapter, is something which is forced from the external to the internal. There is a barrier between what is deemed as knowledge and what is seen to not fit in the paradigm already presented. This is decolonisation of ideas. What this particular section here looks to discuss is actually not in tearing it all down and starting again, because in many ways that is a flawed concept based around the idea that all we need to do is to tear down external structures and that the will not recreate them in the same fashion without realising that we are said structures and that everything new we build will of course hold massive parts of the internalisation of the external systems (this is why repetition compulsion is also a systemic concept and not just a psychological one).

Decolonisation of psychotherapy, although presented as something which is massive and which needs to be undertaken in steps as I am presenting here, is not as difficult as people make out. What there is though, is a great resistance to doing so. One of the reasons for this, as I have already explored in this chapter, is that there is a comfort with remaining within said system of colonisation. There is a comfort in knowing, or in believing that we know, what it is to be black, white, male, female, securely attached, ambivalent attached, or schizoid or any such other concept placed before us; and yet within us all there is always that drive to know a bit more, that actually there is an understanding that actually we do not know it all, that actually truth does not exist, that on some sort of deeper level there is something within us which always recognises that actually truth is a mirage; it is out there in the distance, somewhere where we can never get hold of it, but that we will always strive to walk towards it. Human nature, our inner self, knows that truth does not exist.

It is our egoic sense of self that actually tries to pin truth down time and again and within this rigidity comes an internalised and externalised distancing of the curiosity, the internal wisdom, the intuitive sense that we all have, that there is more out there, more to discover, more to realise, more to obtain, incorporate and grow from. Truth suggests that we have come as far as we need to go and that there is nothing else for us to learn, develop and understand, but that inner quest for truth, recognising that that is a flawed and dangerous concept, that actually this journey of ours is an ongoing one and as human nature evolves, so does our understanding of what it is to be counsellors and psychotherapists alike.

Decolonisation therefore involves not only the reintegration of theorists along-side their theoretic presentations, some of which will also offer a greater and deeper understanding of just where these ideas and ways of being have come from. This will also lead to a greater inter-connectiveness of our ideas as we trace the historical narratives that have run from our professional's formation through the last 100 years, with different splinter groups, directions and the multiversal attempts to understand the complex nature of human nature. This inter-connectiveness also has the potential to counter some of the splintering mentioned earlier on, through the capitalist sort of lens, whereby the more we can actually look at the relational nature of the work we all chose to do, through our training groups and also as ways of working, the more likely it is that practitioners, through their very natures, can then work with a wider range of clients because they, themselves have taken on a more integrative or pluralistic approach to the work of being a counsellor and psychotherapist.

What I am suggesting here in some ways already happens. Many a theorist will get their qualification, do their work and then venture out into the world to actually then become the psychotherapist they want to be, because they have realised that the courses themselves not only teach them the basics but also teach them a way of being that can run counter to their own sense of self. Psychotherapy and being a psychotherapist (an area which I will discuss in more depth in Chapter 5) can often mean that when one is on training courses that one must adapt to a way of being and way of acting to pass the criteria laid out within said institution. It is the pain of this inauthenticity which many students feel they must put to one side to complete the requirements presented. This is particularly prevalent for students of difference, be they gender, race, sexuality, ability of even age and so on.

Returning to my idea though, that we build into our trainings some way of understanding the cross-sectional nature of theories and theorists, presentations and schools of thought, what we end up creating is a lattice work effect within our profession. Now, when we talk about maps and territories as ways of understanding the psychology of our clients, what we often have is one map of one, one inch map of a 100-mile area of humanity. What I am proposing here, though, is that in this exploration of inter connectiveness and decolonisation, what we end up doing is creating a lattice map which covers a greater area laid out before us, and therefore runs a greater risk of actually working to the benefit of our wide range of clients who we might meet accordingly.

The lattice effect in psychotherapy as I call it, means practitioners get to experience the inter-connectiveness of our ideologies, for the first time in their careers. This lattice also leave space, it should be said, for other ideas to come into being. It creates areas of knowledge and of dissonance, which also leaves space for where greater, new research and ideas can come into play. This lattice effect does not centralise knowledge in one particular area; it does not pinnacle the ideas of one particular theorist, but it recognises that actually all theorists have something to offer, be it large or small and that this crossover lattice effect replicates the incompleteness, not only of the work that we do with our clients in understanding them, but also of the theorists and their ideas themselves. It offers space for the diverse voices of other groups and nationalities and cultures to come forward and try and fill that aspect of psychology for themselves. It allows us to build within this lattice patchworks of knowledge which can fill up the spaces left through our lack of understanding.

Summary

This chapter has tried to lay the groundwork of just what has happened to our profession as seen through the lens of an outsider, such as myself. I though, must admit to having been as colonised as anybody else within the worlds of psychotherapy and counselling. Like I stated earlier on, I trained in an institution which was very much built around a particular model and a way of working, something which ran all the way through the course and has benefited me to a greater or lesser degree throughout my career.

What has also happened is that it cost me an awful lot of money to train within said institution. The immense amount of money spent on trainings, psychotherapy, supervision, on travel and so on, meant that I left my course tens of thousands of pounds in debt. I was caught up within the capitalism of psychotherapy. Choosing then to work and see clients at the same institution, whilst grounding myself in a way of working, also felt in some ways that I had become institutionalised because it was exceedingly difficult to leave and separate out from the psychological mothership I had become wedded to.

Ways of being, being seen as not transpersonal enough by my peers, were messages I often received along the way, as if there was a singular way of being which I needed to adhere to. It was therefore difficult to challenge any of that through my own sort of work, my own sort of understandings and my own readings. And yet, there was always within a calling to be something more, to be a different, diverse voice to the world of the transpersonal. That I have had the pleasure of doing that, both within and without the institutions I have worked within, says a lot about my own eventual inner resistance to my own complicity, as well as the sometimes-projected super-egoic sense that I had to conform to a way of being.

What I am saying in this example, and what I have said in this chapter, is that stepping out, outside of these structures and ways of being, is often quite difficult for practitioners. Out in the world, we are used to being told how to be, what to do, how to perform, how to act, how to write and what to believe most of all. This is no different within psychotherapy. Even if we believe that we are being told otherwise, if we are being told that there is no one truth, it can often feel as if there kind of is, and we must listen to that.

The ideas here, about decolonisation, therefore lead, I will suggest, to a greater level of anxiety within training courses and within the practitioners themselves and yet, as existentialists have known from time immemorial, that anxiety is a constant, it is always there and in the search for certainty, what we have tried to do more often than not is to create spaces within our psyches whereby certainty and knowledge settle down a sense of self which is quite fragile at the best of times and quite destructive in its search for certainty at the worse.

These next chapters will go into a lot more detail as to how psychotherapy, our trainings, our placements, our charity work, our research and ourselves as practitioners, might work to decolonise across the board. As I said in Chapter 1, this idea that decolonisation is just about reading a distinct set of books, is really quite basic at its best and does nothing to prevent the re-institution, or the unconscious reconstitution of oppressive positions that we all reside within (Table 2.1).

Table 2.1 Decolonising theoretical approaches

	Modality	Theorist	Historical context	Contemporary context
Colonised Approach	Core Themes and Practical Appliances	Very little background or critique is ever provided to where these ideas came from or how they were birthed	The historical context of the time is often ignored, or not known by the practitioner. The ideas have become sanitised by this absence	This is often left to the designs of the practitioner as to whether they wish to engage with the contemporary perspectives around an identity. Often this leads to a rejection of said theory.
Decolonising Theories	Core Themes and Practical Appliances	Closer consideration of the theorist and their influences	The socio and political eras which both influenced the theorists and moulded/ created the theories themselves	Contemporary contexts, meaning the closer consideration of feminist, black, LGBTQ, Disability theorists and their angles on these contemporary theories
Role of Continued Professional Development	• Continued Profession Development Courses have a huge role to play here in teaching practitioners about contemporary ideas around psychoanalysis, CBT, trauma work, Internal Family Systems and others means of working, thereby addressing some of these colonial ideas. • Encouraging the creation of trainings which present a different lens on theorists and theories brings a reality and honesty back to the theories, which their colonisation erased and purified out of them.			

References

Abd Elaziz, H. G. (2021). Against white feminism: Notes on disruption, by Rafia Zakaria. W. W. Norton, 2021. 256 pages. *Women's Studies, 51*(2), 268–270. https://doi.org/10.1080/00497878.2021.2014837

Asante, M. K. (1998). *The Afrocentric idea*. Temple University Press.

Asante, M. K. (2008). *An Afrocentric manifesto* (2nd ed.). Polity Press.

Barenboim, D. (2009). *Everything is connected: The power of music*. W&N.

Beardsworth, S. (2005). Freud's Oedipus and Kristeva's Narcissus: Three heterogeneities. *2Hypatia, 20*(1), 54–77. www.jstor.org/stable/3810843

Benjamin, J. (1990). An outline of intersubjectivity: The development of recognition. *Psychoanalytic Psychology, 7*, 33–46. https://doi.org/10.1037/h0085258

Benjamin, J. (1998). *Shadow of the other*. Routledge.

Bhabha, H. K. (1985). Signs taken for wonders: Questions of ambivalence and authority under a tree outside Delhi. *Critical Inquiry, 12*(1), 144–165.

Bhabha, H. K. (2004). *Location of culture*. Routledge.

Butler, J. (2003). Violence, mourning, politics. *Studies in Gender and Sexuality, 4*(1), 9–37. https://doi.org/10.1080/15240650409349213

Carter, R. E. (2013). *The Kyoto School: An introduction*. SUNY Press Ltd.

Cesaire, A. (2000). *Discourse on colonialism*. Monthly Review Press.

Davies, D., & Neal, C. (1996). *Pink therapy*. Open University Press.

Davies, D., & Neal, C. (2000). *Therapeutic perspectives on working with lesbian, gay and bisexual clients*. Open University Press.

Diangelo, R. (2011). White fragility. *International Journal of Critical Pedagogy, 3*(3), 54–70. file:///C:/Users/CSWAC/Documents/CSWAC/Research articles/White fragility.pdf

Ellis, E. (2021). *The race conversation: An essential guide to creating life-changing dialogue*. Confer Books.

Eminem. (2009). *Eminem: The way I am*. Plume Books.

Freud, S. (1924). The disillusionment of the war. In *Thoughts for the times on war and death*. (Z. Psychoanal (ed.)). Der Untergang Des Ödipuskomplexes G.S. *10*(13), 245–252.

Freud, S. (1930). *Civilisation and its discontents*. Penguin Limited.

Frosh, S. (2005). *Hate and the 'Jewish Science' – Anti-Semitism, Nazism and Psychoanalysis*. Palgrave Macmillan.

Harvey, J. (2022). 'The kaleidoscopic conditions' of John Akomfrah's Stuart Hall. *Transnational Screens, 13*(2), 83–95. https://doi.org/10.1080/25785273.2022.2061130

Haug, F. (2008). Memory work. *Australian Feminist Studies, 23*(58), 537–541. https://doi.org/10.1080/08164640802433498

Hauser, T. (2021). *Muhammad Ali: His life and times*. Portico.

Havsteen-Franklin, D. (2007). Re-visiting Freud, Jewishness and the other. *Psychotherapy and Politics International, 5*(2), 116–129. https://doi.org/10.1002/ppi.130

Homo, E. (1992). *Friedrich Nietzsche*. Penguin Classics.

Inayat Khan, H. (1996). *The mysticism of sound and music: The Sufi teaching of Hazrat Inayat Khan*. Shambhala Publications Inc.

Jacobs, M. (2003). *Sigmund Freud – Key figures in counselling and psychotherapy* (2nd ed.). Sage Publications.

Jefferson, M. (2015). FGM/Cutting: Contextualising recent legal developments. *The Journal of Criminal Law, 79*(6), 411–421. https://doi.org/10.1177/0022018315614447

Kakar, S. (2012). *The inner world: A psychoanalytic study of childhood and society in India* (4th ed.). OUP India.

Karatzas, K. D., & Каратзас, К. Д. (2015). *The use of passive resistance during the civil rights movement: An interpretation [ИСПОЛЬЗОВАНИЕ ПАССИВНОГО СОПРОТИВЛЕНИЯ В ХОДЕ ДВИЖЕНИЯ В ЗАЩИТУ ГРАЖДАНСКИХ ПРАВ: АНАЛИЗ].* https://doi.org/10.15688/jvolsu4.2016.1.5

Kernberg, O. F. (2002). Unresolved issues in the psychoanalytic theory of homosexuality and bisexuality. *Journal of Gay & Lesbian Psychotherapy, 6*(1), 9–27. https://doi.org/10.1300/J236v06n01_02

Kirschner, S. R. (2012). How not to other the other (and similarly impossible goals): Scenes from a psychoanalytic clinic and an inclusive classroom. *Journal of Theoretical and Philosophical Psychology, 32*(4), 214–229. https://doi.org/10.1037/a0030158

Kitaro, N. (1989). *Last writings: Nothingness and the religious worldview* (D. A. Dilworth (ed.)). University of Hawaii Press.

Laub, D., & Lee, S. (2003). Thanatos and massive psychic trauma: The impact of the death instinct on knowing, remembering, and forgetting. *Journal of the American Psychoanalytic Association, 51*(2), 433–464.

Litvinova, D. (2018). *LGBT hate crimes double in Russia after ban on "gay propaganda."* Reuters Online. www.reuters.com/article/us-russia-lgbt-crime/lgbt-hate-crimes-double-in-russia-after-ban-on-gay-propaganda-idUSKBN1DL2FM

Lynn, M., & Adrienne, D. D. (2013). *Handbook of critical race theory in education.* Routledge.

Matias, C. E., Viesca, K. M., Garrison-Wade, D. F., Tandon, M., & Galindo, R. (2014). "What is Critical Whiteness Doing in OUR Nice Field like Critical Race Theory?" Applying CRT and CWS to understand the white imaginations of white teacher candidates. *Equity and Excellence in Education, 47*(3). https://doi.org/10.1080/10665684.2014.933692

McCann, H. (2019). *Queer theory now: From foundations to futures* (1st ed.). Red Globe Press.

Memmi, A. (1974). *The colonizer and the colonized.* Souvenir Press.

Merrick, R., & White, N. (2021). *United Nations experts condemn 'shocking' race report and call for commission to be scrapped.* Independent Online. www.independent.co.uk/news/uk/politics/race-report-un-boris-johnson-commission-b1833671.html

Messner, M. A. (2011). The privilege of teaching about privilege. *Sociological Perspectives, 54*(1), 3–13. https://doi.org/10.1525/sop.2011.54.1.3

Mignolo, W. D., & Walsh, C. (2018). *On decoloniality: Concepts, analytics, praxis.* Duke University Press.

Monteiro-Ferreira, A. M. (2005). Reevaluating Zulu religion: An Afrocentric analysis. *Journal of Black Studies, 35*(3), 347–363. https://doi.org/10.1177/0021934704263127

Moon, D. G., & Holling, M. A. (2020). "White supremacy in heels": (White) feminism, white supremacy, and discursive violence. *Communication and Critical/ Cultural Studies, 17*(2), 253–260. https://doi.org/10.1080/14791420.2020.1770819

Moore, G. (2010). Imperial white: Race, diaspora and the British Empire/enacting Englishness in the Victorian period: Colonialism and the politics of performance. *Journal of Victorian Culture, 15*(3), 409–413. https://doi.org/10.1080/13555502.2010.519548

Morland, I., & Willox, A. (Eds.). (2005). *Queer theory: Readers in cultural Criticism.* Palgrave.

Nishitani, K. (1981). Ontology and utterance. *Philosophy East and West, 31*(1), 29–43.

Ogden, T. H. (2004). On holding and containing, being and dreaming. *The International Journal of Psycho-Analysis, 85*(Pt 6), 1349–1364. www.ncbi.nlm.nih.gov/pubmed/15801512

Otele, O. (2012). Bristol, slavery and the politics of representation: The Slave Trade Gallery in the Bristol Museum. *Social Semiotics*, *22*(2), 155–172. https://doi.org/10.1080/10350 330.2012.665231

Pereira, J. L. (2016). The Roman Catholic Church and Slavery in José Evaristo d'Almeida's O Escravo (The Slave). *Dialog*, *55*(3), 239–246. https://doi.org/10.1111/dial.12260

Plett Usher, B., & Tawfik, N. (2023). *Tyre Nichols: Mother describes her grief at dying son's bedside*. BBC News Online. www.bbc.co.uk/news/world-us-canada-64428427

Prideaux, S. (2018). *I am dynamite!: A life of Friedrich Nietzsche*. Faber & Faber.

Rutledge, D. (2018). *Neo-Nazis are claiming Nietzsche as their own, but what does his philosophy really say?* News Online. www.abc.net.au/news/2018-10-21/nietzsche-and-the-alt-right/10382460

Said, E. (1993a). Representations of an intellectual lecture 2: Holding nations and traditions at bay. *Reith Lectures*, June, 1–8.

Said, E. (1993b). Representations of an intellectual lecture 3: Intellectual exiles. *Reith Lectures*, July, 1–8.

Said, E. (2003). *Freud and the Non-European*. Verso.

Saini, A. (2019). *Superior: The return of race science*. Harper Collins Publishers.

Sayer, A. (2010). Reductionism in social science. In *Questioning nineteenth-century assumptions about knowledge: II: Reductionism, September 2005* (pp. 5–56).

Schopenhauer, A. (2020). *The world as will and representation*. Cambridge University Press.

Shotwell, A. (2021). *Twitter reminds NYT women exist after H.G. Wells credited with creating sci-fi*. The Mary Sue. www.themarysue.com/new-york-times-mary-shelley-scifi-hg-wells/

Spivak, G. C. (1988). Can the subaltern speak? In *Marxism and the interpretation of culture* (pp. 271–312). https://doi.org/10.1590/S0102-44501999000200012

Spivak, G. C. (1993). Echo. *New Literary History*, *24*(1), 17–43.

Spivak, G. C. (2015). Cultural pluralism? *Philosophy and Social Criticism*, *42*(4–5), 448–455. https://doi.org/10.1177/0191453715602993

Stevens, A. (1990). *On Jung*. Penguin Limited.

Tanaka, Y. (2010). Philosophy of nothingness and process theology. *Diogenes*, *57*(3), 20–34. https://doi.org/10.1177/0392192111415766

Tomarchio, J. (2002). Aquinas's concept of infinity. *Journal of the History of Philosophy*, *40*(2), 163–187.

Toner, P. (2010). St. Thomas Aquinas on death and the separated soul. *Pacific Philosophical Quarterly*, *91*(4), 587–599. https://doi.org/10.1111/j.1468-0114.2010.01379.x

Turner, D. D. L. (2018). You shall not replace us!: White supremacy, psychotherapy and decolonisation. *Journal of Critical Psychology Counselling and Psychotherapy*, *18*(1), 1–12.

Turner, D. D. L. (2023). *The psychology of supremacy*. Routledge.

Various. (2021). *Defaced Marcus Rashford mural covered in supportive notes*. BBC News. www.bbc.co.uk/news/uk-england-manchester-57806142

Verges, F. (2021). *A decolonial feminism*. Pluto Press.

Wade, L. (2012). Learning from "Female Genital Mutilation": Lessons from 30 years of academic discourse. *Ethnicities*, *12*(1), 26–49. https://doi.org/10.1177/1468796811419603

Washburn, M. (1995). *The ego and the dynamic ground: A transpersonal theory of human development*. State University of New York Press.

Wilber, K. (1989). *The spectrum of consciousness*. Quest Books. Theosophical Publishing House.

Chapter 3

Decolonising training

Introduction

In the year 2000, I started out on my long journey training to become a counsellor and psychotherapist. The initial aim though was not actually to train to become a practitioner at all. In the year 1998, at the end of a long relationship, I had descended down a personal route which had led to behaviours and forms of self-destruction which underlined a deeper level of psychological distress. On one particular day, a former friend of mine on hearing my story and hearing some of the things that I was doing during this period of time, suggested that I seek out some psychotherapeutic help. A bell went off inside my mind on hearing that suggestion because psychotherapy, as it has been for many people, was not something that was ever on my radar as a person or as an individual.

I subsequently sought out therapy from my local GP service and had to wait a mere four weeks to see somebody, a woman who sat me down, did a long and intense assessment of me and decided that, yes, I could benefit from working with somebody over a period of time. That first experience of therapy was so positive that I decided then to explore myself on a course in West London. That exploration was supposed to be just one year but, of course, I did not only that Foundational Year in counselling and psychotherapy, but I enjoyed the self-exploration to such a degree that I decided to stay and see how far I could go, ending up with the career that I have now as a counsellor and psychotherapist.

The training doors that I opened up along the way were not based upon some sort of childhood need to become a professional psychotherapist; that access point did not really exist. The need for myself to become a practitioner was driven by something internal. I did not see Therapists of Colour who were doing this great work and were out in the public eye. I did not read many of the theorists of therapists and counsellors of difference, be they feminist, disability theorists, theorists working with class or any other form of difference, to inspire me to therefore become a practitioner myself. My drive to become a professional was very much driven by an inner distress and a need to develop and find myself in a world where I had become quite lost.

DOI: 10.4324/9781032614342-3

There was a massive cost to this though. During the time of my training, although I managed to pay all of my fees eventually, I ended up also incurring debts of around £20,000 which back in 2005, when I finally finished my initial training, was a lot of money. The second cost to this involved the fact that I was absolutely exhausted by the end of 5 years of training. Working full-time, as well as doing a 'part-time course' (a course which although was one day a week needed another day or day and a half to incorporate one's own therapy, placements, reading and essay writing), meant that by the end of my time of training I was pretty much on my knees, thoroughly drained dry and exhausted by the whole experience.

The reason I discuss this is to highlight that whilst part of this exhaustion was psychological, much of it also speaks to the difficulties experienced by persons of difference, be they based around class or of race with regard to accessing courses within the global north.

Our trainings are very much embedded within a capitalist structure. They have very much become a part of the fabric whereby profits need to be made in order to be able to pay for the directors and the shareholders or the superiors of whichever organisation, university or private school is providing said service. This therefore means that our trainings have lost or have sold a bit of their moralistic soul to the highest capitalistic bidder in order for them to survive. This sad state of affairs is one of the reasons why so many trainings marginalise difference and otherness.

As stated in the last chapter, the world of psychotherapy as such, and the theories that we talk about, and the ways that we practice, have themselves become commodified and structured within a colonial capitalist framework. Our trainings are therefore no less susceptible to being manipulated in the same fashion. For example, the costs to study in some modalities, such as EMDR are prohibitive to a good number of therapists of difference, given that they may have already paid out for a first training of some kind and may not have the funding left to finish said subsequent course (Various, 2023a). This therefore limits, and creates an economy of scale, whereby only certain practitioners get to train and therefore get to charge the highest rates for their services, given the lack of people available to provide them.

The reductionism around the types of therapies taught on training courses has also led to certain subgroups within modalities forming, normally around patriarchal structures. To make clearer my point, the fact that the UKCP lists some 70 psychotherapy courses, and that the BACP has many more, whilst probably very useful, also says a lot about how profitable it is to run such courses (Various, 2023c). We are often as training organisations, encouraged to focus in on the next great psychological fad, and in doing so we look to market out great idea, our great adaptation of said psychological theory or system, promoting it through papers, workshops, films and other avenues in order to make a great deal of money for our organisations, whilst suggesting that we also are providing some sustenance and care for those who may well best benefit.

The marketisation of areas of research such as trauma, and the plethora of trauma workshops which exist in the current era, and the preponderance of experts who have emerged accordingly, is perhaps one area where this appears (Bader-johansson et al., 2015; Barnes, 2016; van der Kolk, 2015). This is not to say that trauma is not a key area to look at. My suggestion here is there may be a bit of financial overkill by those who seem to suggest that they have something new to say, when actually all that is being done is a repetition of what has gone on before.

The commodification therefore of psychotherapy education, although suggested here as if it has come from nowhere, is actually nothing new. The world of education in the United Kingdom, for example, has always been embedded within a financial system. The boarding school system, for example, is a perfect example of this and, although used a lot here in Europe, it is something which has been parcelled out to the United States, where they have a suitable number of private schools. The commodification of schooling has become so attractive that often students from parts of Africa, Asia, the Far East, Middle East and the former Eastern Bloc, have parents from these areas who will send their children to western boarding schools because they have been told and encouraged that that is where the best schooling resides (Duffell, 2014; Schaverien, 2004).

I have written in past texts about the nature of boarding schools from a psychological perspective but incorporating some of these ideas now, with regard to the commodification of education, it is important for us to recognise that actually the marginalisation of those who cannot afford said education has been going on for hundreds of years.

For the purpose of this chapter on psychotherapy education, it is important to recognise that any form of decolonisation does not just involve a consideration of the qualification of psychotherapy trainings. It also has to move beyond just the tokenistic attempts to include trainers of colour or of difference on our courses. It has to go that bit deeper and explore just how the various aspects of our trainings have become colonised, and what we might do in order to shift and change the narratives of said colonisation.

This chapter will therefore explore these areas form three different perspectives. The first one will be the trainer. Within this section, there will be a consideration of just how the trainers are chosen, why they are chosen, where they are chosen and what we might do in order to meet the varying demographics our training courses embody within their student faculties. The second part will of course be the training institutions themselves, looking at just how they work, the ways in which they recruit, exploring how these might be in some ways quite exclusive. Whilst also looking at how we might, as a collective, develop ways and means which encourage our training courses to actually bring on board a wider variety of names, faces, voices and ideas. The third part though, will be training post qualifying. This perhaps is one of the trickiest areas to consider. We all need to undertake Continued Professional Development (CPD). Yet, how we do this and what we do is often left in a place of real flexibility and inconsistency as well. There are numerous examples of students who are fairly capable and yet who might like to undertake some of the more expensive trainings that might lead them to obtain places within the National Health Service (NHS). Yet, who are unable to do so because of the capitalising of CPD programmes in and around the country. Firstly, it is important for us to look at how education has become colonised in a bit more detail to set the background to this chapter.

The colonisation of education

On doing research for this book, a few key areas came up which surprised me. For example, in the United Kingdom it was only in 1972 that the school leaving age was raised to 16, having been at 15 before this (Various, 2023b). Going further back, it was only in 1944 when the Education Act was established which thereby made councils put together packages for children to be educated at school up until the age of 15 (Bridges, 1945). All of these moves away from the use of children in workplaces up and down the country, the sweat houses and the exploitation of children in order to create profits for the owners.

The marginalisation of certain groups from education is something which is not just limited to the global north. The fact that in 2020, according to a BBC news report there were up to 130,000,000 girls around the world who had no access to education, is a major factor in the maintenance of patriarchal structures in certain countries (Various, 2020). The wonderful and important Malala Yousufzai has written and spoken extensively around the world about patriarchal structure's fear of an educated, informed and therefore intellectually empowered woman (Various, 2019b).

In the great programme Small Axe, as directed and produced by Steve McQueen, in the episode called Education he explores the marginalisation of the first generation of Persons of Colour from the educational system here in the United Kingdom (McQueen, 2020). He also explores the underlying layers of racism which inhabited and played a leading role in some of the decisions made within education departments in councils and how these would have then had a subsequent impact on those around them from minority groupings.

The weight of these types of interventions around the paucity of education for certain groupings should not be underestimated. Within the United Kingdom, even to this day, the university attainment gaps for minority students show that black students, or for the study students from a Black and Multi-Ethnic background were 13% more likely to drop out from university as compared to their white counterparts (Various, 2019a). Issues of race, class and gender often intersect in the marginalisation of certain groupings from the educational system and it is interesting that on our training courses this pattern is often repeated, whereby a good number of students of colour, and of gender difference, and of sexual difference, and of class difference as well, often struggle more so than any other groups to make their way through the educational structures.

What I am saying here is that education as a structure has always been hierarchical. There has always been the input of the colonial and capitalist systems, together with that of the patriarchy, and this has always led to certain groups of people being excluded. To therefore understand some of the systemic barriers which are already in place around education, and which a suitable number of our students bring onto our counselling and psychotherapy courses, it is essential for us to understand and explore the institutional internalisations they all will walk with.

To emphasise my point about how the colonisation of education actually then impacts on the readiness or ability of various students to access psychotherapy and counselling trainings, I am going to offer you two fairly obvious examples:

> The first one is of a woman named Sarah. She is 43 years of age, the mother of three children. She has worked all her life in social work and was looking to adapt her skills and incorporate counselling and psychotherapy into her working life with the aim of taking on private clients alongside her other work and reducing her social work down to part-time. From a working-class background, the idea of going back to train, although daunting, was not impossible for her, given that she had studied and worked incredibly hard to go back to university in between the birth of her first and second children. The difficulty though, for her was access. Sarah undertook a Level 2 and then a Level 3 counselling course through a major organisation, courses which she struggled to find funding for, having to borrow money from family. The support of her family therefore became integral to her ability to complete said course.
>
> At the end of the Level 3 course, though, Sarah wanted to move onto a postgraduate diploma course at a major university. The problem with this course and the fact it was only a two-year course, was that it meant that she was unable to obtain a student loan for said course as it did not fit the criteria required for her to gain access to funding. Sarah considered her options and went back to undertake a Level 4 course which she could find funding for and where the course allowed her to pay in regular instalments, so she was not left too much out of pocket.
>
> This contrasts though with another student's story that I have come across, which is a common one and this is a student, Elizabeth. Elizabeth was the same age as Sarah, in her early forties and had two children. She had worked successfully in a major organisation within London and had taken time out to care for her children who were both still quite young. Her decision to retrain meant that the family, including her husband, had to re-organise their finances to provide for the course that Elizabeth wanted to undertake. This was no problem for them because her husband, who had a fairly well-established job in the city of London, was therefore able to finance and support the family whilst his wife retrained. Elizabeth then undertook a four-year course in a training organisation which she completed successfully.

The issue with these examples is not to ascertain who would be the better counsellor or therapist, it is not to say that one route is better than the other. It is to provide evidence of the fact that there is a certain financial benchmark which potential students' needs to achieve or hit before they can even access our courses here in the United Kingdom. The commodification of education at all varying levels, including at the university level, is something which is exclusionary and leaves a good number of potential students fighting and struggling or, like myself, incurring huge amounts of debt in order to obtain access to the courses they so wish to inhabit and the careers for which they are probably perfectly well suited.

In doing this to our profession, in allowing our profession and our trainings to be co-opted by capitalism, then what we are doing is not just denying access to those who might be good practitioners, but we are also playing into something I discussed in Chapter 2. We have ended up preventing those of difference who could benefit from counselling and psychotherapy, the right to be seen and in a psychotherapeutic relationship with, those practitioners from similar backgrounds. The number of students, practitioners of colour who want to know how I did it, how I got to this stage (and they are not just talking about the psychological challenges, they are talking about the financial and other structural challenges which we all have to undertake), is astonishing. The number of working class clients who discussed with myself the fact that they often felt that there would be nobody like themselves in the psychotherapy field because it was always seen to be so elitist, so they are so incredibly surprised when they encounter therapists from working class backgrounds who have similar experiences to themselves, not always the same because that is not what this is about, but who they can relate to, and this is important, who they feel safe with.

In the commodification, the capitalisation or the commercial colonisation of psychotherapy, what we end up doing is recreating from the very first stages that a person (potential student, or potential client) walks into the door, the exclusion and the marginalisation they have experienced on the outside, within our very institutions.

The colonised trainer

Interestingly, one of the more extraordinary experiences that I have had whilst exploring this book, is having to recognise that a sizeable number of the people that I was taught by whilst on training were middle class and older, white men. Given that the profession here in the United Kingdom in the majority is female and white, it is extraordinary that this should happen at all, and makes me wonder what happens at a certain level that perfectly acceptable women educators therefore find it very difficult to establish themselves on training courses in psychotherapy and counselling, given they are as educated in their own right. A mirror for other industries I would.

This is perhaps more pronounced when we come to other forms of difference and diversity, where around the country the number of trainers from the LGBTQ community, or of colour, or another ability, in no way reflects the wider societal structures within which our profession is embedded. Our trainers and our training organisations have therefore, for some reason, positioned themselves as statutes of marginalisation, therefore leaving on the outside those of difference who could diversify the profession to some degree. The importance of this though, should not be underestimated because it is not just about who we have on our training courses, and what their backgrounds are, it is also about the types of theory that they teach and also how it is taught. What I mean by this is explained in the following example:

> Joe was a practitioner at a university in the north of England. He told me a story whereby him and his three male colleagues were teaching on a course in an area of the country where there was a high preponderance of working class and minority students. They were often questioned as to why it was that the teaching faculty at said university was all white and male, yet given that the person in charge of the counselling service was in his late sixties, the questions were often batted back and used in a more pathological way to explore meaning and difference within the group and cohort itself.
>
> When it came to the teachings themselves, although there was an effort to discuss issues around say LGBTQ experiences through a psychodynamic lens, what would often happen is that these heterosexual older, while men would frame the exploration through a psychodynamic lens which was also quite heteronormative and marginalising. These experiences, on occasion, led to students from the LGBTQ community deciding to leave or to seek out assistance and help elsewhere because they felt unseen and therefore unsafe on their courses.

The importance of this, and the importance of recognising the trainer as the coloniser, is not so much to critique the trainer, Joe, but is to recognise the limitation of the trainer and therefore the training itself. I sometimes get asked, for example, to speak about issues of working with children and difference and diversity, more often than not by women who have far more experience of working with children than I do. My answer is always that I am not the right person. My statement being to empower those who have far more knowledge than I do in this, or in any other, particular area. In the opposite way to that of Joe's colleagues, who decided to take it upon themselves to deliver a lecture on a topic area that they knew little about and has no personal experience of, the limitations of the training therefore would lead to a sense of marginalisation.

The second part to it is this, trainings have an obligation, I will suggest, in fact a moral obligation if I go that bit further, to provide trainers who model and inhabit the training areas for which they are proficient and which are being taught on said courses and for which they want their trainees to learn from. This is no different to practitioners working within their own areas of expertise, and being required to clearly state to clients when they are not experts with certain presentations, as per the BACP Code of Ethics (British Association for Counselling and Psychotherapy, 2018). Otherwise, what happens is the trainings themselves, through the lens of the trainers then becomes tokenistic and tick-boxy and miss the point to some degree whilst also reinforcing structural and institutional issues of power, prejudice and marginalisation that have been experienced by varying groups accordingly.

As an example, in 2021, I did some work for a small private centre in Somerset, who were running a special day on intersectionality. Having done a presentation and answered some questions around privilege and otherness, in a break a student of colour came up to me and said,

> Dr Turner, that is the first time in my 40 years in any environment, that I have ever been taught by somebody of colour.

His statement is not an uncommon one, but what touched me in particular was the tears in his eyes, as he then went on to tell me about how much it mattered to him that I was there and also how deeply impactive it was, not just to see a person of difference, a person of colour, a person from a similar racial and cultural background as himself, talk and act in a way which was authentically himself and not perform to try and be a white, middle class, older lecturer psychotherapist. The tears in his eyes spoke to me also of that deep seated longing to be witnessed and mirrored in such a way, that we often as persons of difference repress, without even realising we are doing so, in order to fit in with some other kind of cultural narrative.

The importance of this example is obvious. A student of colour, although not from the same city as myself, had incorporated for the very first time in his career a lecturer of colour and this unknown desire had come to the surface and burst like a bubble from the base of a can of Coke. The emotions that I experienced on standing with this man will stay with me forever. The fact that I am a role model for students of colour around the country is not lost upon myself. In the same says that I am sure that some of the more prominent names in the LGBTQ community provide a beacon for students on varying courses round the country, in the same way that feminists within our profession are standard bearers from a variety of backgrounds across our organisations, and in the same way that those who are otherwise able, or who are neurodiverse, provide a framework and a way of being and understanding for others within our profession.

This is vastly different, though, to how our profession has performed in many of the generations gone. As stated early on in this book, often what we are taught is from a very white middle class, patriarchal perspective, and whilst there are a number of women presented as well, the Melanie Klien's, the Anna Freud's and the Emma Jung's, these are very much few and far between. Our training courses do not always explore the words of the Jessica Benjamin's, the de Beauvoir's and the Judith Butler's (Beauvoir, 2010; Benjamin, 1990; Butler, 1999).

The same could be said for how we recruit trainers, in that we are still very much unconsciously enticed to recruit from within that patriarchal structure of white heteronormative masculinity. Looking at how this can actually happen, before developing ways and means to counteract some of this, is central so that not only we are diversifying the range of trainers on our courses, so shifting the narrative towards a more diversified profession which reflects the greater range of Others within our client pools, plural.

The second reason for this is the systemisation of psychotherapy trainers then becomes a bottle neck to knowledge, as anything that we discuss and explore will always be filtered through that same white, male, patriarchal lens. We may also want to look at not just recruiting a more diverse range of trainers, but also providing training for said trainers so that they too could understand the internalised systems which inhabit their identities. The sheer number of courses that I have been invited to explore these issues since George Floyd was murdered in 2020, suggests to me that there is a move towards doing this, whereby training courses are starting to explore systems of whiteness, for example, within their training cohorts, systems of exclusion and how they might better work with issues of privilege and otherness in a holding and contained fashion. This is not to say that myself and others have all these answers to hand. What it is to say, though, is that we recognise that there is an effort being made to actually address a massive problem which had sat on the table, clearly seen but unseen until we all had to slow down and take a good hard look at our racism, our misogyny, our homophobia and other isms and obias.

It is also important to recognise the role of prejudice in all of this discussion. As discussed by Weil and Piaget (1951) in his work in the early days of psychotherapy, prejudice forms our identity. We learn to know who we are by our prejudices against the other, and we go through varying stages of development from childhood onwards all through our lives, where we form in groups and out groups accordingly as we simultaneously form and deconstruct and reform and deconstruct identities ad infinitum. This will be no different for any trainer on our courses. They too will have been moulded, formed, reconstructed and formed before they came through their own trainings, whilst they were in their own trainings and beyond their own trainings as they develop and become psychotherapists and lecturers.

As McDermott (2008) states in his original paper published in The Psychotherapist, that most often for students their idea of training is that you study, get your certificate, and that is it. His reality, and I agree with this, is that it is at the stage of qualifying that one starts to really learn what it is to be a Psychotherapist. There is a vast difference from that beginning state of being a neonate, a student, to becoming a Psychotherapist with 20- or 30-years' experience. One's identity would have changed and developed at numerous stages through that full process. Yet, what it also states is in order to achieve that initial goal of gaining one's certification, that one has to jump through a certain number of pre-determined hoops which show that we are capable of maintaining the basic standards within our profession. This though does lead to a sense that we end up churning out a systemised production line of similar characters if we are not careful. It is only post that qualifying stage, that a sizeable number of practitioners find themselves and bring themselves back into the game of what it is for them to be a practitioner and therefore what it is for them to work with certain demographics and types of clients that they resonate with in that more authentic state.

So, when I say that it is the same for trainers, it is for them to actually explore how they have become systematised over time in what ways might they put down their unique perspectives on counselling and psychotherapy in order to fit in within the systemic nature of psychotherapy trainers. So, if that is the case what is it that then gets lost or put to one side that students, or that their faculty, their colleagues, could use when working with fellow students and practitioners. Any sort of decolonisation of the trainer has to involve not just brining in diverse faces to meet quotas as pre-described by the organisation. It also has to recognise that those voices, those faces, may also have been colonised themselves because they are part of said system, as none of us are separate from it. So, only by actually working on those systemisations within ourselves can we then fully embrace and be the diverse names and voices and faces that our professions needs, deserves, and actually really, genuinely wants, under the surface. Otherwise, what we end up with is a tokenisation of training diversity, where we go from just having one or two hours on a training course to do with difference, to providing one non-white face who will provide a lecture on difference or providing just one person of sexual or gender difference to talk about their issues, never to be seen again.

There are many ways to fully embody this.

I met a lecturer whilst running a course in the north of England. This lecturer was a white man who told me of his fear of getting things wrong when talking about difference and diversity on his course. He said that being seen as a white man meant that he often got a lot of vitriol from not just some of his colleagues, the majority of whom were female, but also from many of the students on his course. When we looked at this, one of the things that struck me was the strength of this gentleman, his manner and mannerisms, the way he carried himself and so onwards.

At some point, I asked him to tell me a bit more about his background and the gentleman actually informed me that he was from a working-class town in the northwest of England. His father had worked away a lot in the mines in Yorkshire and had suffered an awful lot during the Thatcher years when she fought against the miners' strikes in an attempt to break the backs of the unions. Their family grew up fairly poor subsequent to that and he was fortunate enough to get good enough grades to go to a decent secondary school, leading him to get himself a good enough degree when he went to university.

I asked the gentleman what was it about his story that mean he did not feel able to bring his working-class background to his course, because that sort of story would have been massive for his cohort to hear about. The gentleman talked about his own shame at some of the narrative, at some of the story. His sadness of what he watched his parents go through, their struggle to provide for himself and his sister and yet his pride at them for actually undertaking such a long and ongoing struggle and getting to the end of said line.

My encouragement for that gentleman was to be slightly braver in framing any sort of expression or exploration around difference, around his own personalised experience of being an outsider. 'We all have one', I said to him and when we leave it to one side then what we are often left with when working with students and also our colleagues, is to hold their projections upon us as to who we represent and what we might be. 'In my own talk', I said to him, 'When I speak about the pain of Blackness, the pain of what it is to be a man of colour, the times I have been let down, the endurances of racism, and so on, what often happens is it touches people. So, through touching others, be they students or colleagues, what we end up doing is building a bridge of empathy between them and us. And those who refuse to feel that empathy for the human suffering of another person? Fuck 'em!'

The importance of an example like this is that when working with difference and decolonising the trainer, what we are starting to do is to rehumanise who we are as trainers. It is not that we are going to be able to get away from the level of projection that is placed upon us as trainers in counselling and psychotherapy, because that needs to be there, and we often need to be seen as the negative parent. What we also need to be seen as is a human being and that is important for those of us, or the parts of us, which have endured marginalisation.

The other side of the coin though is also important, and that is when we consider the colonised nature of being the other and how, when you are a lecturer or tutor of difference, old messages may still reside under the surface or behind the persona. These may well inhabit or inhibit one's ability to actually stand up and be a lecturer in organisations and institutions which are seen as predominantly patriarchal, predominantly white.

To offer you an example from my own experience, I remember a respectable number of years ago now, being invited to give my first ever lecture on a course. Not knowing how to give a lecture, not knowing if I should give a lecture, I was flattered to even be asked to provide information around a certain topic area. Even that flattery talks a lot about how disempowered I was, newly entering this game of being a lecturer. My preparations for said lecture were poor; I drew up some very brief handouts, I used some flipchart paper which I wrote on as part of the lecture, and I tried to impart some knowledge in as ill-prepared a way as I could have done. When I sat and gave the lecture, I was incredibly anxious and nervous, being the only non-white face in a room full of white men and women and finding it incredibly difficult to express myself. Even my body reacted. I broke out in a sweat which mean that I had droplets of water dripping from my armpits and across my forehead in a way that was probably not that attractive for those sitting and watching me in those moments. The two and a half hours were some of the most painful hours of my life. I never wanted to give a lecture again.

The feedback from the lecture of course matched my own individual experience. Whereby I was told that although the student cohort liked me, they felt I needed to be better prepared to give a lecture in the future on any topic at all. It took this all to therapy where we looked at performance anxiety and imposter syndrome.

Considerations of imposter syndrome have ranged within the world of psychology and psychotherapy for a good number of years now (Bothello & Roulet, 2019; Wilkinson, 2020). One angle to consider is that performance anxiety often involves the internalised experience of being an outsider being invited in to provide evidence and knowledge, in contrast to contrast the internalisation that one is not worthy to even hold said information.

The sense that one is already less than, is based around the idea that we have not been mirrored, we do not see lecturers of our own sort of similarity or difference, means that standing up and being 'the first' can feel incredibly daunting for those who were previously sat on the outside. Performance anxiety is another similar facet of this internalised debate, emergent as it has to counteract the aspect of a socially constructed superego which actually believes that one should not have a voice (Egilmez & Orum, 2018). The idea of asking a man of colour to speak up on a topic, like it might be for a woman or for other types of difference to stand and speak in front of peers from a majority culture, invites a certain struggle within the other to actually find that voice and find a way of safely inhabiting and expressing the knowledge from that voice in a way which will not lead for them to be vilified or/and destroyed.

Persons of difference have often been taught from a very early age that they should not speak up, that they should be seen and not heard, that they should know their place, that they should speak softly when in the presence of their elders, their betters, the higher class, or those with better ability (Andrews & Palmer, 2013; Kinouani, 2020; Mazzei, 2008). They may have also internalised other aspects from their own schooling as the outsider, for examples, the sense that they are stupid, dumb, idiotic, because they carry some sort of neurodiversity. So, to therefore to be asked to speak up and talk out and give a lecture can feel like the most challenging thing in the world when you have been marked out as the other and labelled as less than.

To end my own personal narrative, undertaking a course in public speaking as part of my doctorate helped hugely. It was only a one-day workshop, and to be honest although I was given some helpful tips about learning your material and so on, there was very little that really stands out for me, except for one small exercise. The exercise was this: I was invited to do some research and pick out three public speakers that I admired and respected and build my way of working and being as a lecture, around them.

Whilst I was on my doctorate though, I decided to actually tweak the exercise and make it more culturally specific to myself. It would not have served me to track the ways of speaking and talking as used by the Emmy Van Deurzen's, the Mick Cooper's or the Windy Dryden's of the world. It would not have helped me to sit and look at old clips of Carl Rogers or Carl Jung or of R. D. Lang and build myself upon them. It had to resonate from myself. I therefore chose Chris Rock, the comedian, T. D. Jakes, the pastor in America and Oprah Winfrey. I spent time watching their delivery, how they worked, how they looked when they spoke and where they stood, and how they enraptured an audience. This taught me an awful lot about how I might be, how I could be, how I wanted to be as a lecturer going forward. Selecting culturally specific, gender specific, sexuality specific or minority specific idols helps those of difference who are being encouraged to become trainers to be the trainers that they want to be.

Ultimately, being a lecturer is phenomenological. The lecturer is a phenomenological construct, so therefore there is no one way to be that construct. This is why in my talks I try and diversity how I deliver material. This is why in my talks I express myself in a way which is connecting, emotional, fiery and dynamic. But this journey from the timid, colonised amateur lecturer, who could not find a way of expressing himself without breaking out in globules of sweat, to the individual right now who is racked with nerves before he talks but finds the fire and the passion to deliver what he wants to say; that journey of decolonisation for the other as a trainer involves recognising and divesting oneself of the internalisations of whiteness and patriarchy simultaneously.

Decolonising training methods

This then leads into the next stage of this exploration about how we might work with decolonisation on our training. As I have already stated, and am happy to restate again, decolonisation is not just about incorporating one or two key lectures, and also including the rewriting of book reading lists. If we are going to decolonise the trainer, and what it means to be a trainer on a course and if we are going to bring the trainer more into a relationship with the training organisation and the students, then what we also need to do is diversify the ways in which they can deliver their material. Now, this is something which a respectable number of courses in some ways already do. Universities though, in the past, had become a bit staid and caught in bit of a pattern of lecturing, mini workshops, and the occasional weekend in their delivery. There was extraordinarily little space on our training courses within the university sector for a more experiential exploration of what it is to be a counsellor or psychotherapist, something I advocate highly for. But where there is something of benefit, which the university sector has to offer, and which the private sector could perhaps work to incorporate, is the encouragement to diversify ways of teaching in lecture formats, or Blended Learning as it is called.

A fairly recent term, as discussed in a text by Tucker, Wycoff and Green, Blended Learning involves the utilisation of a number of different means and ways of expressing information in the classroom (Tucker et al., 2016). The importance of this involves the recognition that so many of our students absorb information in diverse ways. The more neurodiverse students, for example those who have dyslexia or have dyspraxia may well find creative means of being taught more beneficial to the standard, old fashioned, man at the front reading from a script like of lecture so many of us would have been raised with.

When I was being trained as a therapist, a single person delivered the vast majority of lectures, normally male, who stood or sat at the front of the class, talking for an hour before fielding a few questions for maybe 30 minutes. That is just one way of being taught and sits very much within the very rigid ideals of education which have existed for hundreds of years. Knowledge though can be imparted not just by being talked at by somebody reading a set of papers; it can be imparted through music, through the arts, through small group work, through actually using our creativity as practitioners, as artists and psychotherapists, to therefore work with an impact knowledge in ways and means which students from varying backgrounds will pick up according to their individual learning styles.

Given that there are diverse learning styles, experiential workshops can also become especially useful and important in enhancing the learning experience of students coming through our trainings. This is important to recognise, as I am often astonished and simultaneously pleased by the number of students who perhaps may struggle more with the academic content on a course, but yet who then blossom when they encounter a weekend say on body work or on Gestalt work, Active Imagination or Dream Work, or something a bit more experiential and feeling based (Cheung & Nguyen, 2012; Hamilton, 2014; Jung, 1997; Stein, 2005). This is not to say that they are any better or worse than other students. It is as if in their lane, they are catching up. This contrasts greatly with having 20 odd students all trying to filter through the same lane and none but a few of them getting very far.

Decolonisation also means though, that we encourage our students within our trainings to think. One of the most common problems with the educational system as it is presented is that given the sheer number of examinations and tests from the very earliest ages of one's educational experience, often what happens is that any creativity, any ability to think outside of the box, any ability to actually develop the skills to critically evaluate the material one is being taught, is drawn out of the educational experience in favour of the need for certain students to hit targets at certain points and therefore to learn things by rote (Hall, 2014).

The difficulty with this when students come to a post-graduate diploma course in counselling and psychotherapy, is that that ability to think for oneself, has become cauterised. What often then takes place on our courses is there is a struggle with the anxiety of not knowing which means that students try to cling to certainty about certain topics. This can often flare up as anxiety as they asks questions around certain scenarios for example, normally beginning with 'What do you do if ...?' So, when something more challenging comes through, there is an even greater struggle not to get it wrong.

To counteract that, there needs to be an understanding that in order to get to a place of exploration of process and not just a clinging on to content, that this decolonised way of learning for the student within our organisations, becomes an ongoing process. A process which is greatly encouraged by the witnessing and the mirroring of the lecturers who think in diversified ways. The ability to not have to deliver certainty, the ability to explore material which may be older and holding prejudices by using a more contemporary lens, encourages students to think at a different level and more importantly with a wider breadth and depth. They start to become who they need to be as practitioners. The recognition that there is not one wisdom within psychotherapy. That to decolonise a way of being and deconstruct who we are, is a part of the course that they have chosen to undertake should sit front and centre of any sort of recruitment drive, open day, or interview questioning. This is so that students learn to start to have a sense of just what they have undertaken and the world they are choosing to explore; that it is not all out there, written down in the annals by the Freud's, the Roger's and the Yalom's. That it is contained within the student themselves and yet to get to that space in the deepest depths of their psyches, they have to unlearn what it is to learn and rediscover what it is to hold truth. Their own truth.

Another aspect of decolonising training methods is there needs to be more research done into, and a consideration of the meaning of, how we collaborate with clients. What I mean by this is that often when I have explored and taught ethics on courses, there is draw for students to actually be told what to do and when to do it. This is not to criticise students, but it is to touch on a fundamental aspect of the colonisers narrative which is very much rules based. What I mean by this is within any sort of social structure, be it patriarchy, be it white supremacy or within any sort of religious structure, a church or religion for example, we know what the rules are, we are told how we should be, what we should do and how we should do it. We therefore do not actually have to consider the whys and wherefores of what we are told and why we are told it.

This is vastly different to the world of psychotherapy, whereas to work with difference and diversity and otherness, we are often taught that given that there a multitude of ways of being in the world, that all our clients are very different that we need to be able to engage with difference on a more regular basis (Turner, 2021; Various, 2022; Williams, 1989). This shift can be quite disconcerting for students and also quite problematic for trainers when working with this, so there needs to be greater understanding and research done into what this psychological shift is actually like for all parties involved.

To add to this though, within a colonised, idealised sort of society which is more individualistic, there can be a sense that if one has the rules then one will not get it wrong and that it is all about getting things right and wrong. Whereas within the world of psychotherapy, we are often taught to explore each scenario that appears in turn; why is the client telling me this story, what do they actually mean by it, what is my countertransference, etc.? So, in these explorations what we might have previously seen as right or wrong, is often a lot more nuanced and sits a lot more in the grey areas that sit outside of that idealistic binary of a coloniser's narrative.

As I have said, this can be quite disconcerting, but being able to help all involved to sit with and work with process, and not get so rigidly tied down and preoccupied with the context and what it means, is a learning process in itself and it is also one that a good number of students have not encountered in any way at all since their school days. So, having the ability to actually help our students and ourselves work with the complexities of human nature removes us from the scientific essentialism of a more quantitative understanding of human nature and edges us more towards a qualitative exploratory understanding of a human being's experience.

Decolonising the trainer

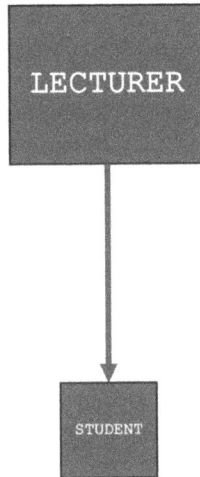

Figure 3.1 Traditional trainer/trainee relationship.

The reason for trainers to become aware of how they themselves may have internalised something of the colonised ways of being is that without doing so what can often happen is there is a set-up of a power dynamic, as presented in Figure 3.1. This top-down way of teaching will though be common to trainer and trainee as, as previously stated, our schooling systems here in the Global North very much projects the power dynamic of expert and neonate into the academic space. There is an expert whose role it is to talk about what they know and pass this onwards, and there is a student whose role it is to just take in said material.

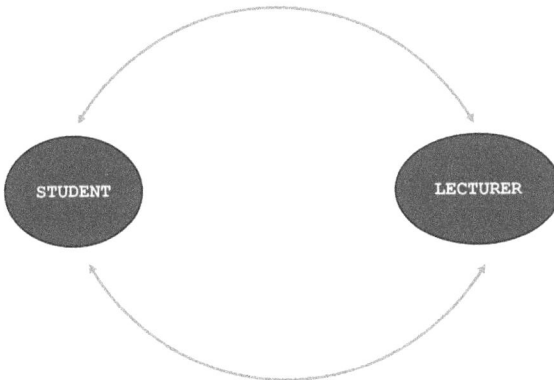

Figure 3.2 Trainer/trainee intersubjective relationship.

This contrasts to Figure 3.2 which talks about the interconnected relationship between the trainer and the trainee. Within this simple diagram, it is very easy to see that both parts learn from each other, and very much mirrors the work of psychotherapy itself. The trainer/trainee dynamic as presented here counters some of the ideas around power which are often traditionally posited as being within this interaction.

This deeper recognition, that trainers themselves, especially on psychotherapy and counselling courses, are always learning, may seem simply stated, but it is often something lost as much on students as it is on lecturers. The development of a lecturer does not end because they have entered into the role of the lecturer or the trainer. Their development is ongoing because that interaction with every new student brings up a different type of relationship each and every single time, and in many ways this interaction speeds up said personal development. The interconnectedness of us all will also bring change within the training course itself. Simple examples will be the feedback that students are allowed to give on numerous training courses and universities and private institutions around the country.

That inter-connectiveness should encourage the courses to grow and develop in connection with the times that they are embedded within, the demographics that they are working within, and also the types of students who are entering through their doors. Every cohort brings in a different flavour and that flavour needs to add a certain taste to the training courses themselves. Returning to the trainer as an individual, their willingness to be challenged and to reflect upon their experience as trainers is a hugely important facet here. I know, I myself will take to my own supervision what it is to be a trainer, a lecturer on a training course, my use of supervision an essential aspect of how I have developed as a trainer.

A perfect example of this is when I was given the role of a course leader for my course at the University of Brighton back in 2021. I spent a long time trying to look at and understand just what it was to be a leader. What does that actually look like for myself and what would I learn about myself along the way in order to better facilitate that role for my students? This involved a good amount of therapy on my part, given that my own experience, my own internalised experience of being around leaders was often that I had to be subservient because my father was so dominant, or that there was a hierarchy given my time in the Royal Air Force. To therefore come to a place now where I had to re-learn what it was to be a leader meant that I had to do a lot of investigative work within myself to work out how I might do that whilst also divesting myself of the internalisations of family, culture, history, of slavery for example and the other ways in which power was something not to pick up and yet to be given away.

In my simple example, there have been a number of others I have looked at with regard to their ways of leading and being in the forward line. The likes of Sir Alex Ferguson (2014) and trying to understand his story and how he worked, both as a leader but also in relationship to those often quite difficult players he managed within the Manchester United football team. Other types of leaders have included the likes of Oprah Winfrey and her ability to use her own talents and skills to lead the way within the media world, whilst also working alongside a number of other names and prominent figures, enhancing their careers as they progressed. Being a leader for myself has then become more about relationship, but the final test was always going to be how would that occur within the framework of a training course.

Some of the things that I have learned along the way are that, although we talk about the relationship as being the core part of being a counsellor and psychotherapist within the therapy room, what we often do not talk about is the importance of relationship as being a course leader and how important it has become for myself to attempt to build interpersonal relationships on an individual basis with each and every student that I come across and I work with. This does not mean that I get to know everybody to their fullest extent, but it does mean that I will attempt and try to understand where they are coming from and give them their own individual guidance if I might be able to do so. This sits alongside my modelling of what it is to be a practitioner, whilst also it sits alongside the fact that I am, in a way, the figure head for a course, but what it does not do is place me head and shoulders above everybody else at a hierarchical pinnacle which will only invite projection and distortions of such in a different way.

The trainer is therefore there to empower and use the differences within a cohort of students and not just shoehorn the diverse ways of being and understanding of each individual person into a colonised psychotherapist framework. The trainer, as I see it, has a role to play in therefore diversifying the profession by actually allowing students to diversify their understanding of what it is to be a psychotherapist. What I am ultimately saying here, is that the relationship between trainer and trainee will involve elements of shadow work for both parties. There will always be projections and transferential relationships from trainee to trainer because there will always be a sense that the trainer is placed in a position of power which may represent a care giver or a form of society or family.

Simultaneously though, there will always been transference and projections from the trainer themselves. It could be that the person that they meet reminds them of somebody they were within a relationship or, if they are older, someone whose is parental or a figure of power in that trainer's life as well. The constant, honest reviewal of what it is to be a trainer and what is being provoked and tweaked within the trainer's own unconscious, adds an extra layer to the honesty within the trainer but also brings the trainer back into a relationship with the trainee and challenges some of the colonised ideas about what it is to be a trainer/teacher.

The other part to this which is important is in a departure away from the colonisation of the mind discussed in an earlier section here, around education. This attempts to actually be honest and reflective around each aspect of the interpersonal relationships, and the studies whilst on training courses, actually helps trainers to model the fact they are thinking through their process whilst also modelling for trainees the fact that they needs to think as well as to what it is to be in a relationship with the trainer, with the course or with the institution.

This ability to think, to feel and to relationally experience one's training, returns to the individual trainer and trainee alike something which has been stolen and co-opted in order to fit into a framework of education many years before. It is not a painless process though and it can often come across as a process which is quite challenging, which can bring up lots of emotions, which can be disruptive to one's sense of being. Yet, for all of us who are psychotherapists and counsellors at whatever stage of our career, be us neonates or experienced and famous practitioners, we all go through this process of dying, death and renewal, which is an important facet of becoming a professional. Those who avoid such a process are often those who are less effective one might add as therapists, although this is not a general rule, because there are many ways to get to the promised land.

The systemic structural decolonisation of counselling and psychotherapy

One of the trickier aspects of decolonisation will come with the range of rules placed around trainings by Governing Bodies. This is not to criticise governing bodies to great an extent, because I believe that they do the best that they can do within the frameworks within which they are embedded, but it is to ask governing bodies to look at just how the structures that they have imposed upon training courses may well reinforce some of the coloniser narrative, as already discussed in this chapter. The different layers of conformality which training courses have to adhere to, whilst both helpful from one angle in that they add a layer of safety and competency within training courses, can also be seen as problematic and constraining by another angle because they sometimes fail to allow for the creativity and the diversity and ranges of thought which should sit central to universities and training courses, and in particular should enhance the art which is counselling and psychotherapy.

Another important aspect for trainings to recognise is their own complicity with regard to the systems of colonisation that we have already discussed in Chapters 1 and 2 of this tome. It is important for trainees to understand that the ideas and the structures that they themselves are embedded within are part of the colonial project. To adopt the ideas and the work of Edward Said and Franz Fanon, trainings need to understand that the education from a colonial perspective often only involved the expression of ideas which would fit the cultural narrative of the global north (Fanon, 1959; Said, 2003b). In his ideas around Orientalism, Said (2003a) explored this even further. His ideas unpicked the narratives that preferred western angles on anything from the arts to science, thereby rejecting anything that was presented for a more diverse indigenous nature.

The only way then for ideas to therefore become incorporated were for those ideas and idealists to then adapt themselves or to in more modern parlance, to code switch to be seen as amenable and non-destructive of what would have been seen as the cultural norm.

What we now see is that understanding is that the pinnacleisation of ideas out of the global north, which has therefore meant that the teaching and the expression of anything outside of these is rejected. This could be seen in anything from literature whereby the majority of writers taught on say English literature courses would, more often than not, be white, middle and upper class men, thereby leaving out the diverse voices of say the Bronte sisters and so on to the incorporation of scientific ideas as presented through a white, male lens, thereby leaving out the ideas and angles of scientists and inventors from other cultures, communities or genders (Mügge et al., 2018).

The need to diversify or decolonise the educational structures even within psychotherapy trainings is therefore another essential facet when it comes to the decolonisation project we are discussing. Returning to Figure 3.1, borrowing a Fanonian lens, another angle to this could well be seen to be the valorisation of the colonised in their attempt to gain some sort of relevance and badge of authenticity within the colonisers project (Fanon, 2005). The drive, for example, for so many from colonised countries to send their children to the global north and to boarding schools, an idea I have already explored earlier in this book, is paralleled somewhat by the needs and wants of so many trainees of difference who find themselves drawn to train at some more established and famous counselling and psychotherapy organisations.

Whilst I may be contradicting myself ever so slightly by suggesting that trainings needs to do more to diversify their student pool, what also needs to happen is that trainees need to do more to challenge the idealisation of certain schools and certain modes of being. This can be done by either attending institutions with a more diverse base or by petitioning governing bodies to encourage other organisations outside of psychotherapy's cultural norm to set up their own organisations and institutions which can then be accredited as pathways towards a more inclusive form of counselling and psychotherapy.

The decolonisation of trainings also has a third strand and this involves the recognition that in order for trainings to move beyond the structures in which they have become embedded and colonised or born from within even, there needs to be a recognition that the trainings, the trainers and the trainees themselves will have been moulded and formed and have their ability to think altered from within the schooling that they would have endured and undertaken previously. This is why the following sections after this are so important. As stated in some of my other work, when we talk about systems of supremacy, there is often the belief that the system is external to ourselves and that it runs of its volition and oppresses and contains those of us who sit outside of it. This is a fallacy and a fraud born out of the failure to recognise that we all play our own individual parts within the collective system.

I, for example, am authoring this book for an organisation that will place this book on the market within a capitalist system. I therefore have to acknowledge that I play my part in keeping said system going in order for myself to survive and live an average life. We all play a part in systems of patriarchy. We all act out our own roles within systems of white supremacy. We all enact some part of the capitalist system and in the same way when we talk about the existence and the constant re-invention of the colonisers narrative within training courses, we all of us, courses, trainers and trainees, are embedded within and play a part within said systems of oppression. The importance of this book though, is the constant re-recognition that these systems need to change, that trainees, trainers, centres of excellence within counselling and psychotherapy, have recognised that actually they co-option has gone too far, has outlived its usefulness and needs to alter, shift and change.

So, the importance of decolonising trainings at this point is to recognise the different intersecting layers of colonisation and how by even shifting all of these a small percentage, you start to set the ball rolling of growth and re-growth over a period of time. Growth which will enhance our trainings and encourages a different range and breadth of understandings and ideas and narratives and theories and research from which we can all benefit. This is the importance of this chapter, and this is the importance of the role that trainees have when we consider where we might go with this material next, because at the moment, what we are starting to have been the regurgitation of ideas, of understandings and with each retelling of age-old stories. It is a bit like gossip which has been passed around the circle, the story not only changes over time and loses its essence but also becomes distinctly watered down and loses its power, will and ability to seem new, intelligent and inspiring.

Colonisation stagnates a culture. By only placing innovation within the hands of a small few, and in the challenge of decolonising our trainings, what we are attempting to do is to place back into the hands of so many the ability, the right, the excitement that comes with learning about human nature.

What I am trying to say here is that critical thinking and feeling when used appropriately, becomes a means of decolonising the institutionalised ability or inability one could suggest, for students to think about the material they are being taught. It allows us to realign the body mind split engendered by our earlier education and reinforced by most institutions.

Decolonisation of thinking and feeling then becomes an essential facet of the whole decolonisation project. To better embed a module where students are encouraged to be with a topic is as much for them as for psychotherapy and to bring their ideas into this module, be they acceptable by the course or otherwise. Whilst being able to also argue theoretically as to where these perspectives are important, or maybe not, then helps the students to reconnect with that ability nay that right, to think outside of colonised narratives prescribed to them at school.

Decolonising training methods

Next must be a consideration of our training methods. This is actually quite a large topic, and it is one that I am not going to be able to cover in as much depth as I would like within this volume, because it has certain ramifications for the practice methods of all modalities in varying separate ways, some more so than others. Yet, it is simply this. Many of our more experiential training methods have been developed within heteronormative, neurotypical, body typical, white supremacist or patriarchal ways of working and understanding the human being.

I can offer several examples and will present some of these in the following which I will consider in turn.

The first one is a client names Jan. Jan was diagnosed with ADHD in his early thirties, a diagnosis which gave him a greater understanding of himself and his environment. Jan sought out some therapy to help with the process of understanding who he was. The issue for Jan though, is that he sought out a cognitive behavioural therapist (CBT) who tried to understand Jan though a series of exercises and techniques given to the therapist as part of his training course. Repeatedly, the therapist was critical of Jan for not hitting and achieving certain goals as laid out in his portfolio. Jan felt very much misunderstood, so much so that at the end of the six sessions, when the therapist had told him that Jan had failed, Jan felt especially ashamed that he had not been able to measure up to the therapy that he had been given.

A friend of Jan's asked him to see a different therapist. This therapist was more person centred and worked with Jan in helping him to understand what the diagnosis of ADHD actually meant to him, whilst also helping Jan to recognise that actually his experience with the previous therapist was about a level of theoretical and emotional disconnection, and also an inability of the therapist to step outside and critically think about their theoretical structures and boundaries. I do not know what happened to Jan in the end, but this story highlights one of the problems with not just CBT, but with other modes of working which are that they are developed in a certain way, for a certain typical, or in this case neurotypical, client bases.

Then there is this second example in the following:

A workshop facilitator was running a Transpersonal workshop which involved a level of body work. There was a trans man on the course who was in their forties. The trans client found a number of the bodywork exercises difficult. The facilitator though, in a similar fashion to the CBT practitioner in the previous example, pathologised the trans client's "inability" to work with body using some sort of theoretical lens which did not really represent the trans student's experience. When discussed with their therapist beyond the training, what became apparent for the trans student was their feeling re-traumatised by the bodywork, give their lifelong difficult experience of the physical and of their body.

This second example is another one whereby we choose to use techniques from a very typical, and in this case body typical way, and struggle therefore to recognise that not all techniques are going to work with all types of students. The level of difference that comes into our training spaces needs to be recognised. So, were we able to think outside of the box a bit more, coming back to my earlier point, where practitioners, facilitators and trainers willing to critically think about the work they are doing in those moments, then it allows a greater level of inclusivity and creativity around the exercises. This could see the methods themselves grow and evolve in a way which allows other to feel that they have felt seen.

I am not immune to having to witness this experience. To borrow from one of my own, on a training course some time ago, I was delivering a workshop on inter-sectional approaches to difference and otherness, I had given my talk as I always do, and I had chosen to do the privilege walk. The privilege walk is an exercise which has been used within my trainings to actually explore the group experience of privilege and otherness. It is a sometimes-contested technique, but it is one that in my experience, as a group sculpt has worked well within a held environment. It is essential that I mention this, to give students or practitioners of experience the sense of just where privilege sits for them, but also where it lies for them and their colleagues or peers.

Traditionally this is a physical exercise where when students are asked several questions they move backwards and forwards depending upon their response to said question. At the end of the Walk, the resulting group sculpt then becomes a way of exploring difference and otherness. On this occasion, there were two students of difference, one who was reluctant to let her disability hinder her from actually taking part in the exercise, so partly chose to hide it, and another one who was quite obviously in a motorised wheelchair. The student in the wheelchair was concerned about the power or her chair running out before she could actually fin-ish the exercise and it fell to myself to then think about 'OK, what is the best way to do this exercise, if that is what I am going to do, but to also keep it inclusive?' Changing the exercise, as I did on this occasion, cost me nothing but also meant that everybody could take part and that no-one got left behind or disadvantaged by doing so. In this case, changing the exercise involved actually asking the same set of questions but asking them all to use a plus and minus scale on a piece of paper to ascertain where they sat with privilege and otherness. Then at the end, the cohort worked in small groups.

Working in these ways, helping students to feel more included and inclusive, involves the trainer thinking outside of their theoretical box, sometimes in quite innovative ways. This also means that we not only critically think about what we are doing, we not only work for more intersectional space, but we also include, innovate and take all of our group of students along a pathway towards becoming de-politicised practitioners.

Decolonising the trainee

If we are going to talk about the trainer, then it is important that we also talk about the trainee. What I mean here is not to look at how the trainee can decolonise themselves because this has already been covered in the previous section but look at how actually we decolonise the trainee as a construct, as an idea and as a way of being on our courses. This will involve explorations of everything from recruit-ment to actually how placements and placement givers and charities might actually assist in providing us with the next generation of trainees. The first thing to con-sider is that in many ways our recruitment processes are disparate across the pro-fession. Whereas plenty of universities have very standardised assessment criteria and procedures for students to get through to an interview stage, in a lot of private organisations this process is more flexible and perhaps a little bit more unclear.

I am not saying here that we need to be standardising everything, because some-times in the standardised way that we assess students what can often happen is that we have already become exclusionary and therefore we leave out or dis-encourage a suitable number of students who might otherwise benefit from being on our courses. A perfect example of this is the ideas that students sometimes have to fill in some sort of application form, normally paper, occasionally online, and often within these is like a statement whereby they talk about themselves and what works for them, who they are and why they have chosen to become a psychotherapist. At this very early stage, given the fact that this is a process which plenty of students might find anxiety provoking, the idea that they are supposed to go through an anonymous hoop in order to access the next stage which will be an interview, pos-sibly, can lead to a lot of students who are neurodiverse, feeling that they cannot at all meet the possibility of even completing said application form, even if they had done so on a previous undergraduate course. There needs to be greater awareness therefore of the obstacles which students might encounter or have encountered in previous forms of education and alternative routes provided for those students who perhaps need a bit more assistance or a bit more diversity around the assessment process.

The recruitment process will always include interviews. Interviews by their very nature are nerve wracking things to consider. I have lost count of the number of interviews that I myself have done over the years, be they for courses, for jobs, for school, and I have not once gone into an interview feeling that I was going to breeze through and feeling myself hugely comfortable and confident. In some ways nerves are a norm when it comes to the interview process, but in other ways they can actually debilitate the potential student from delivering their best. It could be that having a range of interview styles, be they face-to-face, online or even tele-phone, could actually allow certain potential students to find the method that suits them best, whilst also allowing them to give off their best as a potential student for a counselling and psychotherapy course. There would need to be caveats to that though, because of course as counsellors and psychotherapists, when we do our interviews there is often a sense of needing to feel and experience the student in their countertransference. Having a sense of who they are is a key factor, but how we do that can be as diverse as the ways that we work within the profession today.

We may also want to consider at this point the types of questions and the ways those questions are posed. Again, do we need to offer students the chance to read questions in advance and prepare the said interview, or are we really going to expect them always to just think off the cuff and stumble into what we are asking of them, as a means of getting the best out of them? An interview process is not a counselling session. It is an attempt to ascertain the psychological readiness of an individual to undertake a course as rigorous as one within counselling and psychotherapy and therefore our interview techniques and ways of being needed to reflect that. These sorts of things though, as before, should be modular specific. There should be no one way of exploring what this psychological readiness actually means, but there should also be ways which actually allow the interviewer to encourage and entice out the best from the interviewee, even within that 30 minute to one hour interview process, that the potential trainee will undertake.

I have already mentioned the how's and the where's of where these interviews could take place. I have already talked about the whys as well, but the next stage when considering the position of trainees is the level of support given to them whilst on training courses. Most universities provide student support access for trainees. This could range from helping students who have neurodiverse difficulties, for example they may be dyslexic, to providing them with an additional body who will make notes for them in lectures which will then be transcribed, allowing the student to sit and absorb and participate in said lecture without too much distraction. A sizeable number of private organisations though, fall at this stage, meaning that far too many students who would otherwise benefit from their training courses, are unable to take part, because there is not the holding and inclusivity there for them. In many ways, this becomes a form of exclusion and a form of prejudice within the organisation itself, reinforcing the colonised narrative of 'You need to fit a certain neurological way of being in order to access our training course.'

Another way of supporting students comes back to the example I mentioned earlier on in this chapter around the presentation of material through a purely white, male, middle class lens. The sheer number of students who have sought out additional support from groups such as Pink Therapy, BAATN and others, is astonishing. That support often being quested for as a means of presenting the student with additional holding as they work through and do their best to not psychologically split too far whilst in the colonised environments of their training courses.

To present an example of this, a client of mine called Alvin was 40 years of age and had undertaken a training course in the Midlands. He contacted me part way through his training course to say he was struggling with the content of the course and needed some additional cultural support as a means of helping him to just maintain his focus as he walked towards the last year of his course, where he had to submit his thesis. In our first session, Alvin and myself discussed what those problems actually were. He told me these were based around the lack of any sort of work around race and difference, and yet when this was presented in a lecture for two hours it was done in such a poor way that he felt quite insulted. Alvin also felt removed from some of his colleagues at exactly the same time because they felt that they should not have to consider race at all, and wondered why they were doing so given there was only one person of colour on the course.

The hardest part for Alvin was the lecturer agreed with them and verbalised as much in the room whilst Alvin was there. He felt marginalised, not so much by his colleagues who were there to learn, but more so by the lecturer whose inability, in my view, to hold their own perspective to themselves, added an extra layer of harm to said client/student.

Alvin's fear was that, were he to speak up, he would be labelled as an angry, black, man and as he was the only man in the group full of women, that they would find double the reasons to feel afraid of him.

My advice to Alvin was simply to take back this message to the group and to ask the women in the group, who were all white, how easy it was for them to express their anger in their own relationships to their partners. To ask them to think about just what it was like to be a woman growing up in a western culture, whereby one is often labelled either bolshie, sassy, hysterical or some other adjective which has been designed to actually shut down and silence women for generations. Alvin bravely did exactly this and in the following weeks he was told by a colleague of his that it was the best thing that she had ever heard, because it led to her going back to and talking to her own partner and asserting herself in a way that she had not done throughout their own marriage.

The fact that I, in working with Alvin, was able to offer something for Alvin out of a sense of understanding for him to take back in a way that his own tutor was unable to do, in some ways speaks of the colonised nature of the course and the challenge of being a minority. It also speaks of how minorities often have to seek assistance outside of their course in order to feel seen, held and ultimately respected. That is not to say that all remained perfect on Alvin's course, I am sure there were plenty of other issues and problems to come.

The next aspect, though to consider, when it comes to the trainee and how we decolonise the trainees themselves, is also to consider where they come from. I already stated that our profession is majority white, female and middle class in the United Kingdom, with the vast majority of teachers and lecturers being white, male and middle class as well. This therefore means that somewhere along the line trainers of difference, be they whatever the form of difference, have fallen by the wayside or perhaps not even attempted to train at all. Greater efforts needs to be made to remember that often our training courses are embedded within certain communities that could best benefit from the work that we provide. So, to therefore engage with said communities could be an excellent route to obtaining some of the next best generations of psychotherapists who might otherwise have been missed were we unable to lift the veil away from our collective white, colonised eyes.

A fitting example of this came from an organisation that I once worked with a number of years ago, who were very much embedded within Southeast London and yet whose training cohort was from the usual demographic. When asked why they did not do so much within the local community, I was often left with a standard answer of 'Well, that's because of the price of the course and that people cannot afford the training; maybe they are just not seen as intelligent enough' which an actual phrase which was used in this instance.

A change of director within said organisation changed things subtly and in a conversation with the new director, what I was told was there was going to be a greater emphasis on obtaining and working within the local community to access and encourage forward at least a few students from said community. The ways that they did this was to actually engage with a couple of local charities and the engagement with the charities-built relationships whereby through the establishment of a part bursary, both parties, the charity and the organisation, then pitched for potential students, just one or two per year, to come through and train as part of the course, whilst also doing their placement work within the charity. This was one of those rare occasions where a brilliant community-based idea worked really well and led to a steady, yet small stream of future culturally specific and culturally embedded students working within areas that they knew to a certain degree, so that they could enhance the experience and actually lift some of the stigma around counselling and psychotherapy within said community.

This example I have given you just there is not a rare one. I have come across others across the country whereby the organisation's ability to recognise their relatedness within the community has become a huge part of their work and is something which I think needs to be replicated around the country. In some ways, universities used to do a lot of this in the past, but it seems as if some of that has fallen to the side to some degree as the university sector has become more capitalised and more money focused.

The last area I would like to consider within this section though, is actually to move further into the idea of placements and to question and query the placements themselves. On occasion, it has become apparent to a number of students that I have worked with that, where there are placements within certain communities, these are often run from the top downwards by, again, the same demographic of counsellors and psychotherapists. It is even quite difficult, or quite rare, to see on management committees, persons of difference, aka persons that represent the lived experience of those communities upon the management committees themselves. It is essential, therefore, to recognise that when we recruit counsellors and psychotherapists for placements, that the placements themselves have a huge responsibility to ensure that they are not reinforcing the stereotypical imagery of psychotherapy; that it is a white, male or female domain, and that those of difference will not benefit from said experience.

There is a challenge here for all placement services to mirror as much as possible the client base that they work within and the greater the efforts that are made to do this, the more the stigma I have discussed has a chance to dissolve. So, then the greater the opportunity for clients to actually come into therapy and for their mental health to be seen, witnessed, held and helped. Counselling and psychotherapy has a huge role to play in these areas and our trainings are the first point in working with difference and changing the way that psychotherapy has become colonised since its earliest inception over 100 years ago now. I am sure that there are many other ways that the trainer and the trainee and their constructs could be altered to diversify, but much of what I am saying here today is the earliest steps of a deeper exploration as to how we actually have become colonised and what we have left behind ourselves when we choose not to think about what we actually do, why we do it, how we do it and what needs to come next in order to benefit ourselves and those around us.

The role of PD groups in the decolonisation of trainings

One of the most interesting elements of any training course is the group work aspect. A part of the course which has been in situ for several years, the Personal Development Groups were initially more often than not run with group facilitators who were a part of the course structure. Over time, numerous courses have felt that this does not work in the way that it should do as it does not proffer the students the level of security, safety and separateness from the rest of the course material and thereby give them a safe space to explore what has gone on for them whilst engaging with the material they have been taught on a day to day basis.

Group work is an essential part of understanding one's position within the world. It can be a replicant for one's family dynamics and can also be a space where students repair old wounds should they be able to do so. It is therefore a place whereby over time students can experiment with new ways of being. One of the aspects of group work that is often not considered is in the replication of the socially constructed systems within which we are all embedded. It does not always look at how the cultural systems or social systems may also play a role in the student's environment. Given that we are all constructed out of systems such as patriarchy, white supremacy and capitalism, and given that these will mould who we are from very early stages of our lives, it would be important in my view for PD groups to be safe enough spaces for students to then explore the cultural dynamics which they have been moulded by and which may have been re-activated by even being on the course (Turner, 2023).

An example from my own sort of work, as a supervisor, involved working alongside a facilitator who was collaborating with another woman of colour who was often quite deferential towards her. The facilitator understandably saw this as a cultural norm but felt unable and unsure of what to do in order to question it. Interestingly enough, the following years the student themselves came and spoke to me about this issue from their own angle, pointing out how difficult it was for them to find their voice on the course, given that this PD group facilitator was white, and male, and they were a woman of colour from an African background. We often forget that these cultural norms may also be cultural adaptations based around colonialism or one of the other structures of oppression.

So, for PD group leaders, whilst it is important for them to be separate to the courses themselves, it is also important that they are aware of what it is to be a minority on a training course within a mainly white, often western educational system. Other areas where perhaps this happens a lot more readily is where groups are set up outside of the course structures, support groups run by Pink Therapy or by the BAATN Network offer brilliant examples of where persons of difference have often found a safe space to continue narratives based around issues that have been raised within them whilst inhabiting said courses.

The desire for safe spaces is an essential component to this process that we are talking about here and it is not just for the trainee, it is also a safe space for the trainee to explore what is going on for themselves around the course material and the social constructions, but also so that they can take this back into the course and embody a more authentic sense of who they are within said structure. This then may occasionally lead to elements of conflict with the course structure, as the systemised stands up, speaks up and challenges said system. So, it may also involve the system having to review itself and look at itself over and over again; the course having to consider how it is a part of any system of oppression, any system of colonisation, how its comfort in actually being inactive within a certain framework, actually leads to the repression and the silencing of minority groups.

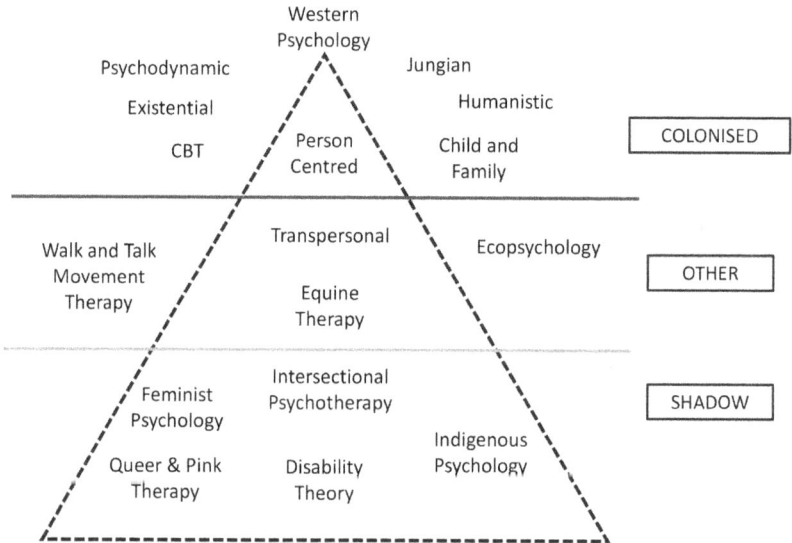

Figure 3.3 Course decolonisation and evolution.

As designated by Figure 3.3, the courses themselves, therefore, have a role to play in this in recognising that actually they are not static beings, but within these elements of decolonisation, there is an understanding that the courses themselves are evolving, they are changing, they are not static. This is because in all of this we are encouraging students to find their own way and because within all of this we are encouraging courses to develop their own means and methods to actually reframe themselves. What we are also looking to do here is recognise that courses themselves are developmental structures. There will also though be resistance to this understanding that courses, like the human psyche go through a constant ebb and flow, a constant growth and regrowth, in structure, in the face that it shows to the outer world.

This is to counter the naïve narrative that suggests that in any sort of course community growth or sense of decolonisation, that this merely happens once, and when it is over and done it will never happen again. This is to recognise that colonisation is so embedded within each one of us, and therefore within the organisations which we inhabit and train, that a process of decolonisation can take generations. These are small incremental starts on a longer journey to making our world within psychotherapy and counselling more inclusive and only when we start to face up to this, only when we start to challenge these processes, do we then start to recognise where we have become oppressive and then start to recognise the humanity of the student other, the course other, the theoretical material as the other.

Decolonising supervision

When I wrote the initial format for this book out, one area that I struggled to incorporate in its rightful place was the role of supervision. As a supervisor, and as well as being a clinician, I was concerned as to whether this section should go into the general section around psychotherapy, if it should be included later on within the section around the practitioner, and the sense of decolonisation, or if it should be included here, within the training segment.

The reason I decided to include supervision here is that my sense is this is a process that is ongoing. Within training courses, there are often spaces provided whereby training institutions review case work and help students to explore the content of their client work as well as the process underlying this. In many ways, this is where, alongside their clinical practice area, or placement areas, or charity work, trainees gather and garner a more well-rounded internalisation of what it is to be a practitioner and what it is to actually set the pilot light going on their own internalised sense of what it is to be a supervisor.

I remember when I was on my training course, many years ago, one of the more fascinating aspects of my evening was that time when I would sit down with a qualified supervisor and willing present a case because I was excited to see what the group was going to come up with and what nuggets of information and knowledge I might glean from the supervisor running the group. Supervision has an enormous role to play in exploring aspects of decolonisation. Whilst there have been attempts within supervision to include areas around diversity and difference, what these have often done is set out an initial framework for how we might address difference, whilst not necessarily going far enough with how we might explore the colonised aspects of the supervisor themselves and also the social constructions of the work within which supervision happens and therefore the client work itself (Hawkins & McMahon, 2020).

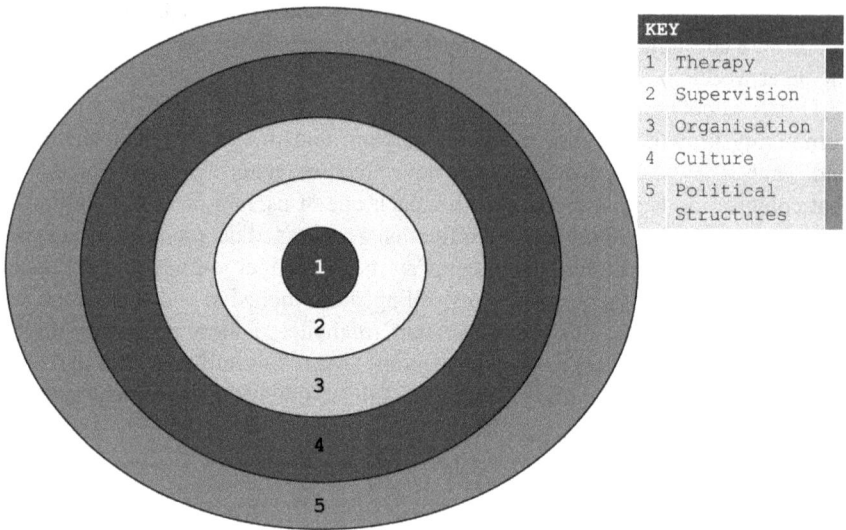

KEY

1 Therapy
2 Supervision
3 Organisation
4 Culture
5 Political Structures

Figure 3.4 Decolonial supervision.

Figure 3.4 though is an adaptation of one proposed by Hawkins and McMahon (2020) in their work around the influences upon supervision. My version though recognises the different intersecting layers which impact upon client work. One of the areas that it does not really look at though is the colonised nature of the organisation, the placement area, as we have already explored earlier on in this chapter, and also how the external world, the colonised environment, may actually play a role in oppressing not only the organisation, but also the supervision and therefore the therapist, the client and the actual work itself. Each client brings in their own experience of colonisation and that needs to be explored, but within that space each therapist brings it in, each supervisor brings that in, and the organisation must deal with their own elements as well.

Perfect examples are the struggles for organisations to gather funding in a world whereby in an environment where there are cutbacks to Social Services to such an extent that even organisations are running on a shoestring, the environmental aspects of capitalism have therefore had an impact on the service themselves. This therefore may well lead to a reduced number of client hours being offered to said client, or certain modes of therapy being valued more so than others. Within the university sector here in the United Kingdom for example, there are several universities who, because of financial constraints and also the impact post-COVID are having to reduce their working model down from six hours of short-term work to a four-hour model. This is sadly becoming increasingly more common.

This is an example of the impact of capitalism and within that there are going to be tensions placed upon the client work accordingly. Supervisors therefore have an essential role in exploring just what those tensions might be and how what we, as practitioners, may look at ways and means to address them and not have an impact upon the client work as much as they might do otherwise.

Given that we have considered the position of the client work within the placement and how the placement itself may also hold elements of colonisation within it, given its finances or its structure or whichever way this may be, it is imperative for the supervisor to then look at not just the conscious narratives around this but also the unconscious ones as well.

The second reason for this is, as we are all born out of a colonised position and as we are all moulded by this, then our clients will also come with similar narrative as well into the therapeutic space. So, a necessary aspect of supervision is for us to look at how that aspect of a colonised sense of self may also appear within the psychotherapeutic dyad, thereby helping our therapists to do the best work that they can do in their placement work.

For example, if I return to the example of the African woman of colour who was working with a facilitator and felt quite deferential towards her facilitator, so much so that the facilitator questioned how easy it was for the student to be authentic in the PD group. Were we to transport that into a therapeutic dyad whereby you have a woman of colour collaborating with a white man, then this deferential side will generate a level of unconscious material which must be experienced by the therapist and/or the trainee. Often though, on training courses, and this is not a criticism of trainees at all, trainees need to be taught and have brought to their awareness, the counter transferential relationship within which they are sat. Trainees may often feel that they want to react against, in this instance, the inauthenticity of the client and it is down to the supervisor in supervision to explore what is generated within them that the trainee is not aware of as yet, and thereby bring it back to the therapeutic work itself.

This may actually mean the supervisor attending to their own cultural or structural biases, prejudices, isms and obias, so that they too can play an active role in exploring the unconscious experience of the client and the trainee. One of the important things about doing this is that this modelling by the supervisor to then explore their own biases and prejudices actually opens the door to an honest conversation about just what it might be to be seen as the more powerful factor within a relationship with a woman of colour in this instance.

This could reveal itself as well through an exploration of what it is like for a LGBTQ+ client to work with somebody who is heteronormative or cisgendered; or it could be the opening doorway to looking at what it is like for therapists who struggle with idea of the use of pronouns, to work with clients whose pronouns sit front and central to their chosen identity.

The world around us is constantly changing and we are constantly being changed and altered to have to adapt to said environments, so any exploration like this must also include where that sits within the therapeutic space.

Another aspect of supervision, and this an important one, is the recognition that we all hold prejudices. We are all at times homophobic, racist, sexist, ableist and ageist. We are moulded from experiences of prejudice, and these play an essential role in helping us to build the social constructionist aspects of our identity. They are embedded very much in the super egoic parts of our psyche, and they inform what is right and what is wrong, who we are and who we are not, and who is in and who is out, group-wise. The fact that we all have these will also appear in the supervision itself; this means supervisors need to be very aware of their own prejudices. This is not to say that a practitioner or a supervisor cannot be prejudice, but what it is to say is that in a way that we do with every other aspect of our work, we are able to acknowledge these parts of ourselves that we feel uncomfortable with, hold them and contain them for long enough to work and provide a safe enough psychotherapeutic space for our client work to exist within.

I am not drafting this book saying that I have all of my social constructionist ducks in a row, to borrow a clumsy metaphor. It is to say that the more that I know who I am, the more likely it is that I will be collaborating with people who will have different views to myself. This brings up one of the core tenants of my way of working as a supervisor, and also as a practitioner. It is that my job is to present an intersubjective space between myself and my clients, so that there can be an intersubjective dialogue between the parts of the client self which disagree.

Often, I have supervisees, who presume that I hold a particular political position. My role as a supervisor is not for me to say actually that is or is not my position at all, but it is for me to explore why they believe I might hold said political positioning. The modelling of this allows supervisees to see that I can both hold my own political and/or a socially constructed position, meaning they can accept a role opposite that and joust in a safe space with myself in order for them to resolve for themself whatever they need to. Change comes in the space in between; it is not built from one aspect or the others. In fact, all that happens, and we have seen this on many occasions in culture and society, in groups, is that when we take up polarised positions, one side chooses not to hear the other or to acknowledge the other or to cancel the other and thereby what it also does is pushes the other into the unconscious.

Supervisors modelling that ability to hold that intersubjective space and create the environment for intersubjective dialogue, then allows change to emerge from the space in between (Buber, 1992, 2010). What that change is, how that change works, what that change might be, will differ from client to client, but it is the change that they need to go through in order to feel healed, heard and whole. Whilst there may be an impact upon the supervisor or the therapist themselves, we have our own avenues to explore this, be it supervision or be it our own personal therapy, but this is not for the client work.

This very Buberian approach to exploring decolonisation actually recognises that the more space and voice that supervisors, that training courses, that trainers and that trainees give to the voices of the other, the more likely it is that change will occur. This, together with training courses and all those who inhabit said space becoming more aware of their role, means that the narratives which have led to the silencing of so many are challenged and decolonisation within said spaces has the ability to bud and flourish, if we let it.

Summary

This chapter has taken an in depth look at the role that training courses have played in re-establishing and maintaining systems of oppression and where some of these ideas may have come from. Training organisations are educational organisations and as such they are as embedded within the structural inequalities inherent within the education systems here in the global north. To therefore explore just where these systems reside, how we have recreated said systems, and where those may have marginalised so many, has been an essential factor within this chapter.

As with each of the chapters in this book, Table 3.1 outlines some of the areas which training courses could use and explore in order to begin the long, slow, painful process of decolonisation of their institutions, or their trainings, and assist their trainees to do exactly the same. There are many facets to decolonisation, as I have laid out here, and as I have always stated from the very beginning, decolonisation was always going to be more than just the re-vamping of varying texts and the inclusion of one or two more lectures around diversity. Colonisation itself was a master project, therefore decolonisation is its' governerness. It is hugely important that we recognise that this relational aspect to the work that we are doing within counselling and psychotherapy, this work of decolonisation, is as mammoth as the work which went to construct it in the first place.

Given that this chapter has looked at training courses and the trainers and the distinct stages that students go through in the process to becoming counsellors and psychotherapists, it therefore makes sense that the next chapter should look at the decolonisation of practice itself. In order to do that, I will be looking at some of the history behind psychotherapy practice and the ways in which we do our work, plus also exploring how some of the ways of practicing and working as a psychotherapist have actually been quite exclusionary from the very beginning of our work. To therefore explore what it might be to work from a more decolonised angle, my sense is that we need to be slightly more open to the evolving world within which psychotherapy is a part.

Table 3.1 Decolonising training

	Colonised	Decolonised
Core Themes and Practical Appliances	Basics of Core Themes are often taught on courses, together with how these are used with a basic diversity of clients.	Broader exploration of the theories and the political and social context they were created within, together with how contemporary approaches builds upon the knowledge borne out of these colonised.
Political Context	Not Considered	Incorporating the political and socioeconomic context to the theories and the trainings.
Lecturers	No real consideration of the impact of the intersections of patriarchy, white supremacy and colonialism upon the identities of the lecturers or on the institutions they work within.	Lecturers paying closer consideration to their own colonised intersectional identities. This is less for lecturers to rid themselves of aspects deemed socially undesirable, but more for them to own these aspects modelling the carrying and holding of one's own views and ideas, whilst holding the perhaps diverse views of clients for their students.
Students	No space for students to explore their intersectional identities. Often students do not feel safe enough to bring their non-colonised identities to their courses.	Spaces created on courses where students look at how they themselves are moulded by the intersections of patriarchy, white supremacy and capitalism, and how these may play a role in their false self.
Student, Trainer and Institution Triumvirate	The hierarchy of Institution, Trainer, Student therefore means that students often do not feel they have a voice in the direction of the institution. Or, in the case of minority students, any challenge of the structural hierarchy often leads to a silencing or pathologisation of the student.	The creation of safe spaces for students from minority groups to be able to meet and discuss their places on the course. These should be created and valued by the institution, recognising the difficulties minority students have in finding and having a voice on courses. Institutions need to do better to challenge the heteronormative, ableist, white, patriarchal, ageist narratives which are deeply embedded within their courses and their teaching.

Placement Providers	Often structured to be run by an elite who are often detached from the community they are embedded within. Then peopled by students and part-time workers who are better situated to work within said communities. Both speak to the systemic hierarchies which created said inequality, and therefore the need for the charity, in the first instance.	Closer consideration of placement providers as to how they populate their management committees so as to better represent their communities and their target demographic. Better recruitment from these communities, thereby challenging the white saviourism of counselling and psychotherapy students coming through their doors. Closer alignment between Institutions and Placement Providers to provide bursaries thereby starting to address the structural inequalities within the profession.
Governing Bodies	Governing bodies are often prone to reinforcing hierarchies and therefore the inequalities already embedded within the profession.	Governing bodies need to do more to address systemic inequalities in the profession, moving beyond performativity with a deeper embracing of just how there are complicit, how their own organisations may themselves be spaces of oppression and inequality, and how they might then address these, thereby modelling this for the wider profession.

References

Andrews, K., & Palmer, L. (2013). Why black studies matters. *Discover Society, 2*, 1–4.

Bader-Johansson, C., Harms, T., Cotton, D., Eichhorn, N., Evertsen, L., & Duclos, M. (2015). The art and science of somatic praxis. *International Body Psychotherapy Journal, 13*(2).

Barnes, E. (2016). *The minority body: A theory of disability*. OUP Oxford.

Beauvoir, S. de. (2010). *The second sex*. Alfred A. Knopf.

Benjamin, J. (1990). An outline of intersubjectivity: The development of recognition. *Psychoanalytic Psychology, 7*, 33–46. https://doi.org/10.1037/h0085258

Bothello, J., & Roulet, T. J. (2019). The imposter syndrome, or the mis-representation of self in academic life. *Journal of Management Studies, 56*(4), 854–861. https://doi.org/10.1111/joms.12344

Bridges, C. E. (1945). Education Act, 1944. *Probation Journal, 4*(10), 106–108. https://doi.org/10.1177/026455054500401003

British Association for Counselling and Psychotherapy. (2018). Ethical framework for the counselling professions. *British Journal of Guidance & Counselling*, 1–35. www.bacp.co.uk/events-and-resources/ethics-and-standards/ethical-framework-for-the-counselling-professions/

Buber, M. (1992). *On intersubjectivity and cultural creativity*. The University of Chicago.

Buber, M. (2010). *I and thou*. Martino Publishing Limited.

Butler, J. (1999). *Gender trouble*. Routledge.

Cheung, M., & Nguyen, P. V. (2012). Connecting the strengths of gestalt chairs to Asian clients. *Smith College Studies in Social Work, 82*(1), 51–62. https://doi.org/10.1080/00377317.2012.638895

Duffell, N. (2014, June). G2: Why boarding schools make bad leaders: The elite tradition is to send children away at a young age to be educated. But future politicians who suffer this' privileged abandonment' often turn out as bullies or bumblers. *The Guardian, 10*, 1–5.

Egilmez, O. B., & Orum, M. H. (2018). Intercourse type of situational anejaculation or inability to ejaculate intra-vaginally: Three case reports from a conservative Islamic community. *Psychiatry and Clinical Psychopharmacology, 28*(4), 473–476. https://doi.org/10.1080/24750573.2018.1468618

Fanon, F. (1959). *A dying colonialism*. Penguin Limited.

Fanon, F. (2005). *Black skin, White mask* (M. Silverman (ed.)). Manchester University Press.

Ferguson, A. (2014). *Alex Ferguson: My autobiography* (revised ed.). Hodder Paperbacks.

Hall, C. W. (2014). *Voices of adolescents: A phenomenological study of relational encounters and their significance within the school setting*. Eastern Michigan University.

Hamilton, N. (2014). *Awakening through dreams: The journey through the inner landscape*. Karnac Books Ltd.

Hawkins, P., & McMahon, A. (2020). *Supervision in the helping professions*. Open University Press.

Jung, C. G. (1997). *Jung on active imagination* (J. Chodorow (ed.)). Routledge.

Kinouani, G. (2020). *Racial trauma, silence and meaning*. Race Reflections. https://racereflections.co.uk/2019/04/20/racial-trauma-silence-and-meaning/

Mazzei, L. a. (2008). Silence speaks: Whiteness revealed in the absence of voice. *Teaching and Teacher Education, 24*(5), 1125–1136. https://doi.org/10.1016/j.tate.2007.02.009

McDermott, P. (2008). *On training psychotherapists*. Paul McDermott Psychotherapy. www.paulmcdermott.org/writing/article-on-training-psychotherapists/

McQueen, S. (2020). *Small axe: Education*. BBC. www.bbc.co.uk/iplayer/episode/m000q fb1/small-axe-series-1-education

Mügge, L., Montoya, C., Emejulu, A., & Weldon, S. L. (2018). Intersectionality and the politics of knowledge production. *European Journal of Politics and Gender*, *1*(2), 17–36. https://doi.org/10.1332/251510818X15272520831166

Said, E. (2003a). *Orientalism*. Penguin Limited.

Said, E. (2003b). *Freud and the non-European*. Verso.

Schaverien, J. (2004). Boarding school: The trauma of the "privileged" child. *The Journal of Analytical Psychology*, *49*(5), 683–705. https://doi.org/10.1111/j.0021-8774.2004.00495.x

Stein, M. (2005). Individuation: Inner work. *Journal of Jungian Theory and Practice*, *7*(2), 1–13.

Tucker, C. R., Wycoff, T., & Green, J. T. (2016). *Blended learning in action: A practical guide towards sustainable change*. Corwin.

Turner, D. D. L. (2021). *Intersections of privilege and otherness in counselling and psychotherapy* (1st ed.). Routledge.

Turner, D. D. L. (2023). *The psychology of supremacy*. Routledge.

van der Kolk, B. (2015). *The body keeps the score: Mind, brain and body in the transformation of trauma* (1st ed.). Penguin Books Limited.

Various. (2019a). *Bame student attainment*. National Union of Students.

Various. (2019b). *Who is Malala Yousafzai*. CBBC, BBC. www.bbc.co.uk/newsround/46865195

Various. (2020). *Reaching 130 million girls with no access to school*. BBC News. www.bbc.co.uk/news/education-51769845

Various. (2022). *Queering psychotherapy* (J. C. Czyzselka (ed.)). Karnac Books Ltd.

Various. (2023a). *EMDRWorks*. https://emdrworks.org/costs/

Various. (2023b). *School leaving age*. Politics.Co.Uk. www.politics.co.uk/reference/education-leaving-age/

Various. (2023c). *UKCP*. www.psychotherapy.org.uk/psychotherapy-training/psychotherapy-approaches/

Weil, A. M., & Piaget, J. (1951). The development in children of the idea of the homeland and of relations to other countries. *International Social Sciences Journal*, *3*, 561–578.

Wilkinson, C. (2020). Imposter syndrome and the accidental academic: An autoethnographic account. *International Journal for Academic Development*, *25*(4), 363–374. https://doi.org/10.1080/1360144X.2020.1762087

Williams, J. C. (1989). Deconstructing gender. *Michigan Law Review*, *87*(4), 797–845. https://doi.org/10.2307/1289293

Chapter 4

Decolonising practice

Introduction

Several years ago, I remember once supervising a student who had come to me whilst studying on a course in England because they were looking to develop their skills prior to finishing their course and wanted to explore in supervision just what their career might look like. This student, a white, English middle-class woman, had decided that one of the things she wanted to do when she finished her training was to obtain a space in a prestigious street in central London from where she would be able to work and charge the highest rates possible for her counselling and psychotherapy practice. Our work together did not last very long, but yet this is what she chose to do and, given the changes that would have occurred around the Pandemic, my hope was that she managed to make the best of some very difficult times which occurred subsequently.

Now, the reason for telling this particular story is less to critique a particular student's desire to work in central London and earn a good living, but it is to in a way open the discussion up as to how counselling and psychotherapy as a practice is very much embedded within systems and capitalism, and is as colonised, as any other aspect of the work described in this book.

To give you another example from my own experience as a psychotherapist:

In the days post my training, I worked for a low-cost housing service in Southeast London. This service received money from the European Union, money which was designated to poorer areas for services that they might need to enhance their livelihoods. I worked within a very poor working-class area of London and the work that we did, which was short-term work providing counselling support alongside one or two other holistic therapies, received a very high uptake within the community from the residents of the local estates. The service itself was populated by a majority of persons of colour, although there were a few white practitioners on the team as well. Yet at some point during this service's short life span, the funding was cut for several reasons and the service subsequently died a death.

DOI: 10.4324/9781032614342-4

On further investigation, one of the reasons given for the severing of the financial stream from the EU was down to financial constraints within the European Government, but this failure of other services or The Charities Commission or our own government to pick up on the good work done in that environment meant that there was nothing left from a counselling or psychotherapy perspective for them to engage within.

This second example, though, has a more personal dénouement. The personal aspect of this was that when I had finished my training, I was very grateful to obtain a job working for a service and using the skills that I had developed and learned over the previous five years. To then have that safety net of an income taken away so instantaneously was one of the more traumatic experiences of my early career and actually led to me deciding that the best way forward for myself was to just go into private practice full-time and make as much of a living for myself as I could do. I chose at that point that I did not want to work within a system which was so inconsistent and so very much driven by financial constraints and reasonings.

Mine is just one simple example, but there are many others out there which hold similar, more contemporary narratives. The number of universities, for example, who were doing their best to offer short-term counselling support to students coming into their services based around the funding they already received. Universities, who in particular post the global pandemic, have had to curb some of that support, for example, reducing their short-term working from six sessions to four, is increasing even as I author this book. The financial pressures on the services that we provide within a capitalist system should not be underestimated, be they based around the university sector, the charity sector or the private sector. How we work as counsellors and psychotherapists is always going to be impacted by the world around us. So, to, for example, simplistically believe that one just has to work a bit harder or that there are not structural or systemic reasons as to why a student cannot obtain enough clients to survive upon, is to be naïve to the fact that we all have to endure a life which is very much driven by the cultural world around us.

These external societal pressures will also have an impact upon how we practice. The number of practitioners who feel that they want to gain as many tools as possible to earn as much money as possible, be they students who have gone to good colleges, have gone off to do even more training say in trauma or Eye Movement Desensitization and Reprocessing (EMDR) work, or have gone off to find work within the NHS, in part shows just how desperate many of our practitioners actually are when it comes to finding work. Then there is the other end of the scale where, even after qualifying, there are a suitable number of therapists and counsellors who remain within the placement arena often doing unpaid work alongside their regular jobs as a means of making a living and obtaining some sort of standard of qualification further down the line. Their efforts belying the fact that they may be very well qualified for the relational work they have trained so hard for.

The other area to explore in this chapter also involves how we do the work. From the earliest days of psychoanalysis, the idea that practitioners should come in to see a therapist four or five times a week was seen as the norm. This though, whilst having some definite benefits to that type of work, often marginalised huge swathes of the population that could have done with psychological support because they could not afford to attend psychoanalysis. This is an increasing problem given that it is still very difficult for a lot of clients to attend therapy once a week for financial and other reasons such as access.

In this the 2000s, how we work also seems to be going through a period of flux. The Pandemic, as previously mentioned, has changed our environment and our working lives forever, where we all ventured out to work in some way previously gave way to online ways of working and connecting with each other. Moving from this more generalised perspective, to then understand how the Pandemic and the upswing in online working has changed the working lives of many practitioners is a topic area which, at the time of writing, is poorly understood and researched. Yet, I suspect and hope this will become more greatly so as we progress through the next few years post the end of this global Pandemic (de Oliveira Cardoso et al., 2023; Duran et al., 2022).

Stories again from the university sector, a sizeable number have gone online at least partially and have adapted their services to meet this new demand. The subsequent uptake from a client generation who are more social media savvy and used to working with computers and technology has been amazing to witness and see and hear about. It is as if in these instances the Pandemic has opened the doorway to younger clients, or those from communities where face-to-face working is just not feasible meaning there is a broader range of clients obtaining the assistance they need. This is not to say that the older ways of working need to die, this is say that psychotherapy and how we work, and how we sit with our clients and so on, has always evolved, from the earliest inception of Freud's idea of having clients lie on the couch whilst he sat behind them which was very much driven by his own wish to not be observed whilst doing the work, for example (Jacobs, 2003). Or to the use of techniques including the Gestalt technique of chair work, visualisations and acts of imagination from the work of Carl Jung, and other areas of expertise, shows that actually how we work is always in a flux, there is not one way to be in practice as a psychotherapist (Cheung & Nguyen, 2012; Jung, 1997).

On an individual level, Yalom (1981, 2002) wrote about his own experience of being a client where he talked about not just staying within the confines of his own modality, but in also undertaking group work, Gestalt and other forms and other forms of psychotherapy as a client, both as a means of understanding who he was on a deeper level, but also in understanding what clients might bring from different phenomenological perspectives. This is the important part to this chapter. Practice, the work that we do, and how we do it, in this evolution is phenomenological. The idea there needs to be one way of doing the work that we do, that this way is the best way, has roots which run all the way back to Freud himself and in many ways sit within the internalised patriarch which speaks away at all of us, given that we are all born within these systems.

This chapter will therefore look at the colonisation of ideas and ways of working within counselling and psychotherapy. It will also look at how, in decolonising how we work we actually open the doors to working with a wider range of clients and client bases. In order for this decolonisation of practice to actually happen, practitioners themselves, and also training courses, need to be thinking a little bit more outside of the box as to what it is that we are doing, why we are doing it and most importantly for this chapter how we can do it better, deeper and more, and this is the important word, broadly. The many ways that we have to understand human nature mean that there should be many more diverse ways to actually explore the experiences of the other. Our clients come and they find us and hopefully we make a good enough match based upon our experiences and their desire. Or we hope that our experiences might match with something within them. Yet, unless we are willing to also broaden out our experiences, then just what are we doing as practitioners? Are we looking for the silver bullet that actually heals all ills, or are we willing to explore aspects of our own psyches in order to work out who we are beyond the five times a week, lying on a couch cliché out of the early days of psychoanalysis?

Colonising psychotherapy practice

When focusing on the colonisation of psychotherapy practice, the first thing to remember is that the ways in which we are taught on our training courses have been very much born out of the world of colonisation. The idea that there are certain things that one has to do, ways that one has to be and a level of authenticity that one has to achieve in order to become a practitioner or counsellor in psychotherapy, will therefore mean that when we come out into the world post our training, we believe that this is who we should be in the world as a practitioner. My earlier use of a paper written by McDermott (2008) actually in a way speaks to this. What I mean by this is that in the need for one to become an authentic practitioner after getting one's certificate, what this involves is that one has to in some ways shake off the systemic shackles which have been placed around oneself as a colonised student of counselling and psychotherapy.

Much of this has to come from the founding fathers and to offer you a couple of examples of what I believe has happened, it is worth looking at the world of Sigmund Freud and the peers that he had around him. Whilst in earlier chapters I have been fairly complimentary of Freud, like with any person in our profession, myself included, there are flaws in the experience of the forebears. Freud was in some ways no different. In his fall out with Otto Rank (1961), whose views Sigmund Freud found difficult to stay with and be with led to the marginalisation of ideas which had a fair amount to say about the psychological world which we walk within as practitioners today. The same could also be said in the marginalisation of Carl Jung which although for a different reason based very much around Jung's perceived mental health, led to Freud actually preferencing acceptance by the already systemised medical community over the authenticity and richness of the cohort of fellow practitioners he had gathered around himself at that point (Stevens, 1990).

Whilst I am not here on this occasion to look at the morality and the issues which led to both types of separation, what I am here to explore is this difficulty within a patriarchal system that some men have in holding any challenge by other men around them. This idea of the patriarch, this idea that there is one way of doing something, is not uncommon in cultures, in families even. The culturally specific statement often uttered by fathers within Afro Caribbean households to their sons a statement along the lines of, 'well if you think you are a man now, it is time for you to get out,' is something which speaks very much to the fear that a lot of men have that their ideas are going to be challenged in some way by those others around them.

This internal patriarchal narrative would also have played a role in the systemic marginalisation of the ideas and perspectives of a respectable number of feminist psychoanalysts in the early days of our profession. These are things which have been countered increasingly so, by the likes of Gilligan, Kristeva and Irigaray, who in particular brought a very thorough feminist angle to ideas routed within psycho-analysis (Beardsworth, 2005; Gilligan, 1982; Irigaray, 1993; Kristeva, 1994). This is massively important because these are ideas and perspectives which often still sit outside of our mainstream courses because they are very much built upon the patri-archal narratives which underpinned the acceptance or not of certain ideas from back in the old days of psychoanalysis. Where there have been attempts to correct these marginalisations, of which these sadly few and far between, include the likes of Laura Perls, Anna Freud, Emma Jung and others who have had to sometimes sit in the shadow of their partners in order to find their space and their voice (Freud, 1992; Jung, 1957; Perls, 1992).

This, though in more contemporary times, has also been challenged, not just by the inceptions of the acceptance of the ideas of feminist scholars, but also of the ideas of scholars from other communities, be they the LGBTQ therapists, therapists of colour and others in order to broaden the range and spectrums of perspectives (Ellis, 2021; McKenzie-Mavinga, 2009; Simpson, 2011; Various, 2022b).

The colonisation of our ideas and therefore of how we work therefore is obvious, as is the need to be increasingly aware that there is no one way to work and that our practice and being a practitioner within said practice is not a fixed point. Counselling and psychotherapy, for both therapists and counsellors, are journeys of discovery, and the colonisation of what it is walk this path to self-actualisation suggests that there is just one set way to do the work.

To discuss decolonisation, I am first of all going to use a couple of metaphors of how I see psychotherapy and therefore psychotherapy practice itself.

I am going to compare some trees. One is the birch tree, common to most of Western Europe and other parts of the United States and so on. This is a tree which grows up to about 30ft tall and around six to nine feet wide, over a span of 60 to 90 years. This is not necessarily a long-lived tree, and it is one which is quite commonly found and for myself represents the individualistic, slim, narrow nature of psychotherapy practices very much, trainings, modalities and how individualistic the world we live within actually is. I am going to compare this though with another tree. This is the Baobab tree, common to parts of Africa. This is a tree which has been called the tree of life, with a life of up to approximately 2,000 years. This tree is 75ft tall in some areas, with a branch span perhaps twice that, and is perhaps even 15-16ft wide in its trunk. An imposing tree, this tree is often one which, in some parts of Africa, is used as the staging post for markets and the sale of local goods.

These two trees though hold contrasts. The birch tree, whilst a narrow tree, is a tree which in Celtic mythology was seen as being part of a metaphor for renewal and purification. Its leaves and branches being used in ceremonies by Celts and others as ways of actually helping individuals and groups find their way and grow accordingly. This though contrasts with the Baobab tree which, as its' name suggests symbolises the life of humankind. This is a tree which is prehistoric in its origins and pre-dates both humanity and also the splitting of continents, over twenty million years ago. Native to the African continent, this is a tree which symbolises life and positivity in a landscape often dry and arid and where little else can often survive.

For myself, this is an even better metaphor for counselling and psychotherapy. Often when clients come to us their lives have taken the most negative of turns and there is no hope. The Baobab tree symbolises this hope from an Afrocentric perspective, and not only does it offer this level of reassurance, it does so with a history dating back millions of years, one where its mere presence has come to mean comfort.

The birch tree in this metaphor symbolises something more Eurocentric. The world that we live within is a lot more individualistic than those on the African continent or in other parts of the world. Therefore, a tree like the birch, with its' narrower waist, its' shallower roots into the ground and its' shorter lifespan, holds a closer similarity to that of psychotherapy in the global north, whereby modalities are created, therapists are constructed and we all walk in this profession in a very individualistic way.

The Baobab tree metaphor sees our work as being something which is ancient, which is deeply rooted and which interconnects all of us in many different disparate ways. Something that Carl Jung (Stein, 2005) talked about when he discussed the process of individuation is that the more that we work on ourselves, the more that we look at our own shadow material, then the more likely it is that we will bring to us not just the world around us that those who are on similar paths towards a moral righteousness and greater good for humanity. Or the work of Carol Gilligan (2014) who in her tearing apart the western patriarchal idea of care being a rational process, brought back the relational more heart centred side of our inter-connectedness.

The birch tree in this metaphor symbolises the separateness of psychotherapy and in some ways the pseudo-colonisation of psychotherapeutic ideas. Whereas, the Baobab tree, in its strength, growth and range, brings with it and brings to it those who would sit in its' shade, eat its fruit, gain health from its' sap and nurture it.

The importance of these metaphorical trees when we consider my ideas around decolonisation is that colonisation narrows things down. It is incredibly reductionistic to colonise ideas, ways of being, ways of acting to a set number of predetermined socially constructed ideas, structures, rules and hierarchical ways by which we are all defined. There is no freedom in this, there is no imagination in this, and although we teach our students that they have to be themselves and perform in a way that is actually more authentically them, often what gets acted out, both within our courses and within our university structures, is that students feel they have to perform to a certain narrative in order to achieve said prescribed goal. The tension between authenticity and achievement within a colonial system of education is a difficult one as discussed in the previous chapter. Yet, this also goes even further when we consider the ideas of what it is to be a psychotherapist and what it is to be in practice, given that often when we leave our training courses, we have become so adapted that it takes a long time for us to work out who we are beyond these structures.

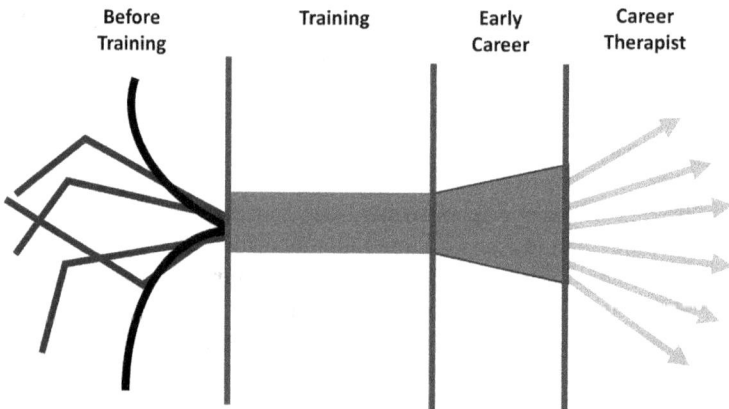

Figure 4.1 Decolonising practice.

This is where Figure 4.1 comes into focus. Figure 4.1 recognises the need for a re-alignment and a re-understanding of what it is to be a psychotherapist. The quest for the truth of what it is to be a psychotherapist is as limited and as reductionist a question as what it is to be a psychotherapist, but our colonised ways of thinking, therefore often suggest that there is just a singular way of being, and when we start to buy into this, we realise that actually we do ourselves, and our clients therefore, a massive, and stereotypical, disservice.

One of the strange experiences of my own training actually involved my trying to dress how I presumed a therapist should dress. My training was transpersonal integrative and, whilst on my training course in a slightly more alternative centre, I went through a whole period in not just embracing my spiritual side but in deciding that in order to fit in I would not only have to wander round the building in my bare feet but would have to dress in a slightly more 'hippy-esque' way than I might have done otherwise. In one way this was an attempt for me to fit in with what it was to be a transpersonal psychotherapist. Yet, after another fashion it was also a way of me trying to show that I was safe as a practitioner, not just by the work I did, but also by how I presented myself to my peers and my teachers.

Whilst I am using a slightly more comical example to make my point, there is a more genuine issue here. Colonisation is not just about what we read, it is also about how we act and how we think about ourselves and how we perform. Dress in an interesting way is one of the core areas that has become colonised over the years with one of the more obvious examples being something I have described in other texts around the colonisation of clothing, the idea being that to be seen as civilised one has to dress and therefore act a certain way in order to fit in (Turner, 2022). The drive to rebel, the drive to separate oneself out from that co-opted sense of being, is something which sits within each one of us. So, it was no surprise that in order for me to establish who I wanted to be as a psychotherapist that I would choose ways of appearing which were more relevant for me than for the service or the environment I had been trained within.

These messages do not necessarily come in overtly from outside. They are there because when we come back to the basics of experiencing difference, what happens when the coloniser sees something which is outside of the norm, is they will either react to it, exotify it or try and eradicate it. So, within psychotherapy, this eradication could actually take the form of the pathologising of the other, or some other means. The pull towards colonisation of practice and in these instances, of how we are as practitioners, is therefore always there.

In my introduction to this chapter, the very first example I gave you was of somebody who, whilst she may have considered herself as a feminist, also wanted to be part of the capitalist needs to be seen as successful, wealthy and so on. The internalised pull towards colonisation in that instance is as much about personal survival, because there is always a survival element built into capitalism, as it is about status and appearance. So, when it comes to practitioners exploring how they might want to be in practice post qualifying, explorations which could happen within their own therapy or within supervision, it is always important for them, the practitioner, and also for those who are supporting them in their work, to start to explore where these driving forces come from.

There is nothing wrong with wanting to make a good enough living from psychotherapy, with wanting to be wealthy or not. What there is alongside that, or what there should be alongside that, is a consideration of which part is actually looking to make that adjustment, to make a leap which will still tie them to a system of capitalism, of white supremacy or of patriarchy. Without that other awareness, then that co-option within said system can actually lead one to feel that there is no other way to be than the way they have adopted or adapted to.

Decolonising psychotherapy

Returning to Figure 4.1, it is essential to see the pathway from trainee to career therapist, because it is here where we are at our most performative as practitioners. From the very earliest stages of our courses, where we undertake triad work, to those students who on person intensive courses will tilt their heads to the side in a sort of Rogerian fashion, performing what they believe it is to be a psychotherapist. We act a certain way to achieve a certain goal and meet a certain target. This is no different to any other profession or any other activity. Learning to drive a car in the United Kingdom, students are often taught to have their hands at the hour points of 10-2, for example, as a means of driving; but in order to be one's own self behind the wheel of a car, one has to risk moving one's hands away from that 10-2 prescriptive ideal to one where there is a chance of actually experiencing and flowing and meeting the need of the car, of the driver, of the experience of driving.

Psychotherapy in some ways is no different. To be a psychotherapist is not to perform, it is to find a way of being that steps outside of the colonised norm and one of the things that I often find as a course leader on training courses is that there is a tension between how a student has been taught to be and how they would like to be as a practitioner, and nurturing that growth. Or, if I put it another way, nurturing the movement from their own individual existential roots into the trunk itself, means that they become something more than whatever I could prescribe, something more ideal, something more real and something truer to themselves.

Psychotherapy has a similar route to follow, as does practice. Much of what we look at in the modern day and age in how we practice is very much formed around previous ways of being. The adaptations we have made in how we practice, moving attendance at sessions five days a week, that traditional psychodynamic model, to some whereby people will attend only once a week, our adaptations were meant to meet the cultural and financial demands of the time. This is not to say that they are perfect. As I have previously stated, some of these adaptations actually cause more harm potentially than benefit for our potential clients. It is therefore down to us, as a profession, to constantly re-evaluate how we work and what we do and to research the best ways that we can move our profession forward given that the world has changed and flowed around us, perhaps in a way that we would not have expected and therefore the needs and dynamic within a psychotherapeutic framework have to change or adapt in accordance with this.

A perfect example is the world of assessments and how we undertake assessments. As I stated earlier on, working online during the Pandemic opened up a whole new area of experience and work for practitioners. This, though raises with it a number of challenges and, whilst I do not have all the answers to these challenges, it is important that we do not reject the challenge laid out before us and that we try and address how best we might meet said challenge as we walk into the future (BACP, 2023).

In the past, 95% of all assessments would have been conducted in a face-to-face environment. These assessments would be to ascertain the suitability of clients for our practices or for our clinical practice areas or placements. They would involve giving the clients a chance to experience some of the skills and techniques the therapists might use, for the clients to actually ask us questions about our work, so that they might themselves feel that bit more comfortable, and for us to set up the boundaries and the framework within which the work would proceed.

This is very different, though, or it changes at the very least, when we actually move this into an online world. An online space then brings with it additional challenges. For example, given the client's presenting issues, let us say they have had early attachment issues, is an online environment the right place for a client to work, versus a client who, for example, may be going through a bereavement or have ended a relationship, and they need some psychological support. These two very different types of client work will therefore generate different ideas about how we should approach and work with our client and the assessment process needs to be very aware of the change in dynamics accordingly.

Doing assessments online brings up a different type of unconscious process and, whilst there are some therapists who find it very difficult to experience the unconscious presence of a client in an online space, there are many others, with myself included, who I would suggest find working online a challenge and different, but note, there is still a strong unconscious process. The body still responds to the vibrations of the client's material, even when working on a screen. Working out, therefore, the types of clients that are better suited to working online versus those who are better suited to working face-to-face, is another core aspect to this.

Another interesting part to it is in working online, is this means that we access and work with a wider range of clients who are not going to be able to sit in a face-to-face environment collaborating with our clients on a week-to-week basis. This is not an adaptation, so much as an adjustment which makes psychotherapy more inclusive. Yet, it does need greater resources placed into research in order for us to understand how it works, why it works and the types of clients and scenarios where this still will be problematic and may not work.

Decolonising practice in the face of greater and newer challenges therefore becomes the next stage of the work that we all have to do as practitioners. Stepping outside of the psychodynamic confines not so much to leave them behind but to realise their limitations and means that we have a chance in a way to be slightly more authentic.

The next area to look at when we consider decolonisation of practice could also be the environment we work within. If we are working online, many of us are working from home in our living rooms or kitchens, or if we are lucky enough in a space dedicated for us to see clients. The Pandemic itself though, brought with it its' own challenges for many practitioners who did not have an ideal space within which to work and see their clients. Many therapists, like our clients themselves, were often working from home in bedrooms, kitchens or living rooms at their living room tables, as they tried to maintain their practices and make ends meet. The existential 'brilliance' of the Pandemic was that it actually shook up a great deal of what we assumed was normal as practitioners. The fact that so many of us would hire room spaces in major cities like London, Manchester, Liverpool, Edinburgh, Glasgow or Dublin, at fees ranging from £10 to £30 per hour in some towns and cities to somewhere in the twenties for a place in Harley Street, meant that we were all caught in the capitalist hamster wheel of trying to make ends meet, to pay big room rents, whilst also charging our clients a great deal more money that we would have done otherwise.

Having the freedom to get off said wheel, and to therefore work in a more authentic and less resentful way, meant that actually our work and our profession, for those moments, became that little bit more separate from a capitalist world where money begets money, begets money. Or where for some therapists the robbing of Peter to pay Paul became a regular occurrence for those who had debts and for those who could not afford to work and just see half a dozen clients per week. Psychotherapy in these instances then became as much about being forced to make a living as it was about trying to help and assist those who were psychologically challenged to find their way forward. In fact, I will add here that for a sizeable number of therapists, the challenges of renting spaces, meeting financial needs and demands, meant that it actually changed the way that many of them were working. This is not to say that loads of therapists out there are working unethically, but it is to suggest, and maybe to ask the profession to think about just how ethical the work is that we do, given that actually so many of us are working within a fairly tight financial framework, especially in here in the United Kingdom.

This is very different to America and across Europe, whereby students of psychotherapy often have to have a first degree, yet where there are similarities is that this first degree in some instances has to be paid for by the student themselves, so they are already carrying a great deal of debt by the time they actually achieve their goal of training to become and achieving said qualification in, psychotherapy. The financial world within which psychotherapy resides therefore becomes a major factor in forcing us to look at how much we charge, where we work, how we work and so on.

As I stated earlier on in this book, I myself exited my training courses with upwards of around £20,000 of debt. On leaving the charity that I worked at for a couple of years, and being made redundant, the one thing that I chose to do from the off at that point was that I decided that I would no longer be working for anybody else. I would work for myself and I had already established that I had enough savings to give myself six months to establish a private practice where I could actually do the work that I wanted to do to my own level of freedom. I am very aware that I am very fortunate to do this job and I do not prescribe that anybody else should follow in similar footsteps to myself. What I am saying here is that trying to extricate oneself from within the social systems which we all work within and reside within is very difficult, but the more aware we are of these systems then the greater the likelihood that one can find a more authentic space within said cultural construct.

Another part of practice that has also arisen and changed things considerably actually ties these two points together. A sizeable number of therapists and psychologists who have now moved their practice online, at least for part of the week, have now found that it is easier for them to work from spaces abroad. The prerequisite message that they should be working and living in a space relatively close-by their clients seems to have altered to a point whereby a respectable number of therapists are now able to see their clients, especially if working online, from either across the country or from spaces in other countries.

The reverse is also true. For example, that a good part of my work is online now means that I have a suitable number of clients and supervisees who are all around the country and in some instances who are British citizens but live abroad. The work has not necessarily changed as such because in many ways this work is still as rich, as fulfilling and as challenging as it has always been. What has altered though, is that in reaching out and working with a wider range of clients, this therefore means that we can all assist a bigger range of people to find their way forward through the psychological maelstroms.

As previously mentioned, when we start to see psychotherapy as a fixed point, when we start to believe that there is a set way to be as a therapist and that our practice has to take on a certain form, then we are falling into the unconscious space of colonisation of our work, of our understanding, of our being and of who we are.

Figure 4.1 challenges much of this, seeing psychotherapy and psychotherapy practice not just as a fixed point but as one which branches off in varying different areas or directions dependent upon the practitioner themselves.

When we talk about other ways in which decolonisation can occur within counselling and psychotherapy, it is also worth noting that there may already be some methods and methodologies and ways of working which reside within our profession that need to be recognised and highlighted. From those within the structures of colonisation, perhaps resisting their more oppressive standards and viewpoints, are things such as pluralism or integrative ways of working. Pluralism is a term coined by Mick Cooper and John McLeod (2010), the idea being that clients should have the chance to work with a therapist who understands a range of relational ways of working, thereby encouraging the therapist to grow in a less colonial and colonised way of being and a more authentic and therefore relational with the client way of being.

Integrative psychotherapy is another strand of this and although different to pluralism, also holds within itself the embers of decolonisation (Faris & van Ooijen, 2011). Integrative psychotherapy courses, a bit like pluralism though, have often been criticised for teaching practitioners a variety of ways of being as a psychotherapist, with a variety of theories, techniques and activities, all of which may work to understand the unconscious process of our clients, whilst also hindering the therapist's chance to become an 'expert.'

The issue I have with this word 'expert' is that it makes what we do into a hierarchy, that one should be the best and at the top of their game and follow a certain path to achieve that. This is another facet of the colonial narrative, the idea that one has to be the best at something in order to meet the needs of our client groups. The fact that there are a range of therapists and counsellors who may have done anything from a two-year post-graduate diploma course, to a four-year Masters course, to an additional year to become a supervisor, to anything between three and five years to gain a doctorate, and that therefore, in my view, brings up an interesting perspective. It is this: if clients only chose to work with those deemed the very best and expert in their field, then theoretically those therapists and counsellors who perhaps had only achieved a two-year course, would not be working in our profession, they would struggle to make a living because clients would not see them as being good enough. This we know, though, to be blatantly untrue.

There are a respectable number of counsellors on two-year courses who come out and achieve important things in the profession. In the same vein, there are a sizeable number of academics who work in institutions and have achieved their doctorates who are often seen as not being the best psychotherapists at all. One of the reasons for this is *the relationship*. The idea that one has to be the best, to achieve the best, to get the best qualification, takes away from the student therapist's relationship with themselves and therefore potentially their relationship with the client as the other. The idea that clients will seek out the best actually denies the fact that more often than not, what the clients are looking for is the best relational fit for them (and I put myself in this category, given that I myself am, have been and will be a client of psychotherapy and counselling). Can I collaborate with this person? Do I actually like sitting with this person? Do I not like sitting with this person but am I open enough to working with them and do I feel safe enough working with them in order to explore why that might be?

Ideas like this help us to then understand that the expertism, which is actually a form of oppression in the form of elitism, which sits within our world of counselling and psychotherapy, is actually part of the colonial narrative to be the best, to be the biggest name.

Offering you another experience from my own journey within psychotherapy, even I have been caught trying to find the expert. On one occasion, whilst I was doing some work around myself, I finished working with my previous therapist who was a female. We had been working together for about five years and I had done a good lot of work around what it was to re-nurtured by a good, positive, female role model. I then wanted to work with a man, to work on my issues around father and the masculine. A recommendation from somebody that I respected took me to see a therapist who I was told was at the top of his game and would be somebody that I could work with on unconscious processes around the masculine. The catch though was that this therapist would charge me £150 an hour (it should be noted that this was back in 2003, so this was a lot of money). Given that I was working as a temporary worker in an administrative capacity at the time, to find £150 an hour for a session was incredibly difficult for me and actually meant that the best that I could do was to see this therapist once a month.

I saw this therapist three times in a six-month period. This was for a number of reasons. The first reason was that he was incredibly busy, he had authored a book, people wanted to work with him, he had people travelling in from all over the place to sit with him. But this led to the second part which was in struggling to get a session and a regular appointment, it then meant that I was unable to build any sort of relationship with him that would have been reparative. There was not the space or the time to actually access those parts of myself which were like my father and in some ways. So, although it was helpful in replicating my experience of my father, who was a very distant man, there was nowhere for me to go with that. I often spent a lot of time on my own chasing the golden dragon and yet not actually getting there. So, whilst on an unconscious level this worked, on another level the fact that this was a therapist who I was told was an expert, although useful for my general process further down the line, did not help my psychotherapeutic work that much I might argue.

The third part is a little bit more interesting; this was a therapist who had written just one book. Looking back on this it was astonishing that I had bought into the idea that it takes one narrative, one book, one text of 60,000 words, to make one into an expert when one is white, male and middle class, as this therapist was. The difficulty here is what we term an expert, as I have stated earlier, is coated within the coloniser narrative. The idea that an expert is a man takes away from the voices of a respectable number of women therapists, such as Luce Irigaray, Jessica Benjamin, Carol Gilligan and many others who are just as experienced and I would argue are more adept at caring for a nurturing client than perhaps this particular therapist was. Subsequent to that experience, although I did not work with a woman for a number of years, what I did do was reframe what I wanted from a therapist and make it more relational. The importance of the relationship is key and to suggest that somebody can be an expert in relating actually misses the point of what it is to be a practitioner.

The colonisation of the psychotherapy expert

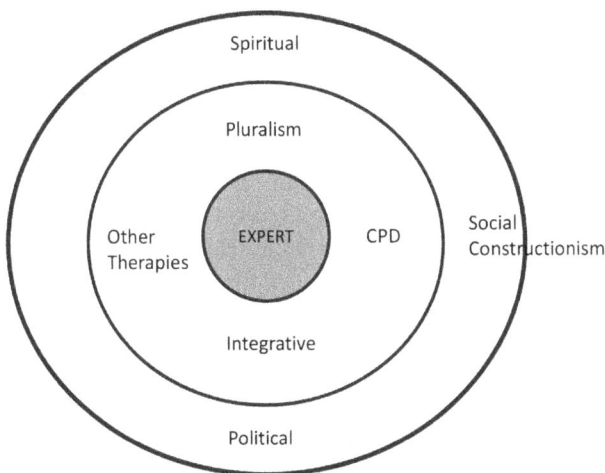

Figure 4.2 The expert in psychotherapy.

Figure 4.2 then explores this to a greater detail. The idea here is that, whilst we might need to have authors, writer, ideologists and theorists who develop ways of working which benefit the wider population, the idea that there is any one particular way of being is at best naïve, at worst narcissistic and destructive. What I mean to say is this, an expert in any particular area is an expert in that area alone and not necessarily in any other ways of working. For example, when we talk about ideas of privilege and supremacy, the idea that there is an expert who holds all the power and all the knowledge then means that it is easier to marginalise other ways of collaborating with clients, ways of using supervision, to the extent that everything else becomes pathologised. Having heard of numerous stories where students, who often come to psychotherapy as a second career, be it from psychology or social work or some other means, have often had their ideas denigrated or had their ideas mansplained, whitesplained or class-splained back at them, shows how easy it is for the expert to become ingrained within both our trainings, in our profession, and even within supervision.

The expert is a myth ultimately. It is one way of doing things and it takes away from the relational needs of our clients. Therefore, when we speak about psychotherapy and we speak about decolonisation within psychotherapy, one of the ideas that we need to challenge is this idea that there is an expert at all. Psychotherapy is not about expertise, it is about the relationship, it is about the ability of one person to work with another to the extent that they may feel and learn that bit more about themselves and therefore develop ideas and coping strategies to help them move through life in a more complete or comfortable fashion.

What I am suggesting here is that the idea of the expert is actually quite reductionist in how we understand human nature and that human nature, which is the map upon which the whole of counselling and psychotherapy is built upon, does not lend itself to a Daily Mail-esque way of pinpointing one or two key areas of development. This also has ramifications for the ways in which we practice psychotherapy. As I have previously stated, although I learned on a transpersonal integrative psychotherapy course what it was to be a practitioner, the fact that I had been drawn at varying stages throughout my career to different ways of being, modalities and structures and identities as a psychotherapist and counsellor, means that my career has taken a good number of different routes and directions that I could never have foreseen when I first trained.

The expert, therefore, as presented in Figure 4.2, in its limitations then misses the wide variety of other ways and modalities and techniques and ways of being in a relationship with our clients, which are always there within our interactions. Were I too have stayed within the narrow confines of a purely transpersonal way of working, then I would have missed out on some of the work of say Martin Buber, of some of the later ideas which involve the spirituality of say a Carl Rogers (Anderson & Cissna, 1997). I would have missed out on reading around issues of race and difference and diversity because those were not included in the reading lists of my transpersonal course (Dalal, 2006; McKenzie-Mavinga, 2009). Being brave enough to step outside of the colonised ideals of the training courses on which I was trained is not necessary for everybody, but it suggests at the very least that there are more ways to do our work than those originally presented.

This then returns us to other ways as presented in Figure 4.2. In some of the wider circles there, I have presented pluralism and integrative ways of working as some of the annals with which we may engage as we, as a profession, look to the next stages of what it is to be a counsellor and psychotherapist. To remain within the narrow confines of just a purely psychodynamic way of working, a purely humanistic way of working, or anything else, denies the developmental needs of psychotherapy as well as the instinctual developmental desires of the practitioner. What it also looks at here, in this diagram, is the fact that through the ethical requirements of continued professional development, we already have in place structures which encourage the decolonisation of ideas and thinking and actually mean that as practitioners we are constantly challenged, not just to update and upgrade our knowledge and understanding, but also to grow and to be 'better' practitioners.

I put the word 'better' in inverted commas here to highlight the idea that this is an insufficient word, it does not quite do what I would like it to, because ultimately better suggests there is some sort of hierarchy that one has to walk upwards of in order to be a good psychotherapist. This too is a myth and actually a better choice of word, or words, would be to say that actually as we grow to become a psycho-therapist, we move beyond this idea that we are an expert and we grow and become more expansive. We spread out, we grow, we become larger than the straight jack-eted perception passed to us through our post-graduate diplomas or our Masters. Whenever I talk to psychotherapists who have achieved a level of knowledge, say through their doctorate, what I always hear back from them is that they are in no way the same practitioner as they were when they first completed their study some years before.

This is not to say that the growth of a psychotherapy beyond the idea of the expert needs to be formalised in some way, because this in its own way is another form of colonisation, but it is to actually look at our practices and how we are, what we understand and how we work, needs to incorporate an understanding of the fact that one's growth does not end with the achievement of a qualification. We become who we are meant to be as psychotherapists by actually following our own routes, meeting varying people along said route, sometimes stumbling as we traverse the dissimilar stages of this route, as well as having intuitive realisations when we take times out along what can be a long and difficult path.

We have, in many ways, models of growth from childhood into adolescence or, using Erikson's model, through the life cycles to old age (Brady & Hapenny, 2010; Ogden, 2004). What we do not have is a generalised idea of what it looks like to become a practitioner and to go through one's career cycle. Again, this is not to say that there needs to be a formalised idea of what that should look like, because then all that happens is that you end up with a whole lot of students who want to map out their journey along the exact same route without recognising that they are unique individuals in their own rights. It is to encourage discussion and research into just what it is to be a psychotherapist in training, on qualifying, after 5 years, 10 years, 20 years and into retirement.

This is also important when it comes to issues of supervision. To borrow from one of my own stories, when I chose my first clinical supervisor, it was on the back of having worked with him in a placement setting a couple of years beforehand. During that process, I realised that I did not really like him very much, although I could not quite pinpoint the reasons as to why. I was a student, I was in the preliminary stages of my training, I had a lot of personal work to do, I was in this place- ment and I was working with a supervisor that I took an instant distaste to. When I chose my supervisor though, for my clinical work, I decided to challenge myself.

We worked together for a respectable number of years until he retired and it was one of the best experiences that I have had as a practitioner developing himself in his career through his supervision. Working through my projected father issues, then allowed me to build a relationship of mutuality and understanding and respect and love with somebody who was incredibly knowledgeable but also encouraged me to pick up my own power and take my own wings.

Supervision therefore plays a massive role in helping the therapist, and also therefore helping their practice, to develop from its original confines to something which is more authentically one's own. Through the relationship with one's super- visor, this can be achieved, or at least explored, should the supervisor and super- vision allow space for it. It is another strand, if you like, of just how important supervision is and how important the relationship with one's supervisor can be. On occasions, these relationships falter and they struggle and they fall, like any other relationship that we have, but by encouraging us to understand what it is about our projected patterns that has led to the disruption in the relationship, that too can be a learning experience.

Within the United Kingdom we have gone down the route of formalising super- vision qualifications to some degree, although not totally. Whilst important to make sure that there are a set level of standards within supervision, or within supervisors, it is also important to recognise again that one of the things that cannot really be assessed is the supervisor's ability to actually build and hold relationships, either with their individual supervisees or with their groups in individual or placement settings. These are things which, hopefully, have been considered within the initial trainings of all practitioners, those abilities to actually build relationships with one- self and with the other. Within supervision this is doubly important as, without the ability to hold the difficult complexities of said relationships from a slightly more removed angle, then what can often happen is things fracture and fall apart and not just harm the supervision and supervisees, but also potentially harm the clients that sit beyond them.

Another important part here comes back to Figure 4.2 and the idea of the super- visor as an expert. Something I often say to supervisees when they first come to work with me, especially if they are still in training, is that I understand that my role will be partly to teach alongside to take clinical responsibility for their client work, but that that role, that power dynamic has to change at varying points in our working relationship. Change to the extent that at some point in the future, when they have their own practice and it is all well-established, or they are just seeing a few clients a week, my role is not to be the overseer of what they do, the arbiter of what is right or wrong. It is to help them to internalise enough of the ethical paradigm within which we are working within and also enough of an understanding of the unconscious processes which go into the work that we actually do, to then see my role as a consultant for their practice.

They do not work for me at any stage in that process and, although in those initial stages I have a role to hold, a bit like a parent with a child, I do not own that child. At some point that child/supervisee will have had enough of me and will move on and do their own thing, and a good parent lets that child go. In the same way, if I am working for somebody else's business, say a limited company around being a practitioner, then I look forward to the day when they can say, 'Actually it is time for me to move on and have a different type of supervision. Thank you very much. Goodbye. It's over.'

The dynamics around power and colonisation are important here, even within the realms of supervision. So, not only do supervisors have to do the reading and the understanding of how their work might be colonised, but they also have to understand the nuances of the relational depths plural which can be explored within a supervised relationship between them and their cohort of practitioners. This then moves us away from that hierarchical one size fits all top dog/bottom dog scenario as often presented within structures of counselling, psychotherapy and supervision.

The expert is therefore just another title borne out of supremacy. In this context, it is not just about class difference in this because what I am actually saying here is that the elite or the expert is something which actually sits central to the coloniser's narrative. For example, many immigrants who were raised during colonial times were raised with the idea that the coloniser, be they the doctor, the politician or somebody else of a certain standard, was not only seen as an expert but was also seen as the elite and therefore as something to be deferred towards. The psychology of elitism hidden in the titles and roles we play is one of those areas of counselling and psychotherapy which is under researched.

Moving slightly sideways but to give a bigger emphasis as to why this challenge towards expertise and elitism is important within the decolonisation sort of narrative for psychotherapy, it is worth exploring that we often valorise those people who have paid the money to the best schools in the country in order for them to lead our country. It is the elite also who are behind such structures as the legal systems, white supremacy, and also definitions of what patriarchy actually is. They are the capitalists of the world and are often tasked with coming up with the best ideas for the industrial revolutions of our time. We exist in a world which is very much filled with an adherence to the work of those who are seen as the elite, as the intellectually superior (Duffell, 2014).

Even within the world of counselling and psychotherapy, we can fall into patterns of deference to those that we perceive as being more psychologically aware than ourselves, the psychological expert, the spiritual expert. These, to borrow from an idea posited by Walach (2008) point to the narcissism held within this sort of elevated position, and also highlights just how these types of positions and people can be used to abuse and destroy the other if we are not aware of the power we are giving them.

So, whilst we look to experts in fields to guide us through such things as pandemics, and so on, it is always worth noting that that guidance is given with, and should be held with, a certain respect as well. The aim here is not to undermine expertise in an area, but it is to question the types of people who are given the role of the expert. Do they all have to be white, middle- and upper-class men? Can they be women, possibly of colour, possibly of another sexuality or persons who are nobinary, or of another ability? When we cast persons who perhaps see themselves as experts but who have not earned the right to be seen as such, then what we are actually doing is playing into a coloniser narrative which actually suggests that a person can be seen as an expert, even if they do not have the wisdom and intelligence to hold such a role.

From a slightly similar angle, the Global North's strange preoccupation with the promotion of celebrities to positions where they get to run countries, is an example of where the idea of an expert has been corrupted to a certain degree. Long gone are the days where being morally corrupt, racist, sexist or homophobic, would actually preclude you from a position of power. Now is the time whereby plenty of people will follow and listen to the faith narratives of influencers that head up the Incel regimes or men who for varying reasons have decided that they are the ones to lead our countries forward (Casciani & De Simone, 2021; Yan et al., 2016).

The expert in a way, and this is another layer of the challenge that lies within Figure 4.2, has become corrupted or more importantly, the idea of what an expert is has become distorted, watered down, and has become nothing more than a social construction. The true meaning of an expert, that person who through pain, effort and suffering, has gotten to a point whereby they understand and they know their environment and the world around them to a degree far greater than anybody else in their field, has not quite disappeared but is very much hidden away. This is very much to do with the age of media that we reside within and is an idea that Stuart Hall (1996) placed in his work when considering the issues of difference and diversity and of the manipulation of the masses through the media.

That it takes a media to elect a Prime Minister or a President says an awful lot about the power that said media outlets actually hold and in the same fashion. That it takes a media to disrupt and discredit those who may hold vital information about the topics of the day of real experts, says an awful lot about the role the social construction of what it is to be an expert and how that can be changed, if we are not careful.

A re-imagining therefore of what expertise actually is, is what sits at the centre of Figure 4.2. it is not the small expert as laid out on the outskirts of this diagram, it is a non-picturesque, plain looking, 10,000 word puzzle of ideas, of experiences, of training, of tears, of pain, of effort, of laughs, of love, of creativity, that have all come together to create innovative new narratives that sit within our counselling and psychotherapy environment today and the wider environment. It is not the purchased power professed by a media outlet which then tells us what we should do and how we should do it. It is the bloodied, guiding hand of those who have suffered in order to achieve their aims and their goals that brings relationship and with it trust and belief in the experience that many of us will choose to follow.

To go a little bit further though, with ideas held within Figure 4.2, as already touched on, social constructionism plays a role here. Not so much the fact that social construction plays a role in the construction of what it is to be an expert, but more so the idea that actually social construction plays a massive role in how we understand ourselves as human beings. Psychotherapy has been and has been mentioned many a time in varying different articles, ignorant of the role of the political within its field of play (Samuels, 2004). This has therefore missed out very much so on how much of who we are is moulded by the world we live within and also the political.

Ideas of what it was to be a gay man changed in 1967 here in the United Kingdom when it stopped being illegal to be gay. This did not though end the story for many clients who were born before that time. There are clients that I have worked with over the years who were raised in a time whereby their sexuality was seen as something not just to be feared and ashamed of, but something which was seen as illegal and therefore immoral. They were impacted by the political narratives of the time and that internalisation would walk with them forever more in many different cases.

Modern versions of this political moulding still exist. For example, ideas about what it is to be of colour have often had their roots in the politics of said times, many of which still rumble on today. Simple ones like the need for students of colour to have a 'tidy' afro hairstyle, and ideas that are often used within schools to marginalise, and in some cases exclude children of colour, again have their roots all the way back in slavery and colonialism and what was acceptable and not acceptable for persons of colour, much of which was actually underpinned by rules and regulations and laws of those times (Akbar, 1984; DeGruy, 2005).

We even have decolonisation of clothing. Having written blogs about this, having talked about it in this tome as well, the fight for girls in school to wear trousers in many ways has its roots all the way back in the idea that actually if you were a girl and you wore anything other than a dress, you could be fined or, in some cases placed in prison (Rovine & Rovine, 2018; Turner, 2022).

These narratives, these ways that define us are as much rooted within the political and the social constructions as they are in the psychological and it is difficult if not nay impossible, to separate one from the other. These are things which will therefore play a role in what it is to be a human being and if we are going to decolonise psychotherapy and the practice that we do, we need to understand much more the role that the political has played in forming our sense of who we are in the world. Otherwise, processes which have been presented as ideas, such as individuation, fall on the rocks of reality as soon as we encounter such a thing as a pandemic where gendered structures which were long thought to have been put to bed during the times of feminism, came racing back into play during the pandemic for many clients (Hennekam & Shymko, 2020).

Exploring the conjunction between the political and the social construction, be they through workshops or by having these further embedded within training courses, is therefore hugely important if we are going to look at how we decolonise counselling and psychotherapy.

Another aspect of this, which ties itself back to the idea of expertise and elitism, and also to power, is that when we look at these constructions, we further help our clients to do the work of decolonising themselves should they wish to do so. The power to self-define, a power which underpinned the feminist movement in its earliest days and has also underpinned ideas of wokeness and the movement towards differing gender identities and pronouns within the black and LGBTQ communities, have their roots in some ways in these decolonial narratives (Cammaerts, 2022; Durant, 1994). Understanding this for our clients then means that actually they too have a choice as to whether they want to remain defined within said social constructions and remain within the political sort of structures, laws and legalities of the time, or should they wish to take on what can be a massive existential challenge by decolonising themselves and walking the lonely, individual, path towards self-identifying who they are.

In many instances in my practice work, people take both. Where in some ways they are happy to remain within said structure, especially cultural or religious ones, whilst in other ways they seek for something more. This not an either/or argument. It is about assisting clients in managing and manoeuvring between two different poles in order to find not just a grey area, but to expand their identification so that they incorporate aspects of both. Ultimately, these simple examples here move psychotherapy away from the idea that as an expert I have to have all the answers in order to define and understand somebody else's process. This then returns our work to that of an exploration, not just between myself and my clients, but also for the client and them in their world, but also for myself and my supervisor as well. The expert is passed around between us. Sometimes, I will hold the knowledge as the therapist, sometimes my supervisor will hold the knowledge as supervisor, and sometimes we both sit back and listen to the client because they hold the expertise on their experience because that is their world.

The political in psychotherapy practice

As stated earlier in this book in Chapters 1 and 2, many of the forebears of our profession were themselves impacted by the political. The writings of Sigmund Freud amongst many others, being much rooted in the antisemitism of Europe during the early part of the last century (Freud, 1964; Jacobs, 2003). It has therefore been interesting to watch as psychotherapy has become colonised to such a fashion that it has lost its political upbringing and standing. There have been numerous moves though, over the years, to re-institute the political back into psychotherapy. In the United Kingdom, for example, psychotherapists and counsellors have a social responsibility as set up by Professor Andrew Samuels and Professor Suzie Orbach and others and who have worked tirelessly over the years to implement and encourage debate and discussion the political within psychotherapy and has invited a number of names, myself included, to come and talk at varying conferences and provide talks to consider just how the political actually enacts on us all psychologically. More modern efforts include Therapists for Social Care, as directed by Professor Mick Cooper (2023) in the United Kingdom and movements already mentioned for minority groups who of course are very aware of how the political impacts upon themselves, because they themselves are the ones who it most affects (Various, 2022a, 2023).

This section here, in looking at the political in psychotherapy, therefore encourages us to look at just how the work that we do when decolonised may actually encourage clients to come further forward into the therapeutic space so that they may feel better heard, respected and empathised with about their issues, not just the psychological ones but also those which are impacted by the socioeconomic status of the worlds around them. It has become too easy for practitioners in the past to pathologise away issues. For example, around say a client's desire to engage in BDSM, which is often presented psychologically as some sort of psychological disturbance. This fails to recognise that in some ways the social constructions around what it is to be 'normal' within a sexual framework actually marginalises and others huge ways of being which sit outside of that principally orientated often, and socially constructed more often, ideal as to how we are all supposed to act and behave (Domingue, 2019; Greenberg, 2019; Speciale & Khambatta, 2020).

This is not to say that anything goes. There are clear demarcations whereby the legal and the moral actually coincide and work closely together. Where there is a divergence between the legal, and the moral, and therefore the psychological, is where distress might occur. The most obvious example is the split between the illegality of homosexuality in this country, a law which was repealed in the 1960s, and a law which also underpinned some of the ideas in the DSM3 of the time, but which did nothing to change behaviours, in fact all that happened with this is that it forced a whole group of people to feel unmet, unseen and to hide themselves away, less they be marked out as wrong or as others.

Morality and culture and the law do not move at the same pace. Often, the morality of a people will move ahead of the structures and the laws which are needed to underpin said ideals. So, when we develop different moralities around things such as sexuality, such as the discrimination against women, or other minority groups, or against the horrors of slavery, what often happens is there will always be people who will want to uphold said legal ideals. These people will state that these old ways are the cultural way forward, instead of seeing them as what they are, which is limited to the cultural structures of the time. Laws, although designed to suggest a moral framework, quickly become dated when that moral framework evolves to be replaced by something newer and more appropriate for the culture within which we all reside. Morality therefore never stays static; it does not stay the same. By the same token, our failure as practitioners to recognise and understand that morality is fluid means that we are only left with the legal frameworks of the times that we live within and much of the questioning about what we do and how we do it fails to occur.

Offering you a client example to make my point helps here:

> A client came to my practice and told me a story whereby they had been to see a previous therapist about an issue to do with their relationship. This young man was married with a young child. His previous therapist was female. When having an assessment with the previous therapist, he had informed her that he was training to become a counsellor himself and was on a course at a prestigious centre. He also informed her that one of the things he wanted to work on was issues around his infidelity. He had on numerous occasions paid for prostitutes. The previous therapist took a very strong line on this and suggested that she could not work with this client unless he sought out some sex and love addiction care, went to regular meetings and acknowledged that what he was doing was wrong. She also went down the route of deciding that he should not be training as a counsellor on his course and would be informing the governing body of the fact that this was a student who "obviously" in her words, lacked the morality to undertake said training. The student felt affronted, stunned, and understandably did not go back. When coming to see myself, what I recognised was that it was not my job to be the moral arbiter for said client. It was my job to actually work with the client to ascertain what it was that was missing for him that he needed seek out other women, therefore leaving his wife and child behind.

The reason I give you this example is when we talk about morality, although what the student counsellor had done was illegal the strong reaction of the previous therapist was less about adhering to certain morality and more about buying into a certain legality and establishing a power dynamic between her and the counsellor, that ultimately pushed him away. There will probably also be issues around just how provoked the previous therapist was by the material that she heard, together with the reasons why, together with a need for that therapist to explore just why they had had such a strong reaction.

One of the things I should express here is that when we talk about social constructions of identity, about the rights and wrongs of what we should and should not be doing, it is worth recognising that this kind of countertransference, when it is raised to the surface, is a very different beast. To say a little bit more about this; countertransference is a term which was originally coined by psychodynamic psychotherapists (Bright, 2009; Ogden, 2016). It was originally used to help therapists to gather information about the client's inner world, which part of the client are they not able to own. For example, when they tell us a story about something difficult within themselves, how we experience said story may differ to, or be similar to, the way it is actually being told to us. Is the client, for example, authentic in their expression? Or is the client inauthentically talking to us about something very difficult whilst say smiling, yet we are left with a sense of just how hard and difficult the experience actually was for them?

When it comes to socially constructed ideas though, around race, around difference, around morality, these are things which are co-created. We are the moral framework of the world around us, the same way that we are the legal framework of the world around us. We either buy into it or do not, but we play a part within in. So, any counter-transferential material, when it comes into the space via our clients, is going to be provocative for both the client and ourselves. What I am saying here is that this is more than just being about therapists attending to their own prejudices; this is a deeper connection to not just the moral framework that we have within ourselves. This is more than just about being provoked by our clients and providing them with a legal or moral standing that perhaps they are not aware of or that they have had to confront or challenge in some way. It is going to be about the therapist attending to their own internalised power structure, be it legal or moral.

There will be plenty of therapists in our profession who will have done something legally wrong or morally challenging in their time, be it having smoked cannabis or slept with prostitutes or have worked in the sex industry. This does not mean that these people should not be practitioners, but what it does mean is that as their therapists, we very much have to look at our own issues around drug use or around sex and pornography. It brings us closer into line with the world around us and makes us actually perhaps for the first time in lots of our cases, come down from the mountain of superiority we have built for ourselves and explore the lived experiences of many of those clients, therapists, practitioners who we meet on this very interesting, yet slightly strange at times, journey.

Working with that countertransference, that deeper embodied sense that we are ourselves being challenged to think about that split between the legal and the moral, then actually moves us out of that sort of colonised space of believing that we know what is morally right for everybody and plants us further into the grey area of trying to work out where are the moral lines that we all need to adhere to? It makes us think, and this is something when we decolonise as I have already stated previously, and this is something that we are all being encouraged to do when we take on the project of decolonisation. The ability to reach beyond knowing and being an expert, a position which does not mean we have to think at all, as we just know, to one whereby we actually work with what is there in the space, where we are actually doing the thinking with our client, co-creating a moral narrative that works for them, is something which needs to be encouraged.

With the client example above, like I stated, my desire was less to judge him on what he was doing, but more so to explore with him the reasons for why he was doing so. In our exploration it was not that he stopped sleeping with prostitutes forever, but in understanding the compulsion to do so, the flaws in his actual relationship with his partner, his sense that he was feeling like he was left outside in a way from the mother/child dyad. These other aspects of his world, helped him move himself from a position whereby doing so was a compulsion to one whereby there was an active choice as to what he could, could not, might or might not do. Ultimately, the need to find somebody else to feel close to diminished greatly and he found himself in a far deeper relationship with both his partner and his child. But, having that insight into somebody else's world and having that ability, perhaps driven by my own dives into the darkness of my own psychological well-being, then meant that I could actually sit with the darkness of somebody else when they are lost, not to bring them out of the labyrinth so to speak, but to sit there with them until they discovered the light and found their own way through.

To understand more the importance of the political in psychotherapy, I am going to offer another client example:

> Frances was a 50-year-old woman who was living on an estate in Southeast London. She had three children and had not been working for several years because she had chosen to dedicate her time to looking after her children. From a Middle Eastern background, she had lived on the estate for a few years, an experience that she found quite difficult given not only its multi-cultural nature but the diverse levels of prejudice that she endure, not just from her white counterparts but also those who were of colour. Frances had previously had therapy with a white, female psychotherapist who was from a middle-class background. Frances found the therapy to be unhelpful, not just because of the modality but because of an underlying sense that she was left with that the therapist was judging her.
>
> When working with myself, although she felt slightly more comfortable, she recognised that the differences between us, given that I am Black British and she was from a Middle Eastern immigration background. This meant that there were going to be differences in how we saw the world. Her fear also being one of me heralding some the same prejudices that she endured whilst living on said estate.

When looking at an experience like Frances', it is worth exploring what I often feel happens with clients of difference who encounter counsellors and psychotherapists who are perhaps from that more mainstream stereotypical band. This being that the client's experiences of deprivation, of living on an estate and so on, is not really held or met by said therapist because there is a difficulty understanding those experiences. Part of the reason for this is obvious, the therapists themselves often, although not always, have no bona fide experience of what it must be like to live on a major estate in southeast London during the years of austerity. Also, because they have been fed a diet of media narratives and therefore of stereotypes, there can be a tendency to believe the stereotypes and see them as a reality, instead of recognising that stereotypes, by their very nature, are limited and can only tell us so much about the person or persons they represent.

The second part to this was the feeling for Frances that she could not bring much of her experience to the therapy. For Frances, being from an immigrant background and having to endure and work within such a deprived sort of space meant that for her a secure base, a term which has been very much used within the world of psychotherapy since its inception, was a very different thing to somebody for whom security and a secure base could be seen as a luxury and where survival is seen as more beneficial (Bowlby, 1988).

A secure base, when explored by the likes of Bowlby and other theorists, is expressed in such a way that it does not really take on board the class or cultural context within which it resides. There is an assumption that all children should be able to have that secure base, although what that might look like will differ from child to child, from family to family. It should also be noted that even with the security of a safe environment, some children may still push back and rebel because that is their nature. Security does not mean that a child is automatically safe and will respond well to said safety.

For Frances, security meant being able to live in a space whereby she felt respected and safe; where she was not going to be shouted at by persons who wanted to pick at her or pick on her when she was walking home from school with her children. Security meant the ability to get things completed through working with her Council on a regular basis when necessary. It also involved making sure that her children were safe, her eldest one being of an age where he wanted to spend more time with his friends, yet for Frances this was incredibly difficult given the environment they lived within.

In many ways, within the world of counselling and psychotherapy, we talk about these things as though they are a given across society and yet when we factor in the socioeconomics of the time, and what these might mean, these things differ hugely across their range. When we consider issues of security and place them in the context of class and socioeconomics, then for Frances in our work our exploration became about how could she provide an environment for her children which was secure and safe. Or, more importantly what was she already doing that meant that she had been able to live in such an environment for such a long time? What qualities had she developed that allowed her to feel safe in said space?

For Frances when she explored some of this same material with her previous therapist, her previous therapist was very much of the mind that she needed to leave the estate as soon as possible, that it was not OK for her to be living there and that she needed to do more to keep her children safe. In our explorations, whilst these ideals were seen as noble, they were also seen as being fairly unrealistic given the financial constraints Frances was under. This whole idea, therefore, that clients often need to look at the psychological reasons for why they cannot earn more money, to place themselves within a better financial position, often denies a reality which is that actually the world that we all reside within, a capitalist environment, needs us to hold a certain level of poverty in order for us to keep running on the wheel like hamsters.

As a side note, this became most apparent as a during the cost-of-living crisis of 2022 and 2023, whereby post the global 2019 Pandemic and with the war in Ukraine, families found themselves financially stretched. Not only would the price of foodstuff rise and in some ways double, but also the cost of fuel, gas and electric also rose by something like 70% (Iacobucci, 2023; Webster & Neal, 2022). So, whilst in many countries across the Global North governments stepped in to assist their populaces to survive the economic onslaught meted out to them by such dramatic and high increases, what this also meant was that for the first time in perhaps a generation, the middle-classes were impacted as well as those from working class backgrounds.

The idea therefore that any one of us only needed to pull up our bootstraps and work that bit harder to make more money to get through what was an incredibly grim time, then denied the reality of the fact that much of what was happening was out of all of our control. That what needed to take place within Frances' experience was more of an understanding of just how powerless she was to affect systemic change. Empathy, sympathy for the predicament that she and others were in, then became massively important in our work and for Frances. Being heard and having some space to actually talk about her struggles meant that she often felt slightly more relieved on leaving the therapy than she did when she entered.

Counter-transferentially that feeling of powerlessness, which I suspect motivated the previous therapist to actually keep offering solutions and examples of what the client could do differently, in my case had to be held and I had to sit with a reality that this is not going to change any time soon. Sitting with the powerlessness of things also meant that I stopped being the expert, or I stopped believing that I had the genuine solution to what was an impossible, economic conundrum. It is important therefore for students, for courses, and for us as practitioners within the profession, to recognise that these realities for all our clients, as well as ourselves, are going to sit within the therapeutic space. So, to pathologise as many of them away as we believe we can do, actually means that we fall into the colonised trap of what it is to be a therapist and reject the decolonisation of our practice.

To add to this, when we come at our practice from a decolonial perspective, we return psychotherapy to the world of the political, including socioeconomic inequalities, racism, sexism, homophobia, ableism, ageism and other forms of prejudice which are not necessarily covered under the Equalities Acts of the United Kingdom. These methods of separation which actually have a broader platform within the worlds of counselling and psychotherapy. This means that not only do we have to attend to our own experiences of these, an area that I will look at in more detail in a later chapter when I look at how, as practitioners and as human beings, we decolonise ourselves, it is about recognising that actually the way that we work with our clients in these instances is slightly different to the more traditional work that we all choose to do.

This re-marriage of the political and the psychological, this recognition that the political has a psychological element and that the psychological holds within it the political, should be more central to how we practice as psychotherapists and counsellors and as psychologists. And, although this might mean that we have to take greater steps in doing research into understanding the worlds that we work within, when we finally chose to do so what we will also start to do is to see ourselves, our clients, and our profession in a far broader and richer way than we have done until now.

For myself in my own experience as a client, even I have experienced therapy whereby experiences of racism that I have endured have been marginalised. Yet, it is strange that in my latest tranche of psychotherapy, having unconsciously chosen a therapist to work with who is also in their own way political, what it needs me to be able to do is to explore issues of difference and diversity through my own lens, but also feel met, respected and encouraged by the political narrative that my own therapist holds. Much of my work over the past five years has centred around the wealth, depth, empathy, kindness, sadness, tears and rage that I have been able to bring into my own personal therapy, to the extent that these are things that have now become central to who I am and I have not been encouraged as I have done in previous therapies, to leave them outside of the therapeutic space because they are not 'seen as psychological enough.'

Decolonising supervision practice

Supervision as per the BACP ethical guidelines (2018) involves the requirement of all practitioners to undertake reflection and consideration of their own practice on a regular basis. What a regular basis could be anything from one and a half hours per month, as per BACP guidelines, and could also be with either an individual supervisor or be in a group of peers with a more experienced supervisor or just purely of peers on their own.

Supervision is an essential aspect of the work that we do as counsellors, psychotherapists and psychologists and offers us the chance and opportunity to understand the theoretical, experiential and ethical issues that might arise in any sort of client presentation. From my own standpoint, it has been an essential aspect of my own work to have regular supervision, so much so that whatever the guidelines state, my own sort of intuitive knowing of what the right amount of supervision for myself is, has always taken precedent.

The problem with supervision is that it is often pitched within the framework of a hierarchy. The student seeks out the supervisor, the supervisor has way more experience than them, and so on. This then sets up an interesting and sometimes challenging power dynamic, whereby the supervisee, be they student or an experienced practitioner, often feels that they do not have as much experience or knowledge as the person that they are working with (Hawkins & McMahon, 2020; Ladany et al., 2012).

The reason for the statement that I made earlier on in this chapter, that at some point my role as a supervisor must change, actually earmarks the various stages of supervision. Figure 4.3 highlights some of these distinct stages as I see them:

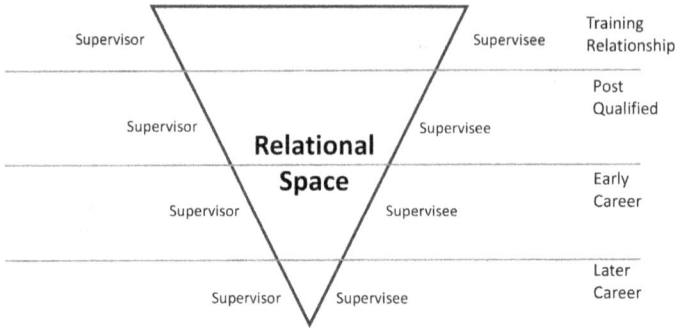

Figure 4.3 Decolonising the supervision relationship.

Figure 4.3 recognises that the relationship between a supervisor and a supervisee is very different in each stage and changes dramatically as the practitioner becomes an experienced counsellor or psychotherapist. It is obvious that even though a supervisor has clinical responsibility for the work all the way through, at Stage 1 there is a very different responsibility which also involves a layer of teaching. This can involve the imparting or helping the students make sense of theoretical material they have been taught on their courses, but it may also involve helping the student to recognise unconscious processes in a way that they have not been able to do so beforehand. The relationship between supervisee and supervisor is still important and still essential but it is a very different beast to later on in the supervisee's journey.

The newly qualified practitioner in Stage 2 and the supervisor I find often have to work to restate the boundaries or, more importantly, the power structure involved in their relationship. The person who wants to fly, as per my statement earlier on in this chapter, the student who wants to leave home, often appears at this time. The student who has decided that actually they know enough to start venturing out on their own and at that point, that more parental position of being a supervisor changes. I often find myself asking the simple question *can I, as a supervisor, let that student go and find their own way?*

Stages 3 and 4 have similarities but also differences. My role as a supervisor has to shift and change in these spaces. As I have stated beforehand on many occasions, and this is something that I state in my own work, at this point it is about the working relationship between myself and that practitioner. I am there to help facilitate them and their world and a bit like a parent who has watched his own child leave home and have their own children. I am no longer the parent in charge, I am perhaps the grandparent, or the kindly uncle who is there to offer some advice, support, sustenance and care and holding should things become a bit too difficult. This subtle, but also very important realisation that the role of the supervisor changes throughout the career of the supervisor and the supervisee, actually helps us to move away from this hierarchical idea of it being a static, 'Well you have way more experience than me, and therefore I am going to be less than you for ever more.' Like a wise elder who sees the world has changed and is vastly different for their charge than it was for them, there is a recognition that the psychological landscape has changed, and that the supervisee is the one who has to negotiate these new philosophies and terrains.

The problem with that, when that does happen is for some supervisees, when the supervisor feels the often insecure need to maintain control and superiority, there can be an inherent need to rebel against and push up against that which they perceive as more superior. Whereas for some supervisors, their discomfort with holding that level of power can also become detrimental to the supervisory relationship. Even just exploring this, or broadening it out, actually starts to move us beyond some of the ideas and ideologies that sit within our profession.

Staying within this stage, supervision can also, when it becomes more peer-based or more group-based, run into the problem of colonised thinking. For example, in a peer group, with this being yet another type of group, which may also hold echoes of one's family unit or cultural system, then there can be a propensity to play out similar colonised narratives to the ones that one was raised with from childhood. When looking at understanding our practice as supervisors, it then becomes essential to understand the socially constructed internalised experiences which may lead to a supervisee playing a certain role within a group setting.

I remember being part of a group a number of years ago where myself, and three other women were working with a white, middle-aged man. This was in the early stage of my career. During our interactions, it became quite obvious that one of the working-class women in the group was finding it increasingly difficult to work with the supervisor. She felt picked at by this man and he, consequently, felt he needed to challenge her that bit more about some of her work. In the end, their relationship fractured leading to a meeting that they held outside of the group and leading to this supervisee leaving because she felt that she could not work with this person any further.

Now, whilst I did not know the full details of said meeting, so it is not my place to comment on those. What it did leave me with a sense of in our subsequent meetings where we discussed the absence of the fourth supervisee, was the recognition of the power dynamics held within the space. One of the things that was mentioned was that the supervisee did see the supervisor as a father figure but felt unable to work with the projection that she had placed on this man at that point. Or another way of looking at it was that given that she had chosen to leave she had done something that she maybe had not done beforehand, which was to separate herself out from an experience and an environment which was not quite working for her.

This very brief example of just how delicate and how necessary it is for supervisors to understand the systemic group dynamics which can come into the supervisory space, although presented through a psychodynamic lens in this case, will also come up through social constructionist lenses as well. The times where supervisors have found it difficult to hear issues of race, gender, sexuality, ability, as presented by their supervisees, and have reverted back to lazy comfort of a pre-determined theory as a means of understanding why a client is acting or is presenting in the way that they have. As opposed to reaching out and doing yet more understanding and research with regard to just what their supervisors are attending to in the wider socioeconomic landscape, says an awful lot about just how powerful supervisors can be but also how reductionist they can be as well.

So, my next point is that the supervisor's ability to remain open to more than just their modality is of massive importance. As discussed in the last chapter, what it is to be a psychotherapist in the modern era is a very diverse thing, it does not follow one route and one pathway only and too many psychotherapists who are so wedded to their own modality, believe that to be the route to the psychological Narnia, or the pathological promised land. The same can be said for supervisors. The natural curiosity of all of us which has brought us to this job, I would suggest, should also be there within supervision to the extent that it allows us all to develop and to grow and to come across new and improved ways of working that inform our practice and our supervision and our supervisory ideas.

The willingness to be open to a supervisee's experience of their clients which does not necessarily resonate with a psychodynamic or an existential perspective, but perhaps sits within more of the realm of Pink Therapy and their theories or of black psychotherapists and some of their ideas, means that actually the supervision becomes a growing organic beast which allows for greater exploration of the nuances of the relationships (Davies & Neal, 1996; Hocoy, 2005; McKenzie-Mavinga, 2009; Various, 2022b; Wilkinson & Kitzinger, 1996). What I am ultimately leaning towards here is a movement away from the expert in Figure 4.3 as discussed, as presented through the supervisor lens and supervision being more relational and exploratory and investigative, allowing supervisees the chance and the modelling whereby they start to critically think about the work that they are doing, not just through a theoretical landscape, and not just through a psychological one, but also through a social constructionist lens as well.

The number of times I have encountered stories of supervisors who have totally reduced down an idea to *well, it's got to be something to do with their parents*, or, *are we sure that they don't just need to try and work harder in order to achieve their goals*, is astonishing and being aware of the power dynamic that goes with that is hugely important as well, because what it can also lead to is a supervisee feeling unseen, unheard and unsafe, to the extent that they end up shutting down and not exploring what is being presented.

The next part, when we consider supervision with just peers follows on from this to a certain degree and whilst these environments can feel like uncontained groups at times, often where they are very beneficial is that they are constructed with likeminded people who work well enough together to explore and investigate whatever is going on in the therapeutic space. The other part to this is the importing of knowledge into the supervision space. My idea here is that instead of supervision always being encouraged as a top-down endeavour, whereby the knowledge is imparted by the supervisor, be it in an individual or a group space, supervision needs to re-imagine itself as a space of co-created knowledge development. This means there are echoes of Figure 3.2 here from the previous chapter.

What this also means in a way is that a supervisor should be encouraged to use the reading and resources that all students, all practitioners encounter on their journeys to become qualified and bring that into the supervisory space. Co-created meaning then means that we see our clients through a co-created lens, it is not just one way or the other and a co-created element as understanding then means hopefully through this more phenomenological lens that we see the client in a more complete fashion. This takes away if one likes from the idea of the supervisor being all knowing, but it also challenges the notion that a supervisor who is not in the room with a client, should know anything more about the client than the supervisee, than the therapist, than the student. This gentle challenge then allows space for the supervisee's own knowledge and unconscious experience of said client to become centre stage. It also helps them to develop the ability to critically think about their work and also to decide what it is of supervision that they want to use or discard, because they ultimately are at the coalface of psychological exploration.

Summary

One of the things this chapter has aimed to do is to consider the colonisation of counselling and psychotherapy practice over the years and also look at the ways and means in which might benefit from taking a closer look at how culturally and systemically co-opted our profession has become, together with just how exclusionary this has made our environment as well. By doing this reflection there is also the chance for counsellors and psychotherapists to better consider and analyse just how they might themselves decolonise their practices.

The reasons for this are actually quite simple. In my own work I have come across a sizeable number of activists, be they from the LGBTQ community, feminists, persons of colour, disability activists and others all of whom are working incredibly hard to consider ways and means in which their lives might benefit from greater levels of equality and equity. For our profession to then encourage these potential students to leave those aspects of who they are outside of the courses, seems incredibly naïve at least and psychologically destructive at best. The idea that feminists attending training courses in the United Kingdom must put to one side their own feminist ideals in order to adhere to theories and ideas which have become colonised and patriarchal, then actually causes psychological harm, an issue that I will discuss in the next chapter. So, to therefore dis-encourage our profession to not be political, then takes away a large amount of potential for our profession.

This last point is really quite important. In the colonisation of counselling and psychotherapy, often what can happen, and this has taken place I would argue within say the Employee Assistance Programmes framework, is an idea that the work that counsellors are doing is actually to help clients fit back into systems of oppression and distress. Our forebears in our profession saw this and realised that there was something wrong with this approach, and it is actually since then that these ideas have gradually been challenged over the years. For example, R. D. Lang in some of his writings recognised the societal and the behavioural constructs which, when not adhered to, can be seen as forms of psychosis or, to put this a better way, could be marked down as forms of mental illness, even when they are not (Laing, 1969).

The obvious examples, hysteria in women and how that was seen as some sort of psychological disorder; homosexuality is another one and the inability for slaves to know their place is a third (Kernberg, 2002; Lev Kenaan, 2021; Willoughby, 2018). Some types of neurological condition which have been greatly considered in the modern era have often been characterised as psychological disturbances of some type. The fact that actually our world has a great deal to offer to challenge some of these narratives, suggests that we have a greater role to play in bringing this power to bear and our failure to do that has actually made us complicit in the marginalisation and the oppression of varying groups accordingly. This part here in how we practice and what we have to offer through our practice, needs to become a central aspect of the work of counsellors, psychotherapists and psychologists.

The next chapter, though, takes us in a slightly different direction. Whilst looking at far psychotherapy as a profession, psychotherapy as a practice, and our training courses, there is another area of consideration which is essential, and this is actually the psychotherapist and the individual themselves. There are a respectable number of books and texts and so on out there which offer a mirror of understanding for those of us whose identities involve us being the other. Yet, it is also essential for all of us, irrespective of our gender, sexuality or any other type of difference to look at how the wider societal rules and frameworks have moulded us in our thinking, in our ways, in our beings and have colonised us as such.

To paraphrase the words of the great bell hooks, decolonisation is not just about incorporating reading lists on courses, it is not just about changing teaching frameworks so that you have more persons of difference. It is also about looking at the little aspects of the coloniser's narrative which have become internalised within each one of us and enact upon us at any moment of time. Because, in only exploring these external frameworks, these systems which have become embedded within psychotherapy, we find that we are only fighting half of the battle. This is because in not facing down these internalisations within us, we allow to remain internalisations which will at exactly the same time undermine our own efforts and reenforce what we already know. The system is not separate to us, we are the system, so even though we challenge the system, unless we challenge the systemisation within ourselves, the system continues afresh (Golash-Boza et al., 2019; Hooks, 2016) (Table 4.1).

Table 4.1 Decolonising practice

	Colonised	Decolonised
Practice	Narcissistic belief in one model and one way of working. Preferential treatment of their own method as superior to other methods.	Research into, and the implementation of, innovative technologies which assist practitioners in meeting the growing needs of a diverse client base. Recognition that the growth of a practitioner is often from that singular trainee/qualitied perspective towards one which is more pluralistic and/or integrative.
Practitioner	Often does not question their own method. Sees own method as an absolute, often marginalising and denigrating other trainings and methods as the other. Tendency to pathologise through a colonised lens.	Creativity and a questioning of own method, not necessarily to debunk own position but because of an awareness of change and developments in own method. Engagement in own Continued Professional Development not just as a self-selected add on, but as a community encouraged motivator to engage with newer ways of working. Questions clinical diagnoses through an intersectional lens thereby seeing the other.
Supervision	Recognition that individual supervision is often embedded within a colonised hierarchical structure.	Regularly reevaluating the supervisory relationship, with a recognition that this is increasingly relational, and transitionary to a point where the supervisee outgrows the supervisor.
Reaccreditation	No consideration or reflection on the continued ways in which the wider political landscape influenced client work or client presentation.	Reaccreditation to include practitioners needing to evaluate their therapeutic position in the context of the social and the political. This consideration to include how these impacts upon themselves, their own work, and their client base.

References

Akbar, N. (1984). *Breaking the chains of psychological slavery*. New Mind.

Anderson, R., & Cissna, K. N. (1997). *The Martin Buber – Carl Rogers dialogue. A new transcript with commentary*. State University of New York Press.

BACP. (2023). *Working online in the counselling professions: Good practice in action 047*. BACP Publication.

Beardsworth, S. (2005). Freud's Oedipus and Kristeva's Narcissus: Three heterogeneities. 2*Hypatia, 20*(1), 54–77. www.jstor.org/stable/3810843

Bowlby, J. (1988). *A secure base: Parent-child attachment and healthy human development*. Basic Books. https://doi.org/10.1097/00005053-199001000-00017

Brady, L. L. C., & Hapenny, A. (2010). Giving back and growing in service: Investigating spirituality, religiosity, and generativity in young adults. *Journal of Adult Development, 17*(3), 162–167. https://doi.org/10.1007/s10804-010-9094-7

Bright, G. (2009). Regression in the countertransference: Working with the archetype of the abandoned child. *Journal of Analytical Psychology, 54*(3), 379–394. https://doi.org/10.1111/j.1468-5922.2009.01786.x

British Association for Counselling and Psychotherapy. (2018). Ethical framework for the counselling professions. *British Journal of Guidance & Counselling*, 1–35. www.bacp.co.uk/events-and-resources/ethics-and-standards/ethical-framework-for-the-counselling-professions/

Cammaerts, B. (2022). The abnormalisation of social justice: The 'anti-woke culture war' discourse in the UK. *Discourse and Society*. https://doi.org/10.1177/09579265221095407

Casciani, D., & De Simone, D. (2021). *Incels: A new terror threat to the UK?* BBC News Online. www.bbc.co.uk/news/uk-58207064

Cheung, M., & Nguyen, P. V. (2012). Connecting the strengths of gestalt chairs to Asian clients. *Smith College Studies in Social Work, 82*(1), 51–62. https://doi.org/10.1080/00377317.2012.638895

Cooper, M. (2023). *Home page*. Therapy and Social Change Network. https://therapyandsocialchange.net/

Cooper, M., & McLeod, J. (2010). *Pluralistic counselling and psychotherapy*. Sage Publications.

Dalal, F. (2006). Racism: Processes of detachment, dehumanization, and hatred. *Psychoanalytic Quarterly, 75*, 131–161.

Davies, D., & Neal, C. (1996). *Pink therapy*. Open University Press.

de Oliveira Cardoso, N., da Rosa Tagliapietra, K., Salvador, E. Z., & de Lara Machado, W. (2023). Adherence to online psychotherapy during the COVID-19: A scoping review. *Psico-USF, 28*(1), 117–132. https://doi.org/10.1590/1413-82712023280110

DeGruy, J. (2005). *Post traumatic slave syndrome*. Joy Degruy Publications.

Domingue, C. J. (2019). A journey in kink: From shameful fantasy to self-actualization. *Journal of Humanistic Psychology*, 1–26. https://doi.org/10.1177/0022167819873238

Duffell, N. (2014, June). G2: Why boarding schools make bad leaders: The elite tradition is to send children away at a young age to be educated. But future politicians who suffer this' privileged abandonment' often turn out as bullies or bumblers. *The Guardian, 10*, 1–5.

Duran, É. P., Hemanny, C., Vieira, R., Nascimento, O., Machado, L., de Oliveira, I. R., & Demarzo, M. (2022). A randomized clinical trial to assess the efficacy of online-treatment with trial-based cognitive therapy, mindfulness-based health promotion and positive psychotherapy for post-traumatic stress disorder during the COVID-19 pandemic: A study protocol. *International Journal of Environmental Research and Public Health*, 19(2), 1–15. https://doi.org/10.3390/ijerph19020819

Durant, S. (Ed.). (1994). *The war of the words: The political correctness debate*. Virago.

Ellis, E. (2021). *The race conversation: An essential guide to creating life-changing dialogue*. Confer Books.

Faris, A., & van Ooijen, E. (2011). *Integrative counselling and psychotherapy: A relational approach*. Sage Publications.

Freud, A. (1992). *The ego and the mechanisms of defence*. Routledge.

Freud, S. (1964). The disillusionment of the war. In *Thoughts for the times on war and* death. Hogarth Press.

Gilligan, C. (1982). *In a different voice: Psychological theory and women's development*. Harvard Publishing.

Gilligan, C. (2014). Moral injury and the ethic of care: Reframing the conversation about differences. *Journal of Social Philosophy*, *45*(1), 89–106. https://doi.org/10.1111/josp.12050

Golash-Boza, T., Duenas, M. D., & Xiong, C. (2019). White supremacy, patriarchy, and global capitalism in migration studies. *American Behavioral Scientist*, *63*(13), 1741–1759. https://doi.org/10.1177/0002764219842624

Greenberg, S. E. (2019). Divine kink: A consideration of the evidence for BDSM as spiritual ritual. *International Journal of Transpersonal Studies*, *38*(1), 220–235. https://doi.org/10.24972/ijts.2019.38.1.220

Hall, S. (1996). *Critical dialogues in cultural studies*. Routledge.

Hawkins, P., & McMahon, A. (2020). *Supervision in the helping professions*. Open University Press.

Hennekam, S., & Shymko, Y. (2020). Coping with the COVID-19 crisis: Force majeure and gender performativity. *Gender, Work and Organization*, *27*(5), 788–803. https://doi.org/10.1111/gwao.12479

Hocoy, D. (2005). Art therapy and social action: A transpersonal framework. *American Art*, *22*(1), 7–16.

Hooks, B. (2016). Feminism is for everybody. In *Ideals and ideologies: A reader*. Pluto Press https://doi.org/10.4324/9781315625546

Iacobucci, G. (2023). The BMJ interview: How the cost of living crisis is damaging children's health. *British Medical Journal*, *380*(3064), 1–2. https://doi.org/10.1136/bmj.p5.2

Irigaray, L. (1993). *Je, Tu, Nous*. Routledge.

Jacobs, M. (2003). *Sigmund Freud – Key figures in counselling and psychotherapy* (2nd ed.). Sage Publications.

Jung, C. G. (1997). *Jung on active imagination* (J. Chodorow (Ed.)). Routledge.

Jung, E. (1957). *Anima and animus*. Spring Publications Ltd.

Kernberg, O. F. (2002). Unresolved issues in the psychoanalytic theory of homosexuality and bisexuality. *Journal of Gay & Lesbian Psychotherapy*, *6*(1), 9–27. https://doi.org/10.1300/J236v06n01_02

Kristeva, J. (1994). *Strangers to ourselves*. Columbia University Press.

Ladany, N., Mori, Y., & Mehr, K. E. (2012). Effective and ineffective supervision. *The Counseling Psychologist*, *41*(1), 28–47. https://doi.org/10.1177/0011000012442648

Laing, R. D. (1969). *Self and others*. Penguin Books Limited.

Lev Kenaan, V. (2021). Digging with Freud: From hysteria to the birth of a new philology. *American Imago*, *78*(2), 341–366. https://doi.org/10.1353/AIM.2021.0015

McDermott, P. (2008). *On training psychotherapists*. Paul McDermott Psychotherapy. www.paulmcdermott.org/writing/article-on-training-psychotherapists/

McKenzie-Mavinga, I. (2009). *Black issues in the therapeutic process*. Palgrave.

Ogden, T. H. (2004). On holding and containing, being and dreaming. *The International Journal of Psycho-Analysis*, *85*(Pt 6), 1349–1364. www.ncbi.nlm.nih.gov/pubmed/15801512

Ogden, T. H. (2016). Destruction reconceived: On Winnicott's 'The Use of an Object and Relating through Identifications.' *International Journal of Psychoanalysis*. https://doi.org/10.1111/1745-8315.12554

Perls, L. (1992). *Living at the boundary*. Gestalt Journal Press.

Rank, O. (1961). *Psychology and the soul* (W. D. Turner (Ed.)). Perpetua Books Ltd.

Rovine, V. L., & Rovine, V. L. (2018). Colonialism's clothing: Africa, France, and the deployment of fashion. *Design Issues*, *25*(3), 44–61.

Samuels, A. (2004). Politics on the couch? Psychotherapy and society—Some possibilities and some limitations. *Psychoanalytic Dialogues*, *14*(6), 817–834. https://doi.org/10.1080/10481881409348809

Simpson, M. K. (2011). Othering intellectual disability: Two models of classification from the 19th century. *Theory & Psychology*, *22*(5), 541–555. https://doi.org/10.1177/0959354310378375

Speciale, M., & Khambatta, D. (2020). Kinky & queer: Exploring the experiences of LGBTQ+ individuals who practice BDSM. *Journal of LGBT Issues in Counseling*, *14*(4), 341–361. https://doi.org/10.1080/15538605.2020.1827476

Stein, M. (2005). Individuation: Inner work. *Journal of Jungian Theory and Practice*, *7*(2), 1–13.

Stevens, A. (1990). *On Jung*. Penguin Limited.

Turner, D. D. L. (2022). *#DecoloniseThis I: Clothing and colonialism*. Dwight Turner Counselling. www.dwightturnercounselling.co.uk/2022/04/28/decolonisethis-i-clothing-and-colonialism/

Various. (2022a). *Bute Park attack: Dr Gary Jenkins left for dead in Cardiff, trial hears*. BBC News Online. www.bbc.co.uk/news/uk-wales-60116759

Various. (2022b). *Queering psychotherapy* (J. C. Czyzselska (Ed.)). Karnac Books Ltd.

Various. (2023). *Psychotherapists and counsellors for social responsibility*. www.pcsr.org.uk/

Walach, H. (2008). Narcissism – The shadow of transpersonal psychology. *Transpersonal Psychological Review*, *12*(2), 47–59.

Webster, P., & Neal, K. (2022). The 'cost of living crisis.' *Journal of Public Health*, *44*(3), 475–476.

Wilkinson, S., & Kitzinger, C. (1996). *Representing the other: A feminism and psychology reader*. Sage Publications.

Willoughby, C. D. E. (2018). Running away from Drapetomania: Samuel A. Cartwright medicine, and race in the antebellum south. *Journal of Southern History*, *84*(3), 579–614. https://doi.org/10.1353/soh.2018.0164

Yalom, I. (2002). Religion and psychiatry. *American Journal of Psychotherapy*, *56*(3), 301.

Yalom, I. D. (1981). Meaninglessness. In *Existential psychotherapy* (Vol. 32, Issue 9, pp. 645–646). Harper Collins Publishers. https://doi.org/10.1176/ps.32.9.645

Yan, H., Ellis, R., & Rogers, K. (2016). *Reports of racist graffiti, hate crimes in Trump's America*. CNN. http://edition.cnn.com/2016/11/10/us/post-election-hate-crimes-and-fears-trnd/

Chapter 5

Decolonising the therapist

Introduction

In 2022, I wrote several blog posts based around the ideas that we are colonised in varying ways. One of these included the fact that actually how we dress and how we present ourselves is very much part of the coloniser's narrative. The general tenet of this short blog was that to be seen as civilised, one had to be wearing trousers and clothes of a certain type and style (Turner, 2022). Things like skirts, dresses or tribal outfits would be seen to mark oneself out as primitive and therefore as inferior in some way. Many of these ideas and rules were actually enforced by law, so much so that in the early part of the 19th century, in numerous countries, there were still laws in place dictating that women should not wear trousers because that denied the position provided for them within society, as to wear trousers marked them out as being more masculine than they were meant to be thereby challenging white male supremacy.

The second part of this story actually involves my own family. My father was a man who came to the United Kingdom in 1944 as part of the Commonwealth Forces which took part in the D-Day landings in World War II. As part of his training before coming to the United Kingdom, my father was taught how to be an Englishman, how to talk like an Englishman, how to act like an Englishman and importantly for this example, how to dress like an Englishman. My father came to the United Kingdom, did his part during the War and with the money that he earned from his time there decided that he would buy the one thing that he truly desired on his arrival in the United Kingdom, a suit from Savile Row in London.

For those of you who do not know much about Savile Row, this is one of the most famous streets in Central London. Not too far from Piccadilly Circus, and established in the early to mid-1700s, traditionally the best tailors worked there and the best suits were made in the United Kingdom. To buy one, in my father's eyes, I could argue marked him out as being English. Strangely enough, in the years since then my father has always maintained these suits to the extent that he still had them as he currently approaches his 95th birthday.

DOI: 10.4324/9781032614342-5

This simple idea around just how much clothing plays a role in colonisation, is just one facet, one simple slither of just how deep the idea of colonisation actually runs. In the story I have just presented, ideas about how we speak, how we present, how we walk, as well as how we dress, show that actually the coloniser had a huge role to play in informing us all of how we should be within their system.

bell hooks (Golash-Boza et al., 2019; Hooks, 2016) in her writing about her own life wrote about what it was like to be colonised from another angle. A woman of colour who was raised in and amongst white people in America, she recognised in some of her feminist writings that actually colonisation was not just of the world around us, that it ran even deeper than this, as it was also in our learned actions and behaviours.

As often stated in this book, it does not need for the coloniser to constantly reinforce the rules of what it is to be an Englishman, a European and such. Often, that narrative has become internalised through one's early life experiences of residing in a foreign land, in an environment which is seen as better than one's own original culture, gender, sexuality or way of being. We are adapted in this coloniser's narrative. We perform to fit in with how we believe we are expected to be and within this adaptation. We therefore assume a level of inauthenticity of which we are not really aware.

The purpose of this chapter is to look at how any sort of movement away from colonisation, is that any sort of attempt to decolonise who we are as psychotherapists, will flounder upon the rocks of the internalised coloniser which sits within us all. In my own book, *The Psychology of Supremacy*, where I look at the role of the activist in helping us to understand who we are in the wider world, adapting the idea presented there recognises that actually decolonisation has to have an internal component in order for it to really take a hold (Turner, 2023). Figure 5.1 speaks to this.

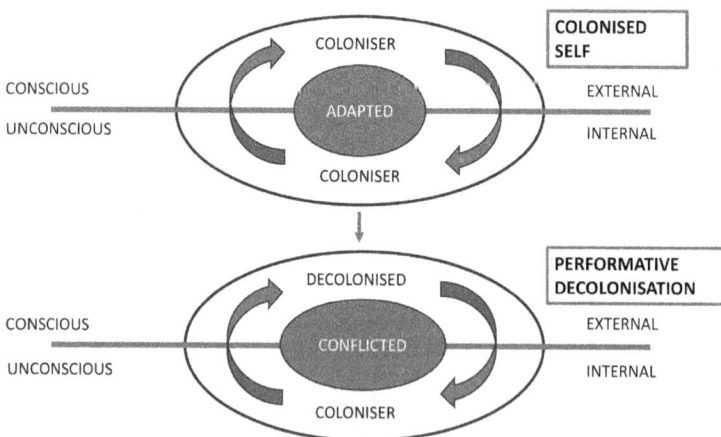

Figure 5.1 The colonised self.

Figure 5.1 sees decolonisation of the self as an important route to establishing lasting change. The idea here is that as we are all part of these systems of oppression, as we are all part of this colonised sense of being, then in removing the structures outside of ourselves, which then seemingly disrupts the systems that oppress us, we are also simultaneously unconsciously guilty of reinforcing said narratives and keeping things in place. We are the system, and we maintain the status quo.

When we discuss Figure 5.1 in a bit more detail, what we start to see is that there is movement in any decolonisation process between the coloniser/colonisation adaptation which we all inhabit, to the external decolonised aspect of oneself and one's world and the internalised coloniser which is more conflicted. This is systemic work, as I would title it, and what I mean by this is this is the external work which a good portion of this book has been concerned with and which was explored earlier in Figure 1.1. This is the externalisation process that sits alongside explorations of what it is to be colonised. It is the understanding of how the structures and the systems that we all walk through, be they the police force, military, the schooling system, all the way down to my original statement of how we all dress and act and behave, are adaptations based upon a set of rules which are not actually of our own. The idea that we are colonised therefore has far broader reach than perhaps many of us actually realise.

The systemic aspect though only challenges the externalisations of decolonisation and this is where the process between the top part of the diagram, the adapted coloniser, and the second part of the diagram, the conflictual decoloniser/coloniser narrative then starts to occur. In many ways, the civil rights movements, the feminist movements and other movements are all part of this process. They sit between that adapted and conflictual state of being but also in many ways there is little movement between the adapted colonised parts of who we are and the conflictual decoloniser aspects as well. Simplistically put, in any rights fight, it can feel a bit like there is no ultimate progress, or that progress is very slow, or that we are yet again trying to prevent the waves from crashing against the shore of colonisation.

A strange example, and yet an interesting one, has happened to myself on a couple of occasions. Recently, I remembered doing a presentation for a group who had invited me on board to raise awareness around difference and diversity. This workshop I had been asked to provide was post the death of George Floyd and the organisation was really quite keen on doing something to facilitate some sort of change of narrative around difference, diversity, race and racism. The original workshop attracted over 100 people and actually went really well. The organisation involved, which was a private organisation, were really quite pleased with the results and decided that they wanted to run a second event the following year, to keep the momentum going.

Agreeing to do so, I myself played into the enthusiasm presented by the organisation, but then things changed within the organisation itself to the extent that the original person that I was working with moved onto a different role and they brought in somebody else less cognisant with the work that I was undertaking. As the new date approached, I started to get slightly concerned that nothing had taken place with regard to organising, the advertising, the set up. No meetings had been organised to discuss the format for the workshop, as there had been the previous year. With literally five weeks to go, I was then contacted by the new organiser to ask if I would still like to run the event, at which point I turned it down, stating there was not enough time to pull everything together and to put on a good enough event for people to attend. Whilst there were apologies for this, there were also attempts to say 'OK, well we will try and do this next year' to repeat the process in the following calendar year. Nothing happened the following year, and the full process fell flat.

The reason I tell this story is that within any system, whilst it will work to do the occasional clever work of challenging something to change, there will always be an underlying resistance to the same said change. An underlying, unconscious belief perhaps that the change has gone too far and too fast. The organisation, in this case presented as a system, then got in its own way and self-sabotaged any sort of movement and continued progress. This is what often happens across different organisations, universities, colleges, centres, when issues of difference otherness decolonisation come up. So that whilst there is often a large enthusiasm to move things forward, when people start to say, 'OK what happens next? What do we do next?,' whilst there is enthusiasm to take another step, at the same time these steps fall on deaf ears, or they fall through the cracks and we end up repeating the same events a second, third and fourth time further down the road.

So, whilst the system reconstitutes itself, remembering that we are the system then says that to change the system we have to look at the internalised coloniser that then drops the metaphorical ball in these instances, reconstituting what the system already knows. This is often the reason when people of difference, be they of colour, of gender, of ability, of sexuality or otherwise, then accept the fight and the struggle to make change on a solitary basis. They will often do so on their own because they tend to rely upon themselves to fight the fight that the system will water down to take away the power and affect which then might lead to change. So, only by challenging the internalised coloniser, can we then start to get anywhere close to recognising and understanding what has become internalised within us all and also looking at just what it might be like to work in an environment where decolonisation is fully functioning and runs off its own steam.

The importance of this chapter is therefore to look at internalisations and how they play a role in understanding who we are from an early age and onwards, and especially looking at internalisations through a social constructionist lens. What this chapter will also do is to look at the developmental stages that we go through when we consider how we internalise the world around us and consider how also the work of psychotherapy, and in particular understanding individuation and personal growth, become routes to internalised decolonisation as well as other forms of psychological growth.

It should be stated from the off that this development is intergenerational, such as the 'rules' of what it is to be a woman have been defined and refined for generations. Just in the same way as the ideas and structures of what it is to be a man, what it is to be of colour, what it is to be white, what it is to be of ability or what it is to be normal. These all mean that when we start to question the rules and structures which we all walk within, which have been passed on to us through the colonial narratives, and which go back generations, that we start to free ourselves up to be more authentically who we are. As well as how this change then allows us not just to embody a more authentic sense of ourselves, but allows space, room and different avenues for our clients to do exactly the same.

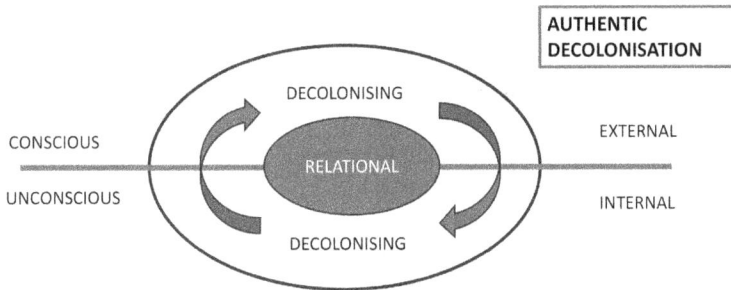

Figure 5.2 Authentic decolonisation.

Figure 5.2 revisits the decoloniser/coloniser conflictual state of development presented in Figure 5.1 and then brings in the idea of shadow work for us to move to an external and internal decolonised sense of self, one which is more relational in many ways. Shadow work here is painful. As I have already stated, many of these structures are transgenerational, have been passed down to us by our care givers, our culture, by those we trust most of all. So, when we try and even challenge them ever so slightly, often the kick back or the fight back from the system itself can be really quite vicious, angry and disruptive. In her excellent book on feminist writers going back generations, Dawson (2023) recognises the struggle of a good number of authors and the resistances they encountered from the patriarchy.

Returning to the differences between Figures 5.1 and 5.2, there is a movement from this conflicted side to a more relationship one, to a more authentic state of being. This must occur for true decolonisation to take place, and much of this chapter will look at the shadow work that goes on when we actually decolonise who we happen to be. The reason I say this is that for us to achieve a real sense of decolonisation, those colonised internalised parts of ourselves do not necessarily have to be removed and exorcised. What they do need is some sort of assertive ongoing challenge so that the power that they hold begins to ebb away and is returned to that true self that sits within us all. My statement here is important. Any sort of idea of a true self, any sort of idea of an authentic way of being, has to recognise that the loss of such a state will also have involved not just the scripts of a negative parent or an abusive situation, but will have perhaps quite early on been impacted by the adaptations placed upon us by the social systems of supremacy embedded within society (Turner, 2021).

The idea follows this path from the moment we are born as we are ascribed not just a gender, but also a way and means of behaving as per the cultural narrative which this gender sits within. We are taught very much how it is to be a boy, a girl and so on. We are passed these ideas on from the moment we are born. In fact, I might argue from before we are born. The clothes which our grandparents buy for the unborn child based upon the results of a gender reveal party are factors which actually play into the colonised narrative, for example. So in many ways, the colonisation of thinking and of being and of our actions happens instantaneously that we are conceived (Aboud, 1988; Beauvoir, 2010; Washburn, 1995; Weil & Piaget, 1951).

The second part to this, though, is that these generalisations, these scripts, these contracts, which we adhere to from that earliest stage of development, are also passed on to us from the system itself, represented by persons that we all love and trust. This is the intergenerational part that I am talking about here and this is one of the reasons why I often say, and I will keep repeating, that decolonisation, especially internally, is a difficult and painful experience. It can lead to what I will term a dark night of the systemic self, borrowing from or co-opting a statement from St John around the dark night of the soul (Marlan, 2005). With this dark night being a recognition that for us to reach a truly authentic internalised state of decolonised development we have to go through the alchemical pain of deconstruction, not just of ourselves but of those intergenerational transcultural strands that bind us to the web of inauthenticity.

The decolonisation of the psychotherapist is probably one of the most key factors in all of this, which is why we are now going to look at the developmental stages of colonisation.

Developmental colonisation

It is important before we look at the decolonisation of who we are as individuals, and as groups as well, that we consider how the adaptation and manipulation of our identities occurs and how there is also a developmental process that we undergo accordingly. The decolonisation and adaptation process that I have already discussed in the introduction to this chapter, starts pretty much before we are even born. Messages are passed to us subtly, familiarly, culturally and in other ways as well around how we should present and how we should be.

In the earlier section, I mention gender reveal parties and offered you an example of this.

My client Frankie and his partner actually told me about an experience that they had had of attending a gender reveal party. Whilst the party was quite a nice, pleasant, summertime affair, what they were most stunned by was that as a gay, male couple, the ease with which the heterosexual couples at the party found themselves engaging with the genderised norms of heteronormativity, sort of surprised and saddened them both. When the child was revealed through the release of several balloons to be blue, and therefore a boy, the number of people who they had previously seen as allies to the LGBTQ cause, who then instantly talked about the genderised things they were going to supply for said unborn child, spoke a lot to just to how easy it was for them to fall back into these pre-conceived, unconscious patterns of systemic behaviour.

For Frankie and his partner, that sense of isolation which they had grown up with was reinforced by witnessing this display or authentic inauthenticity and the difficult experience of watching the conflicts go on for their peers led them to also re-experience the conflictual aspects of their own experience with the same friends and the marginalisation that went with them.

This example here is the first stage as presented in Figure 5.3. Moving from the centre to the external, in Figure 5.3, the first stage is very much from the moment of conception; we are moulded by the messages from family, culture, religion and the intergenerational messages which filter in from all three of these areas. This is how our egoic sense of self begins to be colonised as it takes form.

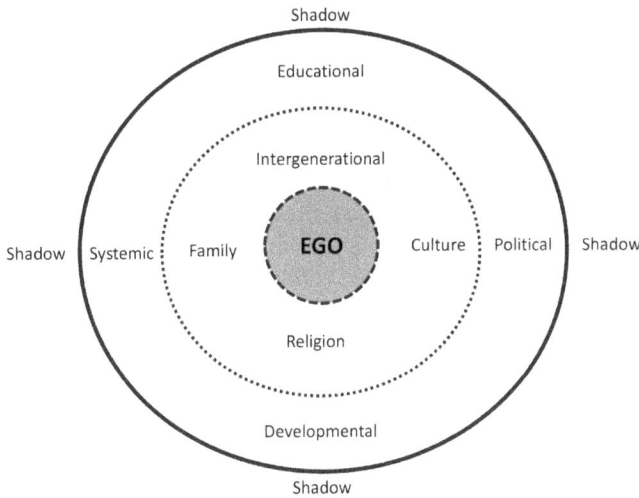

Figure 5.3 Psychological decolonisation.

This stage will continue until not long after the child has actually arrived and will progress until the child perhaps starts nursery. My theory here is that this next stage of interaction with external peers and carers, then brings in another focus and that is which is based around the prejudices and the unresolved scripts of those who care for our children.

These are all influenced by the second layer of colonisation. This involves the systemic, educational, political and developmental ways we are moulded into how we are supposed to be. Often in counselling and psychotherapy there is an attempt to marginalise the political from the social constructions of identity. Here though, in Figure 5.3, there is a clear recognition that the political is a core player in the moulding of who we are within these interlocking systems which colonise us all. The laws which tell us how we should present, and which gender we are supposed to be assigned to. The rules which dictate if it is right or wrong to racially abuse the other at school. The ethics which outline which gender gets to assume which roles in the classroom. All of these three examples will have been influenced by the political and will have their say in the development of a colonised ego within said cultural system of compliance.

In a previous volume, I spoke a bit about an experience of my daughter at nursery, when she was marginalised by a six-year-old child, that example being used to emphasise the developmental stage of a six-year-old whose identity felt threatened when experiencing the other (Turner, 2023). The interesting part for this particular story was when we made a complaint to the nursery about the racist treatment of our three-year-old child by a six year old, the nursery's adaptive safety of taking up the party line, and saying they treat everybody the same, they do not see colour, and so on, then left my child bereft and isolated.

In a similar fashion to Frankie and his partner, the leaving outside of my child and not focusing in on her needs in that moment, plays a role in the reinforcement of the coloniser narrative. The fact that my child came home believing that her hair was ugly, and her skin was dirty, if left unchecked and unchallenged by myself and her mother, would have led to the internalisation of said experience and the reinforcement of a coloniser's narrative that actually Blackness is wrong. This is why, when I hear stories about microaggressions being the small, incremental acts which people of difference, irrespective of what they are, encounter and endure the idea that these are micro is a huge insult to the deep-seated pain and recolonising aspect that sits hidden within them. In fact, I will argue that even using the phrase 'micro' against aggressions as an attempt to show that there is some sort of hierarchical pain, is an consciously inadvertent attempt to reinforce the coloniser's narrative that these are not as painful, even though we all know that they cut incredibly deep and they become internalised to an incredibly deep level as well.

The internalisation of these experiences through forms of bullying, through forms of hate, through the many types of negative experiences that children encounter, both through their peers, at school, and as they get older, through the internet and the wider environment, are all ways of making certain disadvantaged or other groups fit in with an experience or way of being which is built around an idea of what is normal. This word 'normal' comes up time and again in this discussion. We all want to fit in and be seen as normal, and yet at the same time we rebel against the normality of our peers, or our parents, of what they wore, of what they listened to, of the films they liked, of how they act. That constant swing and push and pull between the coloniser and the decolonisation aspect within ourselves is no different to the idea that we want to fit in and below and also separate out and be individual in ourselves.

Decolonisation and the shadow

As we have already seen in the previous section and in Figures 5.1 and 5.2, colonisation involves an adaptation to the structures of supremacy which we are all born into and moulded. This therefore means that the idea of authenticity for all of us is, in our earlier stages of life, a myth and a fantasy. Any process of decolonisation is actually also a process of systemic individuation. It is shadow work.

This crucial factor should not be underestimated when we consider that the decolonisation of our courses, or our therapists, of ourselves as lecturers, as supervisors and so on will always flounder without having attempted or approached the internal work involved in working with the unconscious coloniser. This is the importance of the moment between the two stages as presented in Figure 5.1. The conflictual part, whereby decolonisation is an external process, which is the met by the internalised coloniser, means that actually we are our own oppressors. This is a process that we should know as counsellors and psychotherapists. The internalisation of aspects presented in Figure 5.2, of symbols which will silence us, which will adapt us, which will make us perform, is a fact which is discussed within counselling and psychotherapy from the days of the Freudians.

Internalisation is a term which denotes that we take on board the experiences that we have with our primary care givers, be they mother, father, grandparents and so on. We also internalise other aspects as well (Bowlby, 1988). The experiences that we have in primary school or with our peers will all become internalised. Offering a more philosophical exploration which ties into this developmental framework, Freire (1970) recognised that in any process of oppression we will take on board and internalise the oppressor. This is an area that was discussed also in the work of Bell Hooks (2016) who was a woman of colour raised within a white neighbourhood and yet went on to become a very prominent black feminist, and in the writings of Fanon (2005) who saw this as a key aspect of the impact of colonialism.

Stuart Hall (1996) from the United Kingdom saw this from a different angle, recognising that actually the influence of media would also play a role in just how we would interact with the world around ourselves. His ideas sat most comfortably around issues of race, suggesting, for example, that persons of colour, who saw themselves presented in a certain way through the media lens, would re-enact said experiences in other areas of their lives.

He recognised, and I agree, that it is near impossible not to avoid the internalisation of these said systems and this is why it is essential to therefore recognise that within any system of oppression that we are the system, we are the colonisers, we are those aspects which will silence ourselves and which will leave us to perform for our partners, or which will codeswitch given that we entered an area where we feel uncomfortable or unsafe. The messages for many of us do not have to come from external sources. The messages are often, by the time we reach a certain age, very much embedded within the psyches of us all, re-enacting themselves over and over again and manipulating ourselves to become more adapted. That movement as presented in Figure 5.1, where the unconscious coloniser speaks and whispers to us over and over again, when not challenged leaves us evermore increasingly uncomfortable with ourselves, bereft and angry with ourselves, and also unconsciously aware of just how much we have let ourselves down.

There are always hints though in the client work when it comes to how adaptive one has become within said systems, and one of those areas to consider is in the unconscious anger at the system of colonisation. In any process of adaptation, a true sense of who one wants to be and a true sense of one's own morality and worth, has to be put to one side. This is the fire of individuation. Instead of being put out by the system of colonisation, this has to find its way out through a side door somewhere else. This can be, when utilised properly, the route towards one's own activism, but it can also involve a punching downwards upon another group, another person, somebody more innocent than oneself to divest oneself of the guilt and the same and the resentment of having had to adapt to a system to survive.

Lucy was a 44-year-old woman who came to see me for several sessions of therapy. Her presenting issue was that she had wanted to work on her relationship with her father, who was a punishing, emotionally distant man. Alongside this, she had just exited a work situation with a major corporation where she was being picked on by a director and was finding it very difficult to trust other men post the break-up.

She had engaged with dating apps and had gone out on one or two dates during the period before our work together, but each time that met somebody new, she found herself feeling overly critical of that person, even if it seemed they were perfectly nice and reasonable towards her. Now, on one level it is not my place to say whether these people were suitable for Lucy or not, but in our work, what quickly became apparent was Lucy's resentment towards the patriarchal structure and towards the men around her. We explored this in our work and we looked at how the director in her last place of work had held such power and sway over her over such a period of time, that she had found herself adapting to his wishes in those initial stages. We were then also able to relate this back to her experiences with her father where, much like her own mother, they had to adapt to survive his punishing behaviours.

The next aspect of the work that we did together, myself and Lucy, was to look at in her adapted state with this director, what had happened to her true sense of self and what Lucy found was that to maintain the adaptation, to fit in with what this person needed her to be, that what she had chosen to do was to take lots of her aggression out upon herself through an overuse of alcohol. She had applied for other jobs and had rejected them all for varying reasons.

The importance of this example is to emphasise the fact that when we adapt ourselves, we put to one side much of our potential to be happy and to be more content within our lives. Decolonisation in this instance is not about the chasing of the pot of gold at the end of the rainbow, but it is about recognising that there is an inner process of happiness that has to be constrained to fit in and feel adaptive within said system.

The other way of looking at this is that when we perform, when we enact, when we are acting in a way which keeps the colonised parts of ourselves satisfied, then happiness and satisfaction is passed outwards onto another. We are then choosing to make the other happy over ourselves. This is a theme which has come up in feminist literature for generations now (Butler, 1988). The idea that within a patriarchal structure, women often find themselves looking to keep men happy and feel guilt or shame when they feel they are not doing a good enough job. This is something we also see within the class structure. One only has to look at the latest costume drama on television to recognise the front and centre of the working classes' dedication to keeping the upper class satisfied, content and stationery upon their plinth (Fellows, 2010). Within the political sphere, the undoubted ability of those in class and systemic political power to inveigle from the working classes not only their votes, but also their compliance and dedication shows how much this performativity and this sympathy, be it based around class or gender, takes place (Boffey, 2018).

All of these then involve the ridding from oneself or the repressing within oneself of that aspect which would make us more authentic. Yet, for many activists and others, when this is harnessed, used and brought forth, the ability to focus this outward in ways and means which challenge the structural status quo, means that change can occur should one be able to encourage it into being. Any shadow work though has to look at the internalised patriarch, the unconscious supremacist and the undercover classist that sits within all of use and speaks and whispers to us, keeping us small, keeping us contained and keeping us adapted (Turner, 2015; Walach, 2008).

The shadow work that goes with this should not be underestimated because given that these three aspects of our systemic identities are areas which have been imbibed since we are born. To challenge said systems, to challenge the unconscious structures which have already defined us and involves us stripping away our systemic identities and having to walk a path which is less adapted and more individual, yet also quite rich and potentially a lot more fulfilling. This is a path structure which should define the individual within the wider social environment structures as opposed to defining the wider structure with us just as a machine part within it. This is the major difference when we move from Figures 5.1 to 5.2 and when we move from that conflictual place to a more relational one. The internalised coloniser, when worked with frees us up to find our own ways of being, of happiness, of love, of satisfaction, of identity, of dress, of speech, of sexuality and the list goes on.

Autoethnography and decolonisation

In Chapter 6, I am going to be looking in a lot more detail at the role of research in the decolonisation project, and in particularly at how the research methodologies that we have adopted and adapted over several generations, have actually fuelled and reinforced systems of colonisation.

For this chapter, which is about the decolonising of the therapist, I want to use a process of autoethnography as a means of considering my own experience and journey along this path of decolonisation. This will be done through the lens of telling a story which will involve using personal diaries which were constructed between January and April 2023. This will involve exploring and using diary entries and dreams as a means of considering both the reflective aspect of decolonisation, which I believe is an essential facet of any sort of process like this, together with the deeper unconscious awakening that can occur when we start to look at just what it is to decolonise ourselves.

Autoethnography is a means of research evolved out of ethnography. This development is widely attributed to Kenyatta (1962) who wrote an anthropological text detailing Kenyan culture and the structures of its society. A method which was hotly disputed by other anthropologists, many of who were white and European of origin, this methodology has nonetheless grown in importance and been used in a similar vein to heuristics, where there is a more space for the personal narrative of the researcher on the page (Hughes, 2017). A core facet of colonisation as a minority is actually the loss of a voice. When one is colonised, or when one experiences colonisation, say within a patriarchal environment, then the voice, the right to speak up and say what one wants to, is actually sacrificed as a means of fitting in with said system. We have all heard of stories of minorities who have spoken up for their communities or for others, only to be told to know their place or to watch their tongue. These sorts of terms are straight out of the coloniser's narrative of control and power over the voice of the other. This is one of the reasons why choosing an autoethnographic way of working with this material has felt essential in this tome.

There are echoes here of the work important contemporary works such as Queering Psychotherapy and The Race Conversation, together with the many other texts which promote the voices of the other, their importance and their struggles (Ellis, 2021; Various, 2022). These and other semi-autoethnographic texts work to shift the dialogue away from a purely academic, and objective, means of exploring issues of difference and diversity, to ones whereby the utilisation and the forward focusing in on the stories of the other has led to a shift in our understanding of just what it is to be a minority.

A first step in the decolonisation of the other must involve the rediscovery of one's own voice. The ability to express and to move beyond the same of said (non) expression, is a part of this. This is why me using my own voice and placing my own wounds on the pages, has been so important for the moment this book represents within counselling and psychotherapy.

Personal background

To begin with the process, I want to offer a bit of a back story and a few clear guidelines as to where I was in January 2023. At the time of drafting this book,

I was in my mid-fifties. I had been separated and divorced for several years by now and I have a young daughter who is of pre-teens age. I presently live on the South Coast of England and have been working as a psychotherapist at this time for about 20 years. When I trained as a psychotherapist in London, although I enjoyed the training and although I found so much of myself through the experiences that I encountered whilst I was training, there was much of myself which was left behind to create a level of safety for my peers. In the past few years though, my voice as a psychotherapist has changed. I have found myself standing up and speaking up in a way that I could not have foreseen beforehand.

The murders of George Floyd, Sarah Everard and other instances of hate meted out on other minority groups, led me to feel that I could no longer stay silent, that I had to stand up and speak up and say what I so wanted to say (Morton, 2021; Various, 2020). In the year 2022, I received a number of messages, some from former colleagues, stating that I should, for example *get off my high horse*, that *I should stop presenting myself as so angry* and that I should *know my place* and that *I should not be separating people out and actually should fight for the rights of all people to come together*. I never respond to these types of messages. What I tend to do with all of these is to ask myself questions such as *What is it that people see when they see me standing up and speaking out?* or *What is it that people felt and experienced of myself when I was in my training and practising and being a nice, compliant, house-negro psychotherapist?*

The importance of these two last questions is that they highlight the difficulty for persons of difference when they speak out for their communities. The adaptations, as I have already said, are as much externally driven as they are internally so, to the extent that whilst I was in my training, I very rarely spoke up about issues of difference and otherness to keep other people happy. Those messages were far more implicit than explicit, were far more internalised that externally driven, and yet when I did speak out and start to say what I wanted to say, the messages of fear and anger and resentment, and also perhaps shame on the part of the subject, came at myself, and continue to do so on a regular basis.

My autoethnography story of decolonisation

Diary entry 02.02.23 (02:45 am):

This is a long and strange dream. First of all, I am part of an RAF parade team and we are marching up a road. We are told to halt and to do a left turn and to remain in line. We then seem to be in a bar. There is a woman in front of me in this bar who comes over and takes my hand, placing it on her bottom, not so much as she wants me but because this will then make the very tall man behind me jealous. I get angry and I push her away and I try to go back to my room, but I cannot find it. I got outside onto Kensington High Street where I turn right. As I cross a road, I help an attractive Indian woman who is being followed by a menacing blacked out car. I take her back to find my car. At my hotel we cannot find my room, so I go into one on a different floor. I see three Swedish men acting as cleaners and I shout at them with a toy gun and they fire flaming arrows out of a bazooka which goes into a wall and fizzles out. I go into the room to open the windows so myself and the Indian woman can then escape.

As I look through this diary entry, a couple of things that it reminds me of are of my own history and my own background. I am ex-military, I served in the Royal Airforce in the early 1990s, several years of which I was based in Germany. In many ways, the ultimate means of adaptation is through conformity and the military, be it the army, the air force, the navy, the police of even the fire brigade, are all about conformity. You dress the same, you have the same haircut, you eat the same food at the same time, you all interact together as a unit. Individuality does not really exist. Some of the strange things that would happen during my time in the air force were that I would often find myself coming home from time on camp and being teased by my friends because my accent had changed, an accent borne out of a hybrid of accents which had all come together and changed each other on that base. Then, when I went to back to camp after any time of leave, my friends on camp would say that my accent had become 'more London' since I had been away.

That moulding of myself was a normal part of the life of being a military person and the first part of the dream in many ways speak to that. The second part though is also quite interesting. The part with the white woman who wanted me to play a certain role to make her partner jealous says an awful lot about the objectification and the othering of Blackness in white environments. The fetishisation of myself as a Black man, seen through the lens of sexuality and not through the lens of humanity, by that internalised part of myself the white woman, is actually quite terrifying to recognise within myself.

There are positives though. My first job was on Kensington High Street when I was a child, working out of Safeway, so to be there in a dream meant an awful lot to me. To be helping a woman of difference, of colour, to cross a road and then to look after her, also says a fair amount about my own experience of trying to nurture and hold my own sense of otherness. That this part is then attacked by these internalised, unconscious Swedes who want to kill off that part which makes me unique is something which I recognise is a part of the minority experience. That we are often driven to destroy and to self-mutilate that which makes us the other to fit in and be adaptive within systems such as the ones outside of us, are a core part of who we are and a core reason as to why we still survive in these environments today.

Diary entry 01:15 am (16.02.23)

Scene from a longer dream where I am in a house, and I am demanding to leave. My brother in the dream is very upset and will not let me go because if I leave, I will talk about difference etc and will help find peace in the world. I want to go and get my car so I can go to the station and catch my train. He tries to follow me out of the house crying, so I double back on myself, and I go down into the basement where I try and hide. I see him going round the house over and over again attempting to find me. As I pass my mother in the basement, I then try and leave but my mother alerts my brother to where I am and he comes downstairs to get me. We struggle and fight in the basement of the house.

Re-reading this dream is quite upsetting for myself. That the internalised oppressor in this dream is in the guise of my brother, says an awful lot about the conflictual part that goes with being an activist. There is a want to have a voice, to step out into the world, to do more, to fight more, to be seen and to be heard more. Yet, alongside that, there is a fearful part reinvented by my own kin, which wants to resist and struggle against any sort of psychological and therefore systemic and cultural emancipation. That in this dream my own mother, another part of myself, that internalised part of myself, reveals my whereabouts given that I trusted her, also has a lot to say.

My parents are part of the Windrush generation, my mother in particular, and yet one has to remember that the Windrush generation was during a time of the British Empire. The movement of a peoples from the Caribbean to the United Kingdom was a movement of the colonised from the West Indies to the Great British Empire. This was not a step towards freedom, it was actually a step in many ways towards a greater sense of inclusion within the system of colonisation. It is therefore important for me to recognise that that internalised coloniser was always going to reveal the whereabouts of that rebellious part of myself to the adapted part which my brother represents.

The other important thing to recognise in the dream is the divide and conquer nature of the experience. As already stated, in this dream the internalised mother, who as I have stated came across during the time of Empire, is there dividing myself and my brother, revealing to my brother where I am. Any sort of rebelliousness and any attempt to establish a unique way of being around difference and diversity is therefore repressed, suppressed, contained and stamped upon. This is really important to recognise. In the wider political sphere and in issues of colonialism, one of the major ways that political parties maintain their levels of power is by a divide and conquer tactic.

As I have written about in previous texts, it is something we saw in the Brexit debate and it is also an element which has been used and used a great deal in the colonial projects across the world. The use by the colonial powers: France, Britain, Belgium, Spain and Portugal, in their colonies whereby they would either divide the population into two camps, or bring in a middle class to serve them and manage the underclass or the lower class, is a common facet of how power was maintained and how any dissent was suppressed. It is something which of course would become internalised within all of us to some degree and in this internalisation holds echoes of Figures 5.1 and 5.2, when we consider the conflictual nature of the conscious de-coloniser, and the unconscious colonisers within an individual or within a group.

The exploration of this for myself became incredibly important in understanding the unconscious nature of colonisation. The fact that there was a part within myself which had a friendly face upon it, was quite shocking, together with the idea that to work with that part, to move beyond said part, I would have to defeat not only my internalised brother, but also the internalised matriarch in the form of my mother.

When I speak about decolonisation being an incredibly difficult topic, this simple example when matched across whole groups, whole cultures and so on, reveals how incredibly difficult on a wider spectrum decolonisation is. For all the work that we can, and in this case that I can do, in reading the right texts, in approaching people the right way, in understanding the writings of feminists, LGBTQ theorists and disability theorists, and so on, ultimately if I had not approached and addressed this core part of myself, then all my work would have floundered on the shores of my internalised coloniser. I would have reconstituted every single experience of marginalisation, and I would probably have been left with no more than the frustration that would have risen in its wake.

Diary Entry and Dream on 20.02.23 (no time recorded)

I am in a building where I am with a wise, old man. We go into a kitchen together which is in the basement. I go to my parents' old room down in that basement area and I see that an old man is taken away and disappears. Then two Daleks appear, and I have to hide behind the door to the kitchen. The Daleks then come in and take the wise old man away. They turn off the lights, so I sneak out and go up to the first floor. I then sneak into my old bedroom, and I do not want Robert (a former boss) to see me. He is coming down from the floor above. I hide out on the balcony to my old room, and he enters with two other men. I then go back to see them but Robert already knows that the Daleks are in the building.

This dream also holds importance. This recognition that there is a threat in the basement is not a threat to me, it is a threat to the Daleks. It should be stated that Daleks are a popular character in the television show Dr Who. One of the earliest stories that I ever saw involving Dr Who was called The Genesis of the Daleks and involved The Doctor being sent by his people, the Time Lords, back to a time before the Daleks were created (Various, 2023). The aim of the mission that he had been given was to prevent the Daleks creation and therefore halt the ravages that the Daleks were then about to wreak upon the universe. The Doctor encounters their creator, name Davros, and several of his subordinates who are all dressed like Nazis from the World War II. Davros though, in his madness, decides to create his Daleks and manipulates both his own people and the opposition so that both are mutually destroyed, and the only people left are his genetically modified creations, the Daleks. The Doctor in his mission fails to destroy them, deciding that he cannot actually wipe out a whole species. His supposed goodness coming to the fore.

When I first saw this story, it quickly became one of my favourite all time Dr Who stories and seeing the Daleks and understanding what they represented meant that they often played a role in the games that I would play as a child of good versus evil. The Daleks were colonisers. They sought to take over, dominate and enslave populations across the universe. So, in this dream, the internalised coloniser is still apparent. After a fashion there is a similarity between the Dalek of the dream and my internalised mother. She has been colonised and therefore has passed on down the generations the coloniser's ethic. Whereas these Daleks are the colonisers themselves and are looking to suppress anything which might change their power structure and way of being.

In the dream, the wise old man could be seen as the internalised ally, a part of oneself that we all need to find and relate to if we are to move beyond the internalised coloniser narrative to something which is more authentically oneself. Wisdom in this instance is therefore not just about being wise and knowledgeable, it is about an inner wisdom, an inner knowing, an inner morality which moves us beyond the coloniser's structures of what is right and what is wrong, places us back into the realm of doing what is right for our own selves and therefore for those around us simultaneously. In some ways that unconscious, wise person within us brings us closer in relationship to everyone else around us.

The last couple of facets of this dream involve the continued movement downwards. Within dream work there is a belief that movement and the direction of movement is important, and that this movement relates to where we are in our physical self. A way of understanding this is by looking at this as the movement as a relationship between the literal and the symbolic. The movement downstairs into the basement where I must uncover and find the other aspects of myself, suggests a moment down into the unconscious, down into the physical self, the body, the root chakras, the parts of oneself that most activists are wary to go towards because it is too frightening.

It brings to the fore the idea that in colonisation there is also the colonisation of the body. In more obvious terms the rape and pillaging of bodies of minorities, be they gendered minorities, racial minorities or based around ability and class, has left many of us feeling that we do not have as comfortable a relationship with our body as we might like. We are very switched off from our physical self, we repress feelings a lot of the time through substance misuse, or the use of foods to manage and maintain our compliance and our adaptive relationship with the systems of oppression external to us. Alongside this, it is worth noting that only by working with the body and echoing some of the work by trauma theorists do we then start to recognise how the colonisation of our bodies has often led to us holding a certain level and a type of 'Trauma of Colonisation' within the body.

This is a term that I have coined for the purpose of this text, but what it basically means is that to perform within a patriarchal environment, to allow oneself to be physically abused within a racialised experience, and to endure the physical ramifications of existing within an ableist paradigm there is traumatic experience that we mete out upon our physical self which is a cost to this adaptation.

The movement upwards though, which the other part of this story, and the meeting with persons who in the past were the beneficiaries of my adapted self, speaks a bit about the dance between the internal and the external world. There is a recognition here that I do not want to relate to that externalised patriarch and yet also a recognition that actually this part of myself is fearful of what I might bring up from the depths. The fact that I try and hide myself away is also part of the adaptation. I remove myself symbolically from the white patriarch of my dream and in the hiding, I then make myself safe within a white, patriarchal, capitalist world.

Within these dreams thus far, there is always the sense that whatever I might be trying to hide, there is always an ember of something which is trying to emerge and come through and which desires and wants to be seen, recognised and respected by the world around oneself. We are already starting to see here how dreams in their power to offer a symbolic reparation of the repressed part of self that come up in colonisation, then speak to us in ways which we may not have expected and, as I have already explored, the battle between the internalised parts of oneself are laid out bare for myself, my therapist and the reader therefore, to see and sound the experience.

Diary entry (end February 2023)

Every now and again, someone says something meaningful which rings a small bell in my head. I realise that in a relationship I need to be met emotionally, intellectually, spiritually, sexually, and financially. That this realisation appears now is tough for me, but it puts into context both the types of relationships I have had in the past, as well as the levels I have reduced myself to fit into what is expected of me. For example, my ex-wife had none of those areas. There was another former partner who was great sexually but had none of the other areas as well. In my last relationship, I was met intellectually and also financially but the other three areas were missing. There will always be something lacking in my relationships, but what I have realised is that in forming relationships I have often engaged with them from a place of being grateful that they have chosen myself. This is the flaw in my relational thinking, the belief that actually I should not ask for too much, I should just accept what is given to me and accept what little I get, the crumbs on the plate, within my relationships. It is a hard realisation but an important one.

The importance of the above diary entry came to myself when I realised how often gratefulness is used to oppress minority groups. Grateful, which comes from the Latin word gratus, actually means thankful. This edict often used by the coloniser is important as it is often used as a form of subjugation. Most forms of psychology to not go anywhere near to understanding the debilitating influence of such an edict when it comes to understanding difference and diversity and the coloniser narratives.

From this perspective, being grateful means settling. 'These immigrants should be thankful to be here in this country,' is a refrain which is used across the Global

North by countries which have more and want to unconsciously recognise the power dynamic between them and refugees or those who have come to their shores. 'You should be thankful or grateful to have me' is often a refrain used by abusive persons towards their partners inveigling them to actually stay and submit to the power dynamic of the relationship. Being thankful in both these contexts is actually part of the coloniser's narrative; the slave should be thankful that the slave owner gives them anything to eat, any sort of sustenance whatsoever. The woman should be grateful that any man should pick her to marry, have children and build a life. The refugee should be grateful to be in this country given that their own world, their own climate, their own country is war torn and in a state of chaos.

Being thankful in these instances is not a good thing. It is an insult designed to encourage supplication and compliance and in relationships that this internalisation as a part of the coloniser's narrative means that to challenge oneself to become decolonised, one has to also be seen as ungrateful, as unworthy and unsatisfactory as one strides out from the doors of the prison which is compliance.

The psychology of thankfulness, when placed within a cultural coloniser's narrative, therefore becomes one of the core areas for us to consider. Within this will also be ties to issues of shame and guilt, given that actually when we step outside of being thankful and when we are told that we are not thankful enough, there is an element of shame which is encouraged. We are not doing enough to show our gratitude, we are not doing enough to show that we are secondary citizens within a colonised space, and we need to be doing more to play our part within the systemic colonisation of our hearts, minds and desires. That last phrase is perhaps also important here: desires.

Being thankful means that we put our desires down. Whatever we wish for, whatever we hope for, whatever we strive for, in our lives, for our families, for our environments, is rejected in favour of the wishes, the desires and the direction of the coloniser. The dreams of the slave to have their own family are dashed upon the shores of compliance on the land of colonisation where one is left torn between feeling grateful that one still has a life versus possible death should one revolt and stride out for one's own wishes. The being thankful that one should be in a patriarchal space of compliance within a marriage that one may or may not want contrasts greatly against the striding out to have one's own life, perhaps free of the structures of marriage, perhaps free of the edicts that suggest that one should not have the career or the family that one wants or may not want.

The fact that we conform to these ideals all the time forms a huge part of our identities. The fact that when we try and break away from these ideals, we are left with a sense that we are not being generous enough in our supplication, speaks highly of the insidious nature of colonisation and of the whispering creep of compliance and adaptation which moulds and conforms it.

Dream 03.03.23:

In goal for Everton Football Club or a team struggling just like them. We are on the back foot defending against a team of white men who want to beat us badly.

They are about to take a penalty but take so long and are so cocky about it, that I keep rushing out to save the ball time and again. In the end, a scuffle breaks out between me and a couple of Everton fans. I tell them to back me and let me get on with things, as I am running this club and I will turn things around.

Tying this to the previous diary entry, this dream speaks an awful lot to the fight against the internalised oppressor and recognises how decolonisation and the right to win is not just an external thing, it is not just based around the other team, but it is also an internal one as well involving one's own fans, those who are supposed to support myself. That the fans in the dream are white and that the players in the other team are white, highlights this incredibly well and recognises the tussle between both facets of this decolonisation process. That I need to see and recognise the pain of being on my own in this dream is apparent as well.

On the positive side, though there is a large amount of this dream which actually holds power. The fact that the other team do not score, the fact that I save the ball time and again, says an awful lot around my role and how I can be for my own environment, my own team, my own self.

Diary Entry and Dream on 07.03.23 (no time recorded)

A Black South African chap and I are in a room wrestling in preparation for a rugby game to come. We get on well and feel the game should be a combative one. At the end of the evening, as we are preparing to go downstairs to the main room for dinner, everyone else has gone down to eat, I play tickle with the South African guy and then he says to stop. He then tries to tackle me, but I run out of the room and to the stairs. He chases me and cannonballs me down the stairs. We are both laughing and joking with each other as we reach the bottom of the stairs and head off to have our meal with our rugby colleagues from both England and South Africa.

There is something very different in this dream. The importance is that there is a celebratory aspect here. The colonised part of myself, which in this case is me, is willing to play with the more instinctual part which is represented by the Black South African rugby player. That I played a lot of rugby when I was growing up and that it is one of my favourite sports to this day, says a lot about how adapted I perhaps have become to this country. When I was a kid playing rugby at school, I found myself unable to express myself on the field because I was still very much wrapped up in the idea about presenting a certain safe face. The aggression that I might have needed to have on the field was not always there, except for on one occasion when I was playing rugby in the Royal Air Force when I was so angry about something else that I let myself go, scored three tries, was man of the match and had to drink a yard of beer to celebrate. It never happened again.

This dream perhaps speaks to some of that deeper nature that comes up and compares greatly to some of the other dreams which are more about hiding and remaining compliant and a wish to step outside but a fear of doing exactly that. That this dream also involves layers of only partially adapted blackness, this time presented in the formalisation of the clothing worn by both myself, and my South African colleague in the dream, says a fair amount about how actually in any movement from one culture to another, there is going to be an acculturation and therefore an internalisation of what it might mean for one to be part of the new cultural structure.

This is different to an adapted sense of self. This is different to having a father who bought his suits from Saville Row because he wants to fit in. This is more representing myself playing within said structure and still bringing myself to the fore. That the other person is willing to play with me and have fun also says an awful lot about this union of coloniser and colonised and that I already know that when we have our meal. That the two parts which would previously be in conflict, are actually breaking bread together and having a laugh, a joke, a few beers, says something of the movement from that more conflicted part between the coloniser and the colonised, to the more relational part between decolonised and decolonise. This is the stage of movement presented in Figure 5.2, which I have to highlight here in the autoethnographic display.

Dream 08.03.23:

A scene where I am fighting a white man and I am trying to get away from him. Yet in the scene I become like water and he cannot fight me. He tries by punching over and over again but he hits only water, causing me no harm. We seem to be in some type of warehouse and we fight our way through this environment. I then become like a single drop of water, just in case, and this frustrates him even more and he gives up.

The power of the instinctual comes through here in the power of water in how actually it wears down the other over time. Water defeats rock, not so much by pummelling it hard, although it can do that, but by wearing it down over time. The African deity, Mama Wati comes to mind as well in the expression of an instinctual more ancestral aspect of myself which has come up here (Worship, 1988). In this dream, I feel more powerful and yet again a scene like this reminds me of non-violent activism, a process used by many distinct groups over time to actually disempower and yet simultaneously give back the anger of the subject that is has tried to divest itself from and project outwards onto the activist.

In this dream, the fact that I become like a drop of water has very spiritual connotations and shows how deep one has to reach to achieve that process of decolonisation. It also involves the re-emergence of oneself out from behind the projections of the subject.

Diary entry 12.03.23:

I have had an interesting few days. I relise how negative I have been of late. This is what has changed since I left HL. I knew my worth and what I bring to the table and there are an increasing number of colleagues and friends who have become drawn to myself, both personally and professionally, over the past few months. They want me to be part of their collectives, part of their groups, and part of their movements, which is flattering. I am honoured, surprised, and empowered by the fact I am able to sit as a person at the top table within this profession.

The important part of decolonisation in this particular scene, is not just the internal recognition of my own power as projected through the previous scenes, but also the external recognition of my own position accordingly. Of all the emotions though, which are perhaps most quizzical to myself in this story is perhaps that of being surprised; surprised that I am seen with some value; surprised that I am able and allowed and have been invited to join such elite company. So, whilst I am honoured the fact that I am also surprised says an awful lot about an internalisation of, 'I don't belong here.'

I am a person of colour. I know what it is like to believe that I do not belong, that I am an imposter, that imposter syndrome or performance anxiety are going to play a part and wrack me with guilt, shame, fear, anxiety, at any given moment. To then unconsciously be gifted with the honour of being around like-minded people who see my value, my work and my strength, says an awful lot of just how deep I have had to go into this process of decolonisation. Worthlessness or being told one is worth less is part of a coloniser's narrative. It is one of the reasons why so many of us have had to work so hard, strive so long, go so deep, so far beyond our own boundaries and structures to be seen as merely competent. Whilst those who hold privilege and supremacy, and who also often hold mediocre minds and ways of being, only have to turn up a lot of the time to take on roles and positions of primacy. This dream is a welcoming. It is an acknowledgement. It is a cry of celebration and it is not one that should be ignored unwittingly.

Discussing personalised decolonisation

Any process of personal decolonisation is not linear. As presented here, there is a process which moves forward from one stage to another stage, to another. The stages as I will highlight them, and as presented in Figure 5.4 these stages are:

- Stage 1 – Discovering the Unconscious Coloniser.
- Stage 2 – The Coloniser/Decoloniser conflict for control.
- Stage 3 – Decolonising the Self.

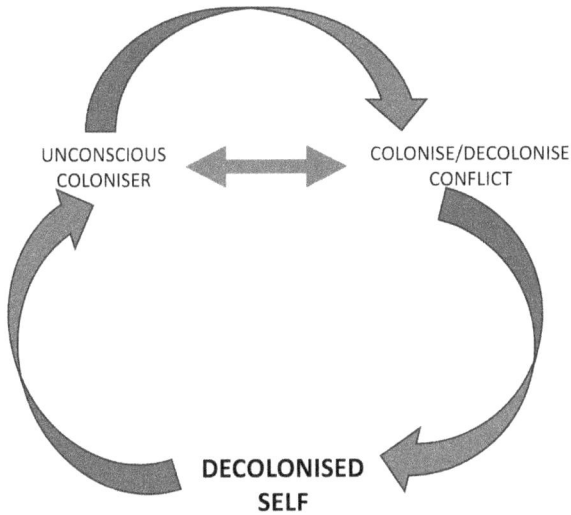

Figure 5.4 The decolonised self.

The reason I am saying that this is not a linear process is because this is a spiral that heads downwards evermore increasingly. In that spiral, as it moves further and further downwards, there is a greater hope that we reach something which is more authentically true. So, as the processes become tighter, and one's awareness's of Self become that ever bit greater. The dreams presented speak very much of these differing stages. Stage 1 being a discovery of the internalisation of a certain aspect which is hindering oneself accordingly. The early dream, whereby the internalisation is performed by my symbolic brother, a sibling, a part of my own blood and of my mother, that the matriarch who was raised during a time of Empire, says an awful lot about how deep and how intergenerational much of this runs (Memmi, 1974).

For those of a different gender, though the internalised patriarch or heteronormative character will also be in there. So for example, for those who have perhaps engaged with level of performance as presented by Judith Butler, the internalisation of a white patriarchal narrative which then encourages that level of performance, will be hidden away somewhere speaking, whispering, encouraging that performance, whilst also manipulating and undermining said person with that sense that they need to be grateful and if they are not, they should be ashamed (Butler, 1988).

For those who have come from a different background or perhaps are from a different class, the sense that they need to play their role in upkeeping the capitalist structures, will be there in the unconscious to some degree (Aosved et al., 2009). We all have these scripts, these whispered voices, these aspects which sit just below the surface, but what we do not tend to do is recognise, challenge and move beyond them. There are many students, for example, that I get to teach who, whilst part of different movement groups often have to be encouraged to look at the part of themselves which has chosen to do so within a capitalist system embedded within a university.

We cannot escape that all of these, and many others, are parts of ourselves. We cannot decide that we are not that part or this one, that we are good people. Because when we do so what we end up doing is projecting said denied part out on somebody else and therefore not interacting with the other not as they are, but as we need them to be. We create an It out of the coloniser we do not want to acknowledge within ourselves (Buber, 2010). The importance, therefore, of much of this is that, as I keep stating, only by working with these unconscious parts do we even start to approach the freedom from the internalised coloniser, allowing us to actually be a bit more of who we want to be and to feel less constrained, less conformed than we want to be as well. Authenticity as a part of the individuation process sits within this framework.

The next issue is that the autoethnographic part of this chapter is incomplete, as it should be. The process of decolonisation, whilst living in an environment whereby it is difficult not to take on board the systemic colonisation of one's own behaviours, ways of being, dress, activities and so on, means that this constant need to decolonise oneself must become a norm for any of us. When we talk about the Jungian terms of individuation we speak about it as if it is a process that one goes through and once one has achieved one's goals, then that process is over and there is nothing more that needs to happen (Stein, 2005; Tyagi, 2008). When we factor in the aspects of one's identity which have become colonised and the fact that we actually still live and reside within the coloniser's environments, then this idea of individuation is actually slightly flawed. Individuation in this process means a constants re-visiting of how we may remain adapted and how we may be re-adapted to said environments. It is a constant checking in with oneself with regard to how those systemic internalisations may re-awaken themselves within our psyche and how they may actually co-opt our identities when we least expect them to. It is, as Lorde (1984) stated, a constant revolution.

This could be when we are at our most tired or when we are, for example, so busy in the world that there is little time to reflect on our experiences. Decolonisation is therefore an ongoing circular process. It needs to be this way for it to really take on the powerful structures which filter down through the superego onto myself, in fact onto any and all of us.

Decolonisation as presented through these dreams and diary entries means the invisibility of so many of us. The subject does not see us, and we often do not see large parts of who we are. Our identity is stereotypical; it is an object; it is othered, and we present these parts of ourselves to be seen as safe as worthy of the position presented before us, the one that we have to play out within said system. Colonisation involves a deep systemic divorce from what we might want, how we might want to be and the things that might potentially drive us onwards to do so much more with our lives. What it is to be a person of colour is not defined by myself, as an example. I am told what it is to be black and a man by the system and

I have a choice to either play that out or to act in a way which makes myself safer within white environments, or I choose to suffer as a consequence.

Personal decolonisation involves a massive change in ways of being. It involves huge shifts in who we are and who we relate to in our relationships, and it also involves the taking back of a lot of responsibly with regard to what we actually want in our lives. In referencing Rousseau's (1998) social contract the idea here is that we are born into an environment whereby the rules and the structures are laid out before us. We are therefore told how to be and how to act and we actively play said role to be seen as part of the system. Decolonisation therefore passes that responsibility back to us. It is not situated within the system itself. This is an existential challenge for all of us and actually brings to mind the ideas of freedom as per the existential lexicon (Bazzano, 2007; Yalom, 1981; Zuckerman, 2015).

Within existentialism, ideas of freedom also tie themselves together with the anxiety that said freedom brings with it. Responsibility and anxiety walk hand in hand here (Buben, 2013; Heisig, 2000). The personal responsibility of not knowing what to do, but having said choice to do what one wants to do, means that there are going to be a number of fears along with way. Firstly, when we have an idea of how we are supposed to be, the direction of travel is laid out before us. Within this sort of more existential framework of decolonisation, that yellow brick road does not exist. For many of us, it may seem that we are carving swathes through the unplanned crops of non-identity to find our way to where we might want to be. Many of us find ourselves wondering who we are and why are we so alone, because this is the second part to this dilemma. The isolation and the loneliness that comes with decolonisation is a massive factor and a reason why so many people choose not to take up such a role (Rosedale, 2007).

Many activists will fight for the rights of their own environment or their own identity, or one particular identity. Yet, because they have not done the internal decolonisation work, or perhaps they do not wish to do so, they do not have to face the existential angst of isolation that comes with working with ridding oneself of the unconscious coloniser that sits within us all. There is a comfort, an intense system comfort, in knowing the rules and knowing where one belongs. Decolonisation challenges this to the extent that we often have to sit with the not knowing, the lack of truth and the responsibility of finding one's own way, which has been discussed both in this chapter and in previous chapters in this whole book.

The next part to this is to recognise the impact that decolonisation of the self has on others around us. In an earlier chapter, we talked about the decolonisation of the trainer. One of the things to explore here is how we as trainers regurgitate and re-express so much of the coloniser's narrative in our teaching. What we teach, how we teach and what we say about it may often be colonised. So, to recognise this adaptation to our modalities, to our way of teaching, to the way of being academic, may actually start the process of recognising ways in which we can diversify how we work, how we teach, how we relate to the material, to the theories, to the ideas which have formed the bedrock of our profession. A second strand to this is when we are facilitating workshops and groups with our students, helping students who are minorities recognise the dilemma that they are stuck within around the coloniser/de-coloniser narrative, can be a fantastic way forward to helping them find their own way to decolonise themselves.

In numerous students across the United Kingdom who when expected to author essays say on material from a Freudian perspective, struggle to bring in their own non-white, LGBTQ, feminist, angle around the material always astonishes me. But part of that dilemma, when explored more deeply, is based around the fear that that student may be labelled as the angry woman, Black person, person of a different sexuality, person of a different ability, because they are not towing the systemic line.

There are numerous courses that do not want to see their students bring in material that sits outside of reading lists, or that might bring to the table their own idealist or activist views; things that brought them to the profession in the first place. The courses involved may want to see students perform a certain type of way, even down to what they reference and how they reference it. Whereas were we more flexible within these constraints because there were always going to be structures and ideas that all students need to achieve. Then we are encouraging students to play within the confines and to bring more of their individualistic Rapinoe-esque way of being (based around the famous American women's footballer, Megan Rapinoe, who was both an activist for the LGBTQ community and also one of the best footballers in the world over the past ten years, and who when invited to the White House, in no uncertain terms told Donald Trump where to go). Rapinoe's example is a perfect one watching a person play within the rules of the game, but also express themselves more fully and take the game on as well (Frederick et al., 2022).

Recognising the internalised struggle within students then helps them to start to spot the route that they might follow to find their own way through. It does not mean that all of them are going to draft the perfect essay where they fully express themselves, but it does give them the chance to look at these internalisations and see where they are self-centring based around either a real or internalised aspect of the coloniser's narrative.

The third part to this exploration of decolonisation then has to be with our clients. Not all clients will come in looking at systemic oppressions, but a sizeable number avoid psychotherapy and counselling because these aspects of the political sphere have not yet found their active space within our profession. So therefore, as clients they feel that they are going to be pathologised for their inability to find work; pathologised for having sexual predilections which sit outside of the medical norm; pathologised for being of a distinct cultural or racial minority and having to struggle with their identity within this. These medical labels therefore separate us from our clients and are part of the reductionist nature of the coloniser narrative. The number of therapists and supervisees who I have come across, who actually find it safer for them to remain within the modality that they have been taught within when encountering difference and diversity, says a lot more about their blind spot and their inability to actually risk seeing something outside of that scope for what it might be, as much as it says about their actual need for the comfort of truth, for the comfort of knowing everything.

That difficulty in sitting with not knowing, in being in a space of investigation, of curiosity, of learning consistently, then actually leaves certain clients sat outside not feeling seen, heard and actually more often than not leaving the therapy. For our clients, when we start to go through the painful process of decolonisation because these dreams presented here are not easy to access and work with, then what we start to do is model and contain the pain and the pressure of our clients doing exactly the same thing. It could be that having to sit with a client's sense that they do not have enough money, enough worth in the world, even though when they came to this country, they came with a medical degree that allowed them to practice where they were. The struggles to find a way of being in this environment, in this new world that they have sought to find themselves within, is then what empathetically understood by the therapist. It does not mean that the therapist has to have exactly the same knowledge, but it does mean that it opens a doorway to empathy which is closed by those therapists who rigidly stick within the straightjacketed confines of their modality out of a fear of an encounter with difference and otherness.

The psychology of decolonisation

One of the most important factors of this whole chapter and in particular the autoethnographic exploration of colonisation and decolonisation and its unconscious processes is that with this deeper dive into the psyche, there comes with it when one returns to the surface, a number of ideas and specifications which will filter back through the other sections of this book.

What I mean by this is that by understanding the internalisations of colonisation, we also have a chance to look at just what colonisation and therefore decolonisation are, from a psychological perspective. This book is very much built around the idea that these instances, these processes, these systems, impact upon us, not just externally, meaning the changes we make involve more than just our reading material. In this process, decolonisation is further and deeper reaching than we could ever have assumed. This does not mean that it is impossible to decolonise a curriculum or a process, but what it does mean is that this process of decolonisation needs to be considered in far more nuanced and wider and deeper reaching ways than we could have originally considered.

In many ways, the worlds of counselling and psychotherapy have an awful lot to offer when we explore decolonisation. As has been expressed in this section here, colonisation by its very nature involves the dehumanisation of ourselves, or our humanity and of the world around us. We become the other to become colonised. We become moulded by systems of oppression which tell us who we should be and how we should be in the wider world. We kill off and destroy that which makes us unique in order of us to endure under these forms of systemic oppression, and we internalise the narcissism of the oppressor when we are moulded and systemised to perform and be a certain way.

In many ways, or from a Buberian perspective, we become an It to survive (Buber, 1992, 1998). We codeswitch, we perform, we find ways of being which will allow us to not feel destroyed. There is an instinctual part to this which I could suggest that Newton would admire, in the form of survival of the fittest (Saini, 2019). To survive we therefore adapt. Yet, for us to adapt, we have to kill of that which creates our potential, which makes us unique, which makes whole and human.

Colonisation creates the other, but it also creates some of the shadow from our very being. So, only by working with this internalised aspect of ourself, by doing something with shadow work, do we then start reach anywhere near our potential as individuals, as groups and as a society, culture planet.

Summary

The way that we form knowledge and who gets to form said knowledge, is an ongoing debate which we still need to have, because it is in many ways rooted in the coloniser's narrative of people owning knowledge. This next section, this final main section for this book, will look at research, how we do research and how we can decolonise research, knowledge and what we believe that we know. Recognising that when we start to do this, that we actually start to make knowledge more inclusive, makes research more of a collective experience. Also, in another way we look at how we can decolonise the researcher, because so much of what we view as knowledge has been gathered from such an objective standpoint that we reject and hide away from the impact that the researcher may have on their whole research environment. This is one of the reasons why I chose in this chapter to use an autoethnographic exploration.

If I am going to talk about decolonisation in this case, if I am going to do the research about what it is, how I understand it, how I view it, how it impacts upon us and so on, of course there is going to be an impact upon myself, upon my client work, upon the way that I write to my friends, my daughter, my family and so on. There is a wealth, therefore, of material, nay of research material, which can be gathered and utilised should we choose to do so. The earliest of our researchers did this work really, really well. The ancient Greeks did not just work from an objective standpoint, they let their perspective drive their knowledge; their ideas being a starting point for deeper, more philosophical explorations around the terminologies that they had come up with.

This is not to say that their ideas were not slanted by their own political perspectives and their life experiences (that has to be there in some ways), but the diving deep for any sort of diamond of knowledge will always bring with it the dirt of the environment in which the diamond has been birthed and it is our responsibility post that discovery to then polish off the ideas and hone them in a way which can then be used by the populous at large. It is not just to accept them as read; it is to do proper research into what these things mean.

The other part to this which I will also explore in a lot more depth in the next chapter, involves the corruption of knowledge and the manipulation of science to make certain ideas, to turn certain prejudicial ideas, into something which then becomes hardened in the oppression of the other. And, whilst I am aware that that last statement sounds quite flowery, it is an umbrella statement for some of the horrors that research and science has also meted out upon the world, as much as it has done in bringing undoubted benefits to many of those around it.

The next section, which is called *The Decolonisation of Research*, will therefore explore all of this material to a far greater depth and understanding (Table 5.1).

Table 5.1 Decolonising the therapist

	Colonised	Decolonised
Performative Decolonisation	The practitioner is not aware of how they have been moulded by the systems of patriarchy, white supremacy and capitalism. In the denial of any internalisations there is a belief that the client is there to reaffirm their own systemic position.	The practitioner may fight for one of the systems of oppression, whilst simultaneously remaining ignorant of their own role within the other two. This thereby means that whilst they may believe they are good people, they are also a part of the problem in their denial of their own 'bad/ wrongness.' There is also an over reliance in the belief that the system is outside oneself, and that there is no need to consider their own experience as an oppressor.
Towards Authentic Decolonisation	The practitioner begins the painful process of recognising that they are the agents of change they so seek. The practitioner contends to their own complicity within the systems of capitalism, white supremacy and patriarchy. The practitioner works with their own shadow and undergoes a kind of Dark Night of the Ego as they contend with their intersectional shadow. There is a growing awareness and acceptance of the therapist's own socially constructed identity, no matter which political position they hold.	Recognition that the process of personal decolonisation is a painful and ongoing one, linked to individuation and personal growth. Working with the internalised oppressor does not mean that one rids oneself of said internalisation, but that one is aware of, and increasingly distant from, the unconscious messages and ways of being which are expressed through this. That the decolonised practitioner is both an ally and an activist, fighting to support the struggles of both those who are the same and those who are different to themselves. Acceptance of the therapist's own socially constructed identities then leaves space for their client to explore their own internalisations in a safe space, free from conflict and judgement.

References

Aboud, F. E. (1988). *Children and prejudice*. Basil Blackwell Limited.

Aosved, A. C., Long, P. J., & Voller, E. K. (2009). Measuring sexism, racism, sexual prejudice, ageism, classism, and religious intolerance: The intolerant schema measure. *Journal of Applied Social Psychology, 39*(10), 2321–2354. https://doi.org/10.1111/j.1559-1816.2009.00528.x

Bazzano, M. (2007). *Brave new worlding*. A response to: Practising Existential Psychotherapy: The Relational World by Ernesto Spinelli, p. 216. Sage.

Beauvoir, S. de. (2010). *The second sex*. Alfred A. Knopf.

Boffey, D. (2018, November). Empire 2.0: The fantasy that's fuelling Tory divisions on Brexit. *Guardian Online*, 1. www.theguardian.com/politics/2018/nov/08/empire-fantasy-fuelling-tory-divisions-on-brexit

Bowlby, J. (1988). *A secure base: Parent-child attachment and healthy human development*. Basic Books. https://doi.org/10.1097/00005053-199001000-00017

Buben, A. (2013). Heidegger's reception of Kierkegaard: The existential philosophy of death. *British Journal for the History of Philosophy, 21*(5), 967–988. https://doi.org/10.1080/09608788.2013.825576

Buber, M. (1992). *On intersubjectivity and cultural creativity*. The University of Chicago.

Buber, M. (1998). *The knowledge of man* (M. Friedman (ed.)). Humanity Books.

Buber, M. (2010). *I and thou*. Martino Publishing Limited.

Butler, J. (1988). Performative acts and gender constitution: An essay in phenomenology and feminist theory. *Theatre Journal, 40*(4), 519. https://doi.org/10.2307/3207893

Dawson, H. (2023). *The Penguin book of feminist writing*. Penguin Classics.

Ellis, E. (2021). *The race conversation: An essential guide to creating life-changing dialogue*. Confer Books.

Fanon, F. (2005). *Black skin, White mask* (M. Silverman (ed.)). Manchester University Press.

Fellows, J. (2010). *Downton Abbey*. ITV. www.itv.com/presscentre/ep1week30/downton-abbey

Frederick, E. L., Pegoraro, A., & Schmidt, S. (2022). "I'm not going to the f***ing White House": Twitter users react to Donald Trump and Megan Rapinoe. *Communication and Sport, 10*(6), 1210–1228. https://doi.org/10.1177/2167479520950778

Freire, P. (1970). *Pedagogy of the oppressed*. Penguin Books Limited.

Golash-Boza, T., Duenas, M. D., & Xiong, C. (2019). White supremacy, patriarchy, and global capitalism in migration studies. *American Behavioral Scientist, 63*(13), 1741–1759. https://doi.org/10.1177/0002764219842624

Hall, S. (1996). *Critical dialogues in cultural studies*. Routledge.

Heisig, J. W. (2000). Non-I and thou: Nishida, Buber, and the moral consequences of self-actualization. *Philosophy East and West, 50*(2), 179–207.

Hooks, B. (2016). Feminism is for everybody. *Ideals and ideologies: A reader*. Pluto Press. https://doi.org/10.4324/9781315625546

Hughes, S. A. (2017). *Autoethnography: Process, product, and possibility for critical social research*. Sage Publications.

Kenyatta, J. (1962). *Facing Mount Kenya*. Vintage Books.

Lorde, A. (1984). *Sister outsider*. Crossing Press Limited.

Marlan, S. (2005). *The black sun: The alchemy and art of darkness*. Texas A&M University Press.

Memmi, A. (1974). *The colonizer and the colonized*. Souvenir Press.

Morton, B. (2021). *Sarah Everard: How Wayne Couzens planned her murder*. BBC News Online. www.bbc.co.uk/news/uk-58746108

Rosedale, M. (2007). Loneliness: An exploration of meaning. *Journal of the American Psychiatric Nurses Association*, *13*(4), 201–209. https://doi.org/10.1177/107839030 7306617

Rousseau, J.-J. (1998). *The social contract*. Wordsworth Editions Limited.

Saini, A. (2019). *Superior: The return of race science*. Harper Collins Publishers.

Stein, M. (2005). Individuation: Inner work. *Journal of Jungian Theory and Practice*, *7*(2), 1–13.

Turner, D. (2015). Breaking free from the shadow(s). *The Psychotherapist*, *61*(Autumn), 13–15. https://doi.org/10.1017/CBO9781107415324.004

Turner, D. D. L. (2021). *Intersections of privilege and otherness in counselling and psychotherapy* (1st ed.). Routledge.

Turner, D. D. L. (2022). *#DecoloniseThis I: Clothing and colonialism*. Dwight Turner Counselling. www.dwightturnercounselling.co.uk/2022/04/28/decolonisethis-i-clothing-and-colonialism/

Turner, D. D. L. (2023). *The psychology of supremacy*. Routledge.

Tyagi, A. (2008). Individuation: The Jungian process of spiritual growth. *Explorations of Human Spirituality*, 128–153.

Various. (2020). *George Floyd death*. BBC News. www.bbc.co.uk/news/topics/cv7wlylxz g1t/george-floyd-death

Various. (2022). *Queering psychotherapy* (J. C. Czyzselska (ed.)). Karnac Books Ltd.

Various. (2023). *The genesis of doctor who*. BBC Online. www.bbc.co.uk/articles/cx8rv vrej7zo

Walach, H. (2008). Narcissism – The shadow of transpersonal psychology. *Transpersonal Psychological Review*, *12*(2), 47–59.

Washburn, M. (1995). *The ego and the dynamic ground: A transpersonal theory of human development*. State University of New York Press.

Weil, A. M., & Piaget, J. (1951). The development in children of the idea of the homeland and of relations to other countries. *International Social Sciences Journal*, *3*, 561–578.

Worship, M. W. (1988). Performing the other: Mami Wata worship in Africa. *TDR*, *32*(2), 160–185.

Yalom, I. D. (1981). Meaninglessness. In *Existential psychotherapy* (Vol. 32, Issue 9, pp. 645–646). Harper Collins Publishers. https://doi.org/10.1176/ps.32.9.645

Zuckerman, N. (2015). Heidegger and the essence of Dasein. *Southern Journal of Philosophy*, *53*(4), 493–516. https://doi.org/10.1111/sjp.12151

Chapter 6

Decolonising counselling and psychotherapy research

Introduction

Since the ancient Greeks, many of our ideas have come out of the personal. The ideas that theorists and philosophers such as Aristotle and others came up with was as much built upon their own experience of the world around them and their place within it, as it was about trying to understand the universe that they were embedded within (Edel, 2010).

For many of us in the modern era, research has taken on a different format, whereby the personal is less apparent and the world outside of ourselves, has become another or a categorisation to be mapped, understood and controlled. The aim of this chapter is to explore just how the colonial ideas of mapping and controlling the world had been influenced by, and influenced simultaneously, the world of research. This chapter will also look at just how, even in counselling and psychotherapy, this drive to fully understand or to work towards some ultimate truth, has hampered the ways in which counsellors and psychotherapists have done their work for over a generation. Psychotherapy and the ways that we work has an awful lot to offer the scientific community, but much like the fear that psychotherapists had in engaging with the political, offering a more relational angle to the worlds of scientific research has often left psychotherapists feeling as if they were behind the curve in some way, or that they did not measure up.

It is as if psychotherapists and counsellors, in their collective lack of self-esteem, have neglected and rejected their rights to have a voice on just what is and what could be research. This chapter challenges some of this and looks to give us back our agency, our weight of knowledge, our weight of understanding, as we explore the world around us, as we understand and map out human nature.

First of all though, in this chapter, it is worth exploring just what it means when we talk about the colonisation of research and one of the ways of doing this is by looking at some of the history behind research and some of the ways in which research, and how we understand human nature, has been co-opted by the narratives of the patriarchy, of white supremacy and of capitalism.

DOI: 10.4324/9781032614342-6

The colonisation of research

In 1851, Drapetomania became a known word in the colonies. This was a word that was designated by Samuel A. Cartwright, who hypothesised that this socially constructed mental illness was the driving factor behind slaves not wishing to be kept in captivity (Willoughby, 2018). Cartwright was a scientist of his time who spent an awful lot of energy and money developing ideas around Drapetomania and coming up with corrective treatments that, for him, were supposed to mitigate and correct these so-called deviant tendencies for Black people to escape from their enslaved confines. That his research lasted for so long and was very much rooted in the ideals of white supremacy and of patriarchy, says an awful lot in this instance of just how easy it can be for a small group of people to therefore use their research, combined with their prejudice, to the detriment of huge numbers of people around them.

There are many papers which look at how Drapetomania was rooted in the political stigmatisation of a racialised group, but many of them do not actually explore and recognise the coloniser's need for control within research (Akbar, 1984). This horrific example of the marginalisation and the vilification and the mentalisation of a whole group is something which in some way still holds some sway in the modern era. When we focus in on more modern considerations of mental health, the idea that persons of colour are close to 17 times more likely to be diagnosed with a mental health illness, the idea that one of the reasons for this is that of the systemic racism which underpins said system (Fanin, 2017).

The development of anaesthesia was built on an idea during slavery that black people, enslaved people, were able to endure more pain and therefore needed less medication to help them get through and survive difficult situations (Saini, 2019). The idea here being rooted in the fact that a Black person's worth during slavery was built upon how much they could endure, how much pain and suffering they could manage and hold on their shoulders, again speaks to the racist ideas which were used oppress a people and were then also used against them in subsequent years. The fact that women of colour to in the United Kingdom are some four times more likely to die in childbirth than their white counterparts holds an intersectional angle, in that it is rooted very much in both issues around race and gender when it comes to the consideration, or mis-consideration, or misdiagnosis placed upon women of colour who are with child (House of Commons, 2023).

There are numerous other examples from the Black communities around the planet the Tuskegee Airmen who were injected with syphilis as part of a medicalised experiment is another example of this. The distorted numbers of persons of colour who were sent to Vietnam to fight the Vietcong because they were seen as being less intelligent and therefore were used as cannon fodder, so that when these rules were changed to enable more persons of colour to be sent to the front line, this was built upon the research of that time and day.

The examples I have given you just here are about colour, but these issues do not reside just within race. The misdiagnosis of hysteria around women within mental health was built upon the research of the day and therefore has its roots very much in the sexism hidden within patriarchal research (Lev Kenaan, 2021).

Noting that homosexuality was a core part of the DSM I and DSM II says an awful lot about the conjunction between the political/moral and the scientific rules of those days. That this changed post the DSM III whereby sexuality was de-medicalised, does not mean that for persons of LGBTQ difference their worlds became that bit more comfortable (McHenry, 2022). The prevalence still of conversion therapy across the global north and the failure of successive governments to ban much of these barbaric treatments meted out on persons of LGBTQ difference, says an awful lot again about just how rooted these ideas become when implanted through a scientific lens (Nichols, 2016; Various, 2017). The idea of just follow the science whilst on the whole well-meaning and correct, can often be flawed when science is seen as an absolute by those who do not understand how it can be used or, more importantly in these cases, misused.

The aim therefore of this chapter is to plan a framework around many of these ideas, to see their limitations and to be able to help people to recognise that science is not an absolute truth. In Figure 6.1, *Inductive Truth*, the movement from ideas towards truth becomes an inducted one.

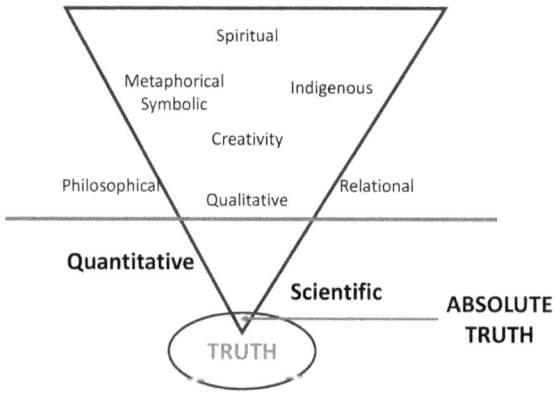

Figure 6.1 Inductive truth.

Ideas are many, ideas are individual, and like the ancient Greeks understood, ideas are quite personal. Yet, the beauty of the work of the ancient Greeks was their ability to take an idea, to turn is around, to come up with a philosophy based around the idea knowing that that philosophy was not an absolute. It was not an ultimate truth. Their idea was a step on a longer pathway towards understanding something more about human nature. Within the research and science of our times, much of it is based around an idea which will always hold its own biases, with this idea then being explored through whatever lens is adopted, be it a more mathematical one or even some of the more basic scientific quantitative/qualitative ones.

One of the beautiful things about the writings and the works of the ancient Greeks was that they rooted their understandings in their environments and their times (McCarty, 2013; Schuon, 2006; Waterman, 1993). For some strange reason, which I have no idea about I will freely admit, that has not happened with modern science. The ideas that science and research and understanding way back when held a more philosophical state, suggests a divorce between the scientific and the philosophical within the researcher that has therefore led them to become more objective in the standpoint of how they view that which is being researched.

The difficulty with this though is that the power dynamics built into the study of the other is in no way considered in so much modern research. Neither is there any awareness of the intersecting prejudices which will influence any decisions upon say Drapetomania whereby white supremacists were able to ascertain and diagnose persons of racial difference are not even recognised. Neither is there a moral angle implanted into the work. These moral and power overlays are present but simultaneously invisible when we explore the patriarchal differences in power between men and women and how these may have influenced the exploration of the uses of anaesthesia on women of colour, or the mental health diagnosis of hysteria. The positionality and the power of whoever the researcher is, is not recognised, is not considered by the researcher, it is not considered as a part of the research, is not considered as a part of the consequences, the results and the explanations given about the success or not of said research project. The relational ultimately is not there and that desire to create, nay to have an absolute truth, holds within it the narcissistic belief that the researcher is superior to not only their research but to that which they have studied.

When we move this narrative further east and into Europe, similar hierarchical ideas around colonialism and research abound. The classic quote 'White Man's Burden' as uttered by Rudyard Kipling speaks a lot to the coloniser's idea of civilising the environments in which they had invaded (Kipling, 1899). This perspective is something which resonated across the colonised countries of the world from North Africa to Australasia, ideas of whiteness colonising, civilising and brining their science to bear on the colonised Indigenous nations of the world, formed one of the cornerstones of the colonial project.

Sir Ronald Ross, in a paper that he presented on the fight against malaria saw the success of colonialism as being very much rooted within the scientific, his actual words being that the battle would be won under the microscope (Sinden, 2007). His ideas in fighting malaria though were not so much to help those who were suffering from said illness in the colonised countries but were as much a means of assisting the white European colonisers as they marched their way across indigenous landscapes.

In a great paper written on the Smithsonian Magazine website, by Rohan Deb Roy (2017), there are a number of other ways in which the coloniser's narrative is rooted within ideas of patriarchy and white supremacy. The view of the negro as posited by colonisers, many of whom were very highly educated, meant that they often saw Indigenous peoples as less than, as needing to be civilised and needing to be brought up to a standard which they could never achieve because they were of course colonised.

Perspectives like this, as I have stated, form the bedrock for how we actually view science and it is behoved to us, as researchers, to look at how we research and explore the early standpoints which we research from. So, for example, the idea that we take an ontological or epistemological perspective whereby we look at the world and we look at how we understand the world, therefore denies the fact that we are a part of said world and have a role within it. To understand our place alongside an ontological and epistemological perspective, ideas of which all researchers are taught when they do any sort of research project, be it at undergraduate level, or at PhD level, the leaving out of the philosophical suggests to myself that there is a massive colonial flaw within the work.

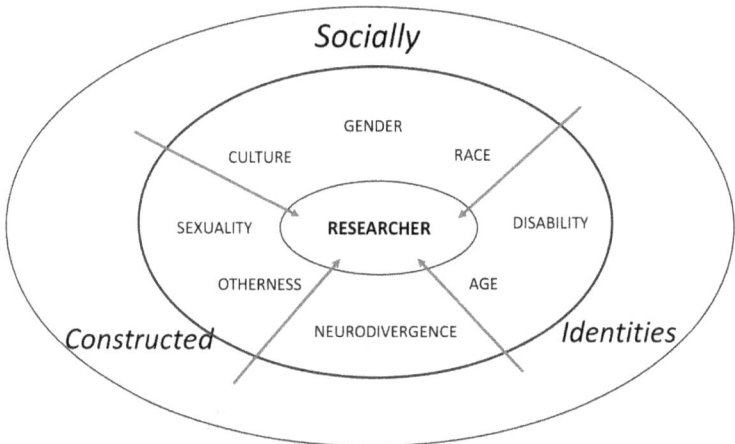

Figure 6.2 The socially constructed researcher.

This is the meaning behind Figure 6.2. In order to better situate the researcher, there needs to be an understanding of how the researcher themselves has been colonised. An exploration of their own philosophical standpoint so that they too can see where their working ideas may hold racist, homophobic, sexist, ageist, ableist or other forms of isms and obias which will therefore slant and tweak not only how they see the world, but also how they then choose to study said landscape. The philosophical as a part of the ontological/epistemological triumvirate therefore helps to balance out and challenges the researcher to bring themselves further into a process of research.

This also has other challenges which I will discuss in later sections to this chapter, but the importance of even recognising this early adaptation when we move from the coloniser's idea of supremacy over the colonised and therefore the researched, to one where one is more in relationship with the researched, therefore actually starts to re-humanise the other, making them not colonised at all, but more a part of said research project potentially. This is where we start to edge towards the decolonisation of the researcher, by understanding that we too, given that we are born and raised within these colonial landscapes, will build our research narratives and frameworks from within said environment.

The colonised researcher

The interesting thing about Sir Ronald Ross and Samuel Cartwright is that these were men of means. They were the elite in their own environments. They were scientists, well-educated, and able and willing to build ideas and structures of truth based upon what they had been taught in some fairly well-established institutions. These were not researchers from the working or lower classes; these were not people who had been raised with Indigenous knowledge, and therefore had a unique perspective on the worlds around them. They were people who had been raised within colonised landscapes where the superiority of men was not just a social construct but was legally defined and also embedded within the religious structures of the days.

Their whole environments, their whole thinking process, their whole research guidance was therefore prescribed within structures of supremacy. So, to therefore expect them to reach beyond said structures, and to therefore be able to see that which has been researched through a decolonial lens, would have been one of the most naïve things of all. The fact that we choose not to recognise the flaws in their make up as researchers, says an awful lot about how willing we are ourselves to buy into the ideas that they raised and posited.

The fact that many of these ideas, such as Drapetomania and some of the other ideas that came up with around the laziness of slaves, for example, and these have been debunked over time, says a lot about the continued quest for truth being ongoing and the continuing need to challenge and sometimes disregard that which has been suggested as an absolute. Yet, the pain and the marginalisation and the vilification of different groups, such as the LGBTQ community for whom it has only been a couple of generations that since the DSM3's death, suggests that we need to be doing more even now to consider not just types of research that we are doing, why we are doing said research, and also who is doing said research.

During the years of Nazism, the range and horrors of research, many of which I am not willing to incorporate in this book here, and also together with how many of these were judged to be correct and assumed to be right and righteous and therefore embedded within the Nazi idea, say an awful lot about the modern era and how even there, there are ways and means in which research can be misused to represent populations, ways of being and behaviours (Weiss-wendt & Yeomans, 2013).

This is why, in my opinion, any sort of work to decolonise research will not just have to involve the inception and the use of other ways of creating knowledge. It also has to look at who is doing the research, why they are doing the research and the scripts which they hold which informed said research. One of the interesting things about my own work over the years has been the constant need to self-reflect at the ways and means in which I too have become colonised in my ways of thinking.

Earlier on in this book, I told the story about how I had been doing my own sort of research and was very much led by the ideas of elderly, white men as I tried to understand the experience of the other. It was only when feminists challenged me to actually find my own way of understanding this, did I realise how much of my thinking had become adapted within the coloniser's idea.

The important part of re-telling that story here is that the deeper psychological work which I discussed in the previous chapter, had not taken part when I first submitted that work for assessment. In order to do so meant a deeper exploration and divestment of what it was for me to be a researcher and to therefore develop a way and means in which I too could research material accordingly. In a similar vein to how I work as a lecturer, whereby my presentations and my techniques and whatever else, are very much built from an implicit knowing of what is right for myself and finding my own style, how I am as a researcher also has to follow a similar path.

This therefore brings up questions when we look at the colonisation of the researcher and of research in the modern era. If we are going to do research, and if research is going to be rigorous, understandable and acceptable in the modern era, then we need to consider how we teach the types of research methodologies that we use, and also, more importantly, encourage types of research which step outside of the collective, westernised bubble of what is scientific knowledge.

Another way of exploring this is possibly through the lens of the regular, and annoying I will say, debate between qualitative and quantitative research and researchers. This need for quantitative researchers to see themselves as better than, or as more than, or as real researchers, holds within its own philosophical framework structures of supremacy, patriarchy and dominance. The inability to recognise that knowledge is not owned by any one person, any one group or any one way of working, says more about those types of people who want to stick their own flag in the sand, that this is the way to do it, as it does about anything else within their frameworks, and holds an element of narcissism within it.

What I meant by that in this instance is this; whenever a person defines a way of being and says, 'this is the way it should be,' what they are often doing is centring themselves in the middle of it. So, where a researcher says quantitative research is the way forward, is often because they have decided that that is the way it works best for them and is the way that everybody should best use it. The secondary issue though is that there are two parts to my last sentence. The idea that a research method is the best way forward for that particular researcher, is actually perfectly fine. The need for that researcher to then universalise that experience like anything, suggests a need for that verification from the external, and a fear of the researcher other.

Should there be any form of difference around the research methodologies that somebody else is using, that their own research idea, methodology, structure or whatever it might be, is then challenged by the appearance of the other. This is the meaning behind Figure 6.3.

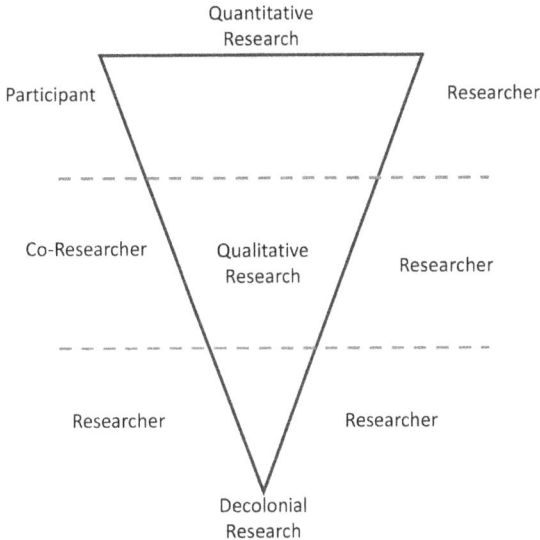

Figure 6.3 Decolonising research relationships.

Psychotherapeutically, the idea of mirroring as posited previously is important. A term used within psychodynamic theory for a number of years suggests that the egos core identity is set up by being mirrored by one's own care givers, primary or otherwise (Mitchell, 1986). And that without that sense of mirroring, one's egoic sense of self may feel fragile, or weak, or not actually exist at all. The same can be said about any part of our egoic sense of self which is newly formed, so that when we become therapists or counsellors of a certain modality, one of the easiest things to do to reinforce who we are, is to recognise who we are not. This is therefore no different to the researcher in their relationship with the quantitative versus the qualitative.

So, for myself when I hear the discussion around which is better, qualitative or quantitative, or when I am asked that wonderful question 'what do you think is the best way forward, is it qualitative or quantitative research methods?' my answer is either that I do not care, or that both matters most. They are both as good and as bad as each other. So, any way forward in any research that I do has to have an element of both, or neither, and also has to be structured around the particular area that I am researching. For me, there is no one way forward because I am able, like many researchers who are not caught in this trap, to hold the relational difference between the two and to work with the grey areas in knowledge between the pair as well. This is shown in Figure 6.3 by the fact that in order to gain greater depth in researching the relational in counselling and psychotherapy there needs to be progression down the triangle.

Showing one means of getting to that more decolonial level, I want to offer one last example. When doing my doctoral research, using a pure phenomenological research method as posited by Moustakas (1994), one of the things that quickly became apparent was that in using phenomenology when working with clients and creativity, was flawed. So, in order for me to do the work that I needed to do, I needed to adapt the methodology to suit the client group and the way of working that I myself had devised. Now, granted this is at doctoral level, but it is not as if I had not come across MA or MSc students who, in their brilliance, have decided to do similar things around their research methods and methodologies in order to adapt them for their environments. This is decolonial research in practice.

Decolonising research

When Glazer and Strauss (Charmaz, 2006) invented grounded theory back in the mid-1960s, their efforts were built from the argument between quantitative and qualitative research. Whilst both men understood and recognised the importance of quantitative research, they felt that the human experience was in some way missed in research and there needed to be a research methodology which explored the human experience of a phenomena but also retained some of the rigour of a quantitative research methodology. Grounded theory, which has in many ways developed ever since Glazer and Strauss' initial input, including the work of Kathy Charmaz has still retained many of these origins, so much so that it can sometimes come across as a qualitative research methodology in quantitative clothing.

The importance of this is that within grounded theory there is this effort to create knowledge, and a truth, and a theory through what can be seen as an inductive methodology. The attempts and the repeated requests for knowledge from participants which, overtime should narrow in on a particular focus or theory, holds for myself some of the problems inherent within western research. The idea that there is a truth, or that there is one truth, even built from the common human experiences that we all encounter and often times endure, for myself I now see is part of the problem with the colonisation of research and research methods.

Research into human nature should by be an exploration. It should not just enhance knowledge, but it should continually clear away the fog of not ever knowing, so that we start to see the general landscape we are all walking through as mental health professionals. The second part to this is a recognition that there is no absolute within this landscape, because not only are we constantly discovering new aspects, new caves, new trees, new fauna, new flora, new animals. We are also recognising that this landscape is constantly changing. So, any attempt at researching and discovering truths is only temporary at best. The idea of not knowing, as discussed in earlier chapters, sits perhaps most prominently within the ideals or research and quantitative research and even those qualitative standpoints which perhaps limit and try and bring in a supposed quantitative level of rigor, therefore miss the point of just how we do research within our professions.

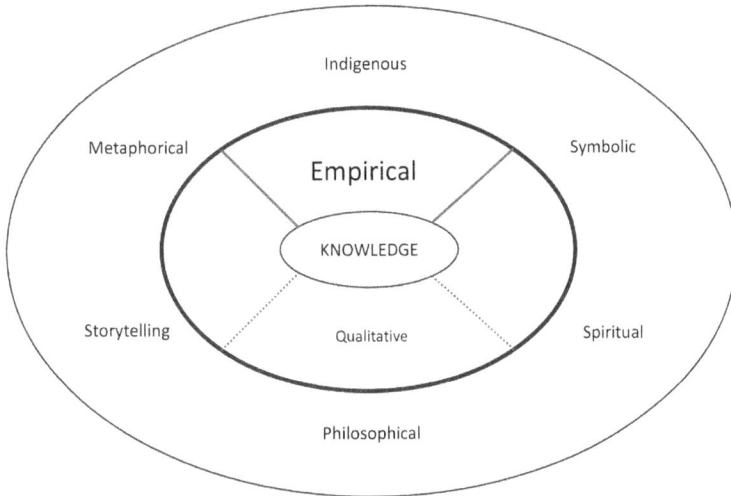

Indigenous

Metaphorical

Symbolic

Empirical

KNOWLEDGE

Storytelling

Qualitative

Spiritual

Philosophical

Figure 6.4 Mapping decolonial knowledge.

Figure 6.4 recognises a few things:

- There is no absolute point of truth. There is no pivotal point as posited in Figure 6.1 which therefore states that actually there is one way of seeing said phenomena, there is one way of experiencing this.
- That there is an absolute, a one way to work with trauma, a one way to work with the body, a one way to work within neuroscience, or diversity, or anything else. That, given our diverse natures, there are many myriad ways of experiencing and understanding the human condition.
- With this absence, there are little pockets of knowledge, and they all inform each other.
- If a client comes in and they talk about their experiences of trauma, then one could work with EMDR to work with the neurological impacts of trauma. One could work with the body using focusing work or somatic experiencing. One can use general psychotherapy, talking therapies, which it is deemed may take a bit longer but could be safe enough for some clients in their experience of working with trauma. There are many ways to work with this material, some more effective than others.

Now, that last statement is also a problem. The idea of what is effective and what is not needs closer consideration because we are setting up a standard point as to what works and what does not based around what? For systems like health services, effectiveness becomes cost effectiveness. The ideas that CBT and the research that has been done around cognitive behavioural therapy makes it more cost effective than say psychodynamic work, or humanistic work, or some other type of work, then makes it more attractive within certain cost-effective systems. So, my statement here about what is effective can be a problem because what is effective is defined from the external by some other system, by some other way of seeing things, and often leaves out the one person, or the one entity, who will define whether something is effective or not and that is the client.

For those clients who do not like CBT work, who find it too prescriptive, does that mean that actually the NHS should not use it? No. What it means is it is not ideal for that particular type of client, and there needs to be another way of working which is more amenable for them. For those clients who work with somebody who is perhaps more transpersonally trained, and yet finds the work perhaps a bit too, to use a common parlance 'woo,' to spiritual, to out there, too disconnected, does that mean that the transpersonal is not the best way forward for all clients? No, again. What it means is that for that particular client a unique way of working is more important.

The idea of what is effective and what is not is something which we need to hold with very tender gloves less we start to define what is right and what is not right for all our clients en masse, not recognising the difference in approaches and more importantly, the difference in needs of our clients.

The next aspect of Figure 6.4 to recognise is that from each point of knowledge, and where each point of knowledge connects to another point of knowledge, we build up a composite map of that *knowledge area, knowledge base* or *knowledge structure*. This then changes as we start to then expand other areas, and we start to see where there are gaps in knowledge, gaps in the spaces between areas, what else could we look at, what else could we research, what other methodologies might actually work to actually explore these areas, because perhaps relying on just one or two key aspects limits the research that we actually do.

A way of considering this is when we look at mixed method approaches to research. The idea that just a quantitative or qualitative way of working is the way forward, as I have already discussed, is incredibly flawed. A mixed method approach then starts to map not just the quantitative experience of a phenomena but also the human interaction that goes within said experience, or the qualitative. We get a more rounded picture of what it might be like for example for clients of colour to be on mental health wards, not just the stats that denote that they are over-represented in the mental health system. By using more diverse and bigger ranges of research methodologies within our profession, we then start to look at our relationship to a phenomenon. We start to approach research from a less inducted standpoint to a more inclusive and phenomenological one.

This next part is where Figure 6.4 holds a lot more weight. As we branch out knowledge, as we stretch beyond what we know, what we start to do is bring into focus other ways of experiencing phenomena and we move from that less inductive standpoint to a more inclusive exploratory, relational understanding of what it is to be of colour, of what it is to have experienced trauma, of what it is to work with the body. Many of the major qualitative researchers have within their exploratory lockers ideas which sit very much within that more phenomenological exploratory standpoint. Yet, what can often happen in that very human need to absolutise their ideas, is that they themselves then become quite reductionist. So, there is even a challenge here for the researcher themselves to remain constantly open to other ways of seeing the data.

The next stage of this is the work that the researcher must continually do upon themselves, to develop their own philosophy of what research is. It is not just about looking at how their ideas have become colonised or how they might colonise their ideas. It is about constantly looking at where their philosophical standpoints are, how their beliefs resonate and what those actually might mean and how that might inform the ontological or epistemological positions that they may accept for future research.

There are many examples of researchers who have been changed by the explorations that they undertook who from their earliest standpoints developed ideas which later on they not so much denounced but recognised that were incomplete. From the flawed origins of someone like Carl Jung to the more existential perspectives of someone like Irvin Yalom, ideas develop and change over time (Stevens, 1990; Yalom, 1981). From Sigmund Freud and his earliest of writings, to Carl Rogers and his inclusion of a more spiritual perspective in some of his later works, ideas develop and it is up to us, as researchers, to incorporate that in some of our thinking (Stephens, 2001). I have already spoken about in earlier chapters how the need for training courses to incorporate not just one aspect a researcher's work, but also some of the wider social context is hugely important to understanding their ideas. What is also important here is to recognise that the most prominent of researchers do so having undertaken a journey of self-discovery alongside the ideas that they present into the public sphere.

That exploration, that recognition, that understanding of said journey must be incorporated because it adds a wholly unique perspective to the ideas that are raised. One of the other reasons is that without that we end up with a snapshot of truth, a lazy opinion-based idea of what a theorist actually means, whereas actually it is worth exploring their relationship to research, their relationship to the philosophy of research, their relationship to themselves and their relationship to their clients, as a composite package.

The last part when exploring Figure 6.4 is the ongoing recognition that research is never ending. The arrows which point themselves further outwards and further forwards talk about this to a great degree. There is no endpoint to research. There is no endpoint to where we might go in our understanding of human nature, of the human experience, of the human condition. As I have already said, our lives, our development will run until the end of time hopefully, so therefore any idea that there is a truth is naïve at best, flawed and at worst incredibly narcissistic. This is the idea hidden within Figure 6.4, that ongoing mapping outwards of what we do and how we actually do it.

Decolonising research methods

It is obvious from this point onwards that although we have looked at the decolonisation of the researcher and at the research conducted, the next thing to consider is actually the methodologies which are used to garner data. I have already talked about, and slightly critiqued, the necessary and unnecessary development of a qualitative research methodology in Grounded Theory which works in some ways to mimic the qualitative research methodologies of the time (Charmaz, 2006). That there was an attempt to not so much broaden out how we do research but to expand research within a colonised framework, says a lot about the unconscious influences placed upon the research method and perhaps the researchers of the time.

The non-reliance or non-acceptance of perhaps more Indigenous or alternative creative ways of working, even at this stage, says an awful lot about the fight which our professions have had to endure to have alternative methodologies seen and accepted. One of those fights is that they are often seen as not being *scientifically rigorous* enough. The issue I have with questioning the scientific rigor of a research methodology is no different to areas that I have raised beforehand, with that being that actually there is a set standard which is built from within a colonised framework, which denotes and defines what is acceptable and what is not; what is rigorous and what is not; and what is the right way to do something and what is not science (Skitka, 2012).

Again, we are tied into a system of truth-ism. A sense that there is a set standard, a set way that we must all do things in order for it to be seen by the research gatekeepers as the appropriate way forward. This co-option and control over what are deemed as right and wrong, I could suggest, adds layers to the coloniser's narrative and control over research, and to challenge that from more instinctual or from perspectives which have originated outside of the global north, can seem threatening to those whose identities are very much embedded within that research framework. Within the worlds of whiteness, in those more binary explorations of what it is to be white and black and so on, the ideas of white fragility as described by DiAngelo (2018) sit there, and whilst it is a flawed sort of turn in some ways, one of the things I would say about it is that it does actually speak to the defensiveness that is encountered when the ego of the subject is challenged by the presence of the other.

I am going to offer the term *research fragility* to the scientific community as an attempt to suggest something similar. To recognise that there are other ways of creating knowledge, of seeing the world, of seeing experience, and that those ways may be no less valid than the ones which have been used for a long time within the global north, suggests to myself that there is a level of research fragility that goes with the mere presence of another type of knowledge. Obvious examples perhaps come from the ideas perhaps of what knowledge is; are the oral stories of are they any less valid than the knowledge held in libraries and places of learning in the global north (Various, 2015)? The way we see the world, the way it is projected, is that these are less valid. But my question is, by who's standard?

Efforts to decolonise research are plentiful and have often incorporated the need for research to involve other Indigenous perspectives and the perspectives of those who are being researched. This is supposed to run counter to what I have already discussed, whereby the power of the research over the researched is often not considered. Offering you an example from a presentation that Laing (1969) did many years ago, whereby he explored the idea that within mental institutions when talking to potential patients about their diagnosis, there needed to be a better recognition that the influence of the psychiatrist on those who are going to be ascribed a mental health diagnosis, may actually be one whereby the patient feels an extraordinary amount of fear. The sense of powerlessness is there within their experience, and they may act in accordance with that sense of fear. This can often be interpreted as a form of acting out by the patient, but without recognising that those certain clients, because of their systemic fear of authorities, or of whiteness, or of men, may actually act in a way which is more defensive and defending of themselves than it is about their own mental health issues.

The importance of this then means that we must do more research, also from the side of those researched, in order to understand their own processes. Ways of working should involve more qualitative approaches. Using Moustakas work around qualitative research, where I explored 25 peoples' experience of being the other, the idea was that they would create the narrative around what their experience was and I would assess and connect the research dots, so to speak (Moustakas, 1994). The words on the page in my thesis at the end of the day were theirs and in the same way if we are going to bring understanding to the experiences of the world around us, then we need to provide a wider space for the words, the language and the experiences of those who are being explored.

Figure 6.4 speaks to this decolonisation of research in a separate way. In taking a phenomenological perspective, one of the things to say from the offset is that phenomenology involves the exploration of a phenomena and also our relationship to said phenomena. It is a twofold approach. Phenomenological philosophy has been around for a while and has been used by many theorists, such as Heidegger, Hegel, Merleau-Ponty and others (Hegel, 1976; Heidegger, 2010; Merleau-Ponty, 2002). I have used it myself in my own sort of research amongst many other research methods and feel that it offers a great non-invasive way to understand experiences.

The more that we approach certain phenomena and the more that we try and involve the *researchee* into the research process, the more that we look to decolonise research. Then the more likely it is that we will have to adapt our research methods in order to fit individual research processes. I am aware that this is a very long statement but Figure 6.4 looks at ways in which we might do this. Yes, there is space for quantitative research. There has to be science in the west is very much built around this, but it should not be the central standpoint in understanding an experience.

The second part to it is we need to better understand and work with more diverse forms of qualitative research. I have mentioned phenomenological research, heuristics could be a way forward for this, as is interpretative phenomenological analysis (IPA). But there are also other ways of working, such as narrative enquiry and some of the more transpersonal ways of working which as well could also garner interesting and valuable information about our clients' worlds. This is where the world of the creative then comes into play.

There are within the worlds of art therapy, for example, and music therapy, and even within some forms of mainstream psychotherapy, schools of thought which have used the creative, be it drawing, be it music, be it sand play, to understand the deeper unconscious layers inbuilt in the experience that our clients may have (Kalff, 1991; Magill, 2002; Schaverien, 2005; Wilson & Ryan, 2005). Understanding the non-literal, more symbolic ways that we make sense of the world around us, then proffers us all a deeper understanding of our clients' world (Cox & Thielgaard, 1986).

In a simplistic way, dream work works in the same fashion (Saunders et al., 2016; Stein, 2005). Using the dreams of our client and helping them to explore the symbolic meanings, means they bring sense to their inner world. Research methods within counselling and psychotherapy need to do more to understand our clients' unconscious, be it through the use of the symbolic, the projections, for example when sand play work is used, we will project onto symbols, and it is up to the clients to discern what those symbols might mean for them, what the projections might be and how they might want to work with those.

Other examples come out of active imagination, whereby visualising a way of encountering the world and reconnecting with this, perhaps even through the body, utilising bodywork and somatic experience, can be ways forward in actually combining ways of understanding knowledge (Jung, 1997; Stein, 2005). If van der Kolk (2015) is correct that the body holds memory, and I believe that he is, then using imagery and visualisation can be a way of accessing and exploring that bodily, imaginal landscape. Our research needs to do more to recognise this.

Indigenous methods are all around us and there are numerous texts out there which look at how we might use and incorporate indigenous methodologies into the ways that we work. Kovach (2021) in her wonderful book, recognises that knowledge is not just a singular path and that actually indigenous methodologies, some of which she talks about in her work, are ways forward in bringing greater knowing and understanding of knowledge, and not without needing to resort to some sort of absolute way of defining the worlds around us.

For example, Indigenous Enquiry recognised that actually the researcher themselves needs to situate themself within said research whilst working in a way which is more relational to the research subjects. There was a chance there to develop a level of self-awareness around the research project, their position within it and, as I have already stated earlier on, in the situating of oneself in the research, there is a change to the epistemological and ontological positions. With indigenous research, as she talks about it, there is a level of creativity and cultural grounding that is hugely important. There is also worth in utilising one's own experience of the research process, and how the research has changed oneself, as a form of knowledge which can be more deeply embedded within the exploration. Therefore, the importance of this, alongside all of these others, is that we then start to bring up composite forms of knowledge around certain areas of experience.

The last part that I would like to add though actually sits outside of our profession. The number of times I have encountered situations whereby it has come down to anthropologists, historians or professions from other disciplines, to offer a narrative or an experience about a phenomenon that I am researching, that has then enhanced my work, is astonishing. The most simplistic of examples that I can offer you came from my own MA research, where I was researching the link that we all have to music, why we listen to music, why we relate to music and why music is a universal force.

In not wanting to root myself purely in the world of music therapy, and wanting to straddle some sort of space between psychotherapy and music therapy, I found myself reading and researching the words of music artists; from Eminem to Daniel Barenboim, their words often resonated and spoke to their intimate connection to this entity called music (Barenboim, 2009; Eminem, 2005). Their ideas, their perspectives, their experiences, tied themselves to Schopenhauer (2020) and his philosophical way of understanding music, but helped me to build a contemporary picture of the world I was investigating and orientate myself as before, as, and after I did the actual research itself, in asking participants about their own experience of music.

Sometimes when we approach research, we hope to find what we need to from within our own profession, school of thought or way of being. Yet, in order to develop knowledge from within, sometimes we need to reach outside and draw in understandings from areas which may not be considered scientific, but they are not anecdotal, they are very personal. So, the words of a rap star, the words of a composer and conductor, the words of a philosopher are all equally as valid in helping to flesh out the world that we are exploring. This is the meaning of the last part of that story, and it is an important one, no less important than anyone else's. It fits in, in a way, with the idea of 'the story' and how important the story is. Yes, within a western paradigm the story is not seen as scientific, the story that somebody has told about their experience of writing a piece of music based upon being excluded from a diner in 1965s southern America. The weight and power of the symbolic, the weight and power of the metaphorical, the weight and power of lyrics of a song, the words of poem or the images painted on a canvas, hold just as much weight as the quantitative understandings that we choose to bring to our research arena.

Re-imagining research

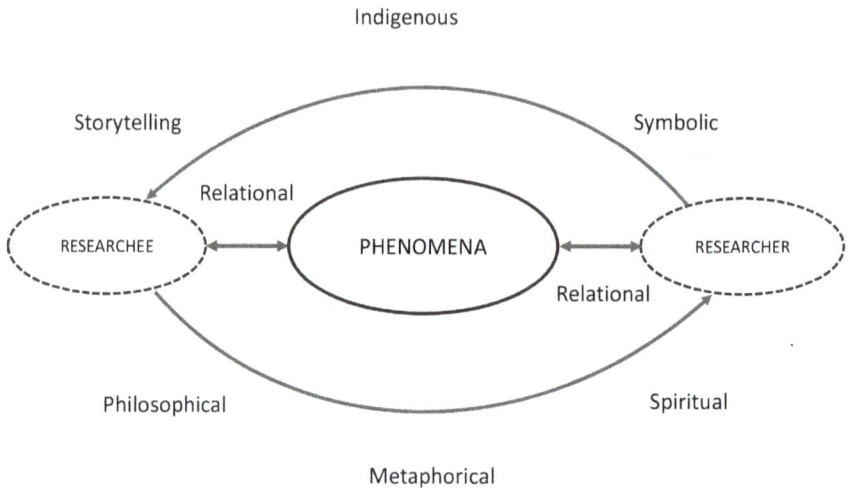

Indigenous

Storytelling

Symbolic

Relational

RESEARCHEE

PHENOMENA

RESEARCHER

Relational

Philosophical

Spiritual

Metaphorical

Figure 6.5 Reimagining research.

Everything discussed in this particular chapter is designed to encourage research-ers to reconsider how they actually conduct research and how research can become more inclusive. Figure 6.4 looks at this from another angle and in some ways builds upon Figure 6.3 before it. To re-state, researching a phenomenon should not be a top-down affair. This much we now see as obvious. We all under-stand the power dynamics which are played out in said research and hopefully can now clearly recognise where these distortions in research have led to a colon-iser/colonised view in understanding the other. This has led to the failure to rec-ognise the distortions in that which has been researched and studied based upon their being observed and studied by a subject which is obviously more powerful than they are.

It is impossible to totally move away from that approach, because with any form of research there is always going to be a power dynamic in play. But there are ways in which we can conduct research, as explored in this chapter, which therefore allow us to re-balance that dynamic, whereby we bring the researcher more into the research process itself and explore their experience of said phenomenon. The other aspect of this is by re-imagining the relationship between the researcher and the researched, and this is the important part of this section.

Figure 6.5 recognises that researcher and the researched both rotate around the phenomena of being explored and only by fully understanding that interplay do we start to gain a more accurate assessment of the phenomena itself. What I mean by this is that by being courageous enough to use the techniques which have been outlined beforehand, in a study of a phenomena by the researcher and the researched, then we end up with a more circular phenomenological understanding of said phenomena. It is not just a research hierarchy whereby the researcher sees the phenomena in the other, and therefore wants to understand the other accordingly. This is to recognise that truly phenomenological research locates the phenomena as both a part of the experience and separate to the experience, of both the researcher and the researched.

This restructuring, in my experience, is why on occasion mixed method approaches have been quite useful. As already discussed in this chapter, in my doctoral process I utilised both a phenomenological research method, as explored by Moustakas and also a heuristic approach, in exploring the experience of being the other (Moustakas, 1994). The reasoning was always that I am drawn to doing research on difference and diversity, but I myself am different and diverse, so therefore there was material placed within myself that could be used to triangulate the experience through to those of my co-researchers. In my doctoral thesis, that experience, that drive to understand both aspects, then brought with it a secondary benefit. In placing myself within the research, and actually recognising my role as part of said research, there was a chance there for me to explore how I might be changed by accessing this information, this material, and working with it accordingly. But does this make research more complex? Not necessarily, but it does make it more relational.

The other beauty in taking on board a more exploratory and less fully defined understanding of a phenomena, is that it leaves room for numerous other perspectives should they come further down the line. The ideas that I am positing here in the co-creation of phenomena are not about absolute truths, they are to echo a point from earlier chapters, about an understanding of a said phenomenon which is always evolving and always changing. How we understand mental health, for example, is very different to how we understood it a couple of hundred years ago and how we worked with mental health issues. Other developments have to come into play, developments in medication and diagnosis. With the DSM V, the latest iteration of the diagnostic manuals, being an example, although perhaps not the best one, of the ways in which we are developmentally moving forward in our understanding of the human condition.

The next part to this is to recognise the fact that I have used a different word for the person we are working with in making knowledge. I am not interested in seeing those who we interview as participants in research. What I am also advocating for here is a sort of psychological buy-in by the other into the exploration of phenomena which resonates for them. My understanding here comes from the fact that they themselves would have been drawn to the topic area being researched for whatever reason. So, when, for example my co-researchers wanted to explore their experience of being the other and of being an outsider, this was because they themselves had a deeper felt experience of something that they wanted to bring to the surface in a non-therapeutic way, perhaps for the first time ever.

The co-creation of understanding and meaning has to involve the neutral revelation of knowledge and experience by both researcher and researched. It is not so much about the researcher being a blank screen for that which is coming towards them, it is about the researcher revealing enough about themselves and inviting in, say within a semi-structured interview, a discussion with the researched which in that interplay works in the same way as it might do within a therapeutic context. Both parties actually build knowledge in that interview space, so how we do interviews, how we approach them, the semi-structured way that we work with them, has to be considered, if we are going to look at decolonisation.

The ideas of lists, charts, tick boxes and so on, placing them on websites is fine for one degree but does it work when we consider actually that we get more information about the other person through our interplay, our interaction, and a revealing of ourselves along the way? The interviews that I did for my own research, for example, would have taken anything between one hour and 15 minutes and two hours, but what I realised as I was doing my research, was that as I became more comfortable with my own process, which was running alongside this one, and as I became more comfortable with the whole idea about interviewing people for my work, those interview took longer and actually went more into depth.

Interviewing is an art form in itself and within the worlds of counselling and psychotherapy, given that we work so much with unconscious process and depth, to be able to hold the person that we are interviewing in a contained space whereby they feel safe enough to reveal parts of themselves that they have not perhaps explored with anybody else, maybe not even revealed in their own therapy, can in itself be really quite empowering and revealing for those individuals. This is something that we need to be very aware of. If we are going to approach the decolonisation of research with any sort of aim to change things, we need to look at the diverse ways in which we marginalise the other in the research process. Interviewing is just one of those.

This is another reason why in Figure 6.5 I have both the researcher and the researched rotating around the phenomena. At certain point should it not be OK for the researched to pose a question back to the researcher, asking them to think about their experience of being the other, their experience of watching the Barbie film (Gerwig, 2023), their experience of being neurodiverse, or whatever it might be? These ideas then bring into a play a lot more material to consider and create a deeper level of safety and containment for both people but also for the phenomena.

Decolonising the researcher again

The final part to this, I think, returns us back to our very first point in this chapter, and this involves a consideration of just who we choose to do research and who might be best placed to conduct it.

Often in universities, there is a drive for academics to look for funding from organisations around the country with regard to doing research. Often those applying for research have an interest in the communities that they are looking to work with but are not necessarily embedded within them. Professional bodies who choose to give out funding for research, in my view, need to consider very carefully the types of people they are choosing to put into communities who might be seen as hard to reach, difficult to engage with and other such stereotypes.

Sometimes this type of research involves an exploration by somebody from majority culture as to why that community is hard to reach. It is not a term that I particularly like, or am particularly fond of, because in my experience there is something objectifying about said community and something that fails to recognise the fear of engagement of some communities, of some environments, of some groups, with the majority, based upon historical colonised narratives.

If we are looking to decolonise research, then also not so much the ways in which money is allocated, but the ways in which those decisions are made and where money is allocated to certain groups and persons, needs to be considered. There are numerous examples of good practice, whereby organisations have given out money to people from a community to do research within their community in a way that perhaps persons from the majority community or from other groups, would not have been able to engage with.

For example, the Aylesbury Estate back in the early 2000s was one of the biggest Council estates in the United Kingdom and across Europe. Funding at one point was given to a group of local practitioners, of local counsellors, and therapists, to provide counselling, psychotherapy and alternative therapies to those people who resided on the estate. This successful project was in part driven by the needs of the community and the fact that that the service, entitled the Aylesbury Centre for Therapy, was peopled predominantly by practitioners from the same community meaning they were better able to work in a culturally sensitive way. This is not to say that persons from other communities could not have done so, but it is to say that you had taken out and challenged some of the power dynamics by actually bringing in people who can actually help on the group and know what they are actually talking about. They have been in those environments.

Research should follow a similar pattern. In 2023, I had the pleasure of examining a wonderful piece of culturally sensitive research which centred itself around the experiences of a counselling service set up in Belo Horizonte, in Brazil. One of the reasons for the success of this doctoral research that I examined back in 2023 was that the researcher in their exploration of the experience of counselling practitioners trained in Brazil was because that person was not only South American and Brazilian, but that they also spoke incredibly good Portuguese. This double whammy of understanding the nuances of a community, of a culture, of a language, then brings with it a better chance to co-create meaning and understanding, and a lessening of the power dynamics and separateness inherent within other types of research.

This is what Figure 6.5 sort of speaks to. It does not run away from the fact that actually there is an intimacy in research which has not really been explored and needs to be there in order for understanding to be raised to the surface.

Summary

The aim of this chapter has been to provide a deep dive into just how we do research, what we consider research, the research methodologies that we use, and the ways in which we can begin to decolonise research and our perspectives.

That this part of the entire process is hugely important is without doubt. The whole idea of decolonisation sort of flounders if we are still producing objective research which does not really look at our experiences as human beings from anything other than a coloniser's perspective. What it is to be a woman when considered by men very much rooted within the patriarchy is very different to that experience when actually raised by women in their consideration of what it is to be a woman. The idea of care as raised by Carol Gilligan in her understanding being very much based around the ethics of care narrative, is an example of research by a woman bringing a very different perspective to the angle of what it is to care and so on, to those posited by men when doing their own research (Gilligan, 2014).

The problem with research, I will argue here, should not necessarily be seen as a problem though. It should be seen as an opportunity to go deeper in our understanding of the diverse range and intersectional identities of those in the worlds that we inhabit, and that when we start to actually widen the range of understandings, that actually we start to witness this grand tapestry of knowledge in a way which actually we have not done ever before.

The ideas of our forefathers, the Freuds, the Klein's, the Winnicott's, Bowlby's and so on, were start points to a greater exploration of knowledge, and the more that we encourage our practitioner, our trainees and students to use their undoubted skills, and imagination to develop new ways of making knowledge, the more likely that it will be that the seeds that were planted in the years long gone, do not have to be the only ones that we relate to in this olive garden of human experience. Research should bring range and curiosity, not certainty and definition and as we are able so much in our work to sit with uncertainty and our discomfort with not fully knowing, that should also play a massive role in how we approach research.

There is an intersectional existential aspect to research which, by its very definition, then challenges the capitalist, patriarchal, white supremacist idea of truth, and it is with these particular hats, worn by myself as by many others, that I encourage us to approach research going forward. This chapter though finally brings to a close in some ways, this round robin exploration of decolonisation within counselling and psychotherapy and, as we approach the end of this tome, the aim has always been to offer different angles and to challenge thinking around what we do, why we do it and the ways in which we can do it more inclusively.

The next chapter is therefore simply conclusion. A tying together of all of the points and all the issues raised in this text. As stated at the very beginning of this text, this is not a definitive statement about how things should be, but it is a start point to a wider discussion about how we do the things that we do, why we do the things the ways that we do and how much those ways of being, those ways of researching, those ways of teaching, of practice, of being with our clients, is actually co-constructed out of a patriarchal, white supremacist, capitalist identity. It therefore brings me pleasure to walk towards the end of this book by letting go of this chapter into research and in conclusion opening up a dialogue as to future ways beyond what I have discussed here in this dialogical work today (Table 6.1).

Table 6.1 Decolonising research

	Colonised	Decolonised
Researcher	Lack of openness within the researcher that there is more than just one truth. Qualitative truth becomes an absolute Absence of the researcher as a part of the research Failure to recognise the unconscious power dynamics when doing research	Consideration of the intersectional identities of the researcher, and how they are themselves moulded by the systems of oppression. Consideration of how these structures can be contained to prevent their influence upon said research. Willingness of the researcher to be a part of the research and to be changed and decolonised by the research process.
Research	Within the Social Sciences the inductive nature of research is to restrictive, meaning there is often an obsession with one truth. The arguments between the prominence of qualitative over quantitative research speaks to a hierarchy within research. This hierarchy is often driven by the forces of capitalism, patriarchy and white supremacy. The hierarchical nature of research often leads to a preponderance of certain types of western research methods placed over other, less known, developing or culturally separate research methods.	Truth is a constantly expanding realisation of what we do know out of what we do not know. This therefore means that there is no singular truth but that there is an ever expanding level of truth which leads to an ultimate, yet utopian, whole. That qualitative and quantitative research methods hold different but equal relational weight within the understanding of human nature. That the research methods utilised to decolonise knowledge need to include Indigenous, spiritual, creative and relational/ phenomenological methodologies.

References

Akbar, N. (1984). *Breaking the chains of psychological slavery*. New Mind.

Barenboim, D. (2009). *Everything is connected: The power of music*. W&N.

Charmaz, K. (2006). *Constructing grounded theory: A practical guide through qualitative analysis*. Sage Publications.

Cox, M., & Thielgaard, A. (1986). *Mutative metaphors in psychotherapy: The Aeolian mode*. Tavistock.

Deb Roy, R. (2017). *Malarial subjects: Empire, medicine and nonhumans in British India, 1820–1909 (science in history)*. Cambridge University Press. https://doi.org/10.1017/9781316771617

DiAngelo, R. (2018). *White fragility: Why it's so hard for white people to talk about racism*. Beacon Press.

Edel, A. (2010). *Aristotle's theory of the infinite*. Kessinger Publishing.

Eminem. (2005). *Curtain call*. Polydor Group.

Fanin, I. (2017). *Is there institutional racism in mental health care?* BBC News Online. www.bbc.co.uk/news/health-40495539

Gerwig, G. (2023). *Barbie*. Warner Bros.

Gilligan, C. (2014). Moral injury and the ethic of care: Reframing the conversation about differences. *Journal of Social Philosophy*, *45*(1), 89–106. https://doi.org/10.1111/josp.12050

Hegel, G. (1976). *Phenomenology of spirit*. Oxford University Press.

Heidegger, M. (2010). *Being and time*. SUNY Press Ltd.

House of Commons. (2023). Black maternal health: Third report of session 2022–23. In *Women and equalities committee* (Issue March). www.parliament.uk.

Jung, C. G. (1997). *Jung on active imagination* (J. Chodorow (ed.)). Routledge.

Kalff, D. M. (1991). Introduction to Sandplay therapy. *Journal of Sandplay Therapy*, *1*(1).

Kipling, R. (1899). The White Man's burden. In *McClure's magazine* (p. 291). https://sourcebooks.fordham.edu/mod/kipling.asp (accessed on 18-02-21).

Kovach, M. (2021). *Indigenous methodologies: Characteristics, conversations and contexts* (2nd ed.). University of Toronto.

Laing, R. D. (1969). *Self and others*. Penguin Books Limited.

Lev Kenaan, V. (2021). Digging with Freud: From hysteria to the birth of a new philology. *American Imago*, *78*(2), 341–366. https://doi.org/10.1353/AIM.2021.0015

Magill, L. (2002). Music therapy in spirituality. *Music Therapy Today, December*, 1–7

McCarty, C. (2013). Paradox and potential infinity. *Journal of Philosophical Logic*, *42*(1), 195–219. https://doi.org/10.1007/s10992-011-9218-y

McHenry, S. E. (2022). "Gay Is Good": History of homosexuality in the DSM and modern psychiatry. *American Journal of Psychiatry Residents' Journal*, *18*(1), 4–5. https://doi.org/10.1176/appi.ajp-rj.2022.180103

Merleau-ponty, M. (2002). *The world of perception*. Routledge.

Mitchell, J. (1986). *The selected Melanie Klein*. Penguin Limited.

Moustakas, C. (1994). *Phenomenological research methods*. Sage Publications.

Nichols, J. M. (2016, November). A survivor of gay conversion therapy shares his chilling story. *Huffington Post US*, 1. www.huffingtonpost.co.uk/entry/realities-of-conversion-therapy_us_582b6cf2e4b01d8a014aea66?guccounter=1

Saini, A. (2019). *Superior: The return of race science*. Harper Collins Publishers.

Saunders, D. T., Roe, C. A., Smith, G., & Clegg, H. (2016). Lucid dreaming incidence: A quality effects meta-analysis of 50 years of research. *Consciousness and Cognition, 43*, 197–215. https://doi.org/10.1016/j.concog.2016.06.002

Schaverien, J. (2005). International journal of art therapy. *The Journal of Analytical Psychology International Journal of Art Therapy, 50*(102), 39–52. https://doi.org/10.1080/17454830500345959

Schopenhauer, A. (2020). *The world as will and representation*. Cambridge University Press.

Schuon, F. (2006). *Light of the ancient worlds*. World Wisdom Books.

Sinden, R. E. (2007). Malaria, mosquitoes and the legacy of Ronald Ross. *Bulletin of the World Health Organization, 85*(11), 894–896. https://doi.org/10.2471/BLT.04.020735

Skitka, L. J. (2012). Multifaceted problems: Liberal bias and the need for scientific rigor in self-critical research. *Perspectives on Psychological Science, 7*(5), 508–511. https://doi.org/10.1177/1745691612454135

Stein, M. (2005). Individuation: Inner work. *Journal of Jungian Theory and Practice, 7*(2), 1–13.

Stephens, B. D. (2001). The Martin Buber-Carl Jung disputations: Protecting the sacred in the battle for the boundaries of analytical psychology. *The Journal of Analytical Psychology, 46*(3), 455–491. www.ncbi.nlm.nih.gov/pubmed/12174548

Stevens, A. (1990). *On Jung*. Penguin Limited.

van der Kolk, B. (2015). *The body keeps the score: Mind, brain and body in the transformation of trauma* (1st ed.). Penguin Books Limited.

Various. (2015). *The oral history reader* (R. Perks & A. Thomson (eds.)). Routledge.

Various. (2017). *Leading UK psychological professions and Stonewall unite against conversion therapy*. BACP. www.bacp.co.uk/news/2017/16-october-2017-leading-uk-psychological-professions-and-stonewall-unite-against-conversion-therapy/

Waterman, A. S. (1993). Two conceptions of happiness: Contrasts of personal expressiveness (eudaimonia) and hedonic enjoyment. *Journal of Personality and Social Psychology, 64*(4), 678–691. https://doi.org/10.1037/0022-3514.64.4.678

Weiss-wendt, A., & Yeomans, R. (2013). Racial science in Hitler's new Europe, 1938–1945. In *University of Nebraska Press – Sample Books and Chapters* (pp. 1–50).

Willoughby, C. D. E. (2018). Running away from Drapetomania: Samuel A. Cartwright medicine, and race in the antebellum south. *Journal of Southern History, 84*(3), 579–614. https://doi.org/10.1353/soh.2018.0164

Wilson, K., & Ryan, V. (2005). *Play therapy: A non-directive approach for children and adolescents* (2nd ed.). Bailliere Tindall Elsevier.

Yalom, I. D. (1981). Meaninglessness. In *Existential psychotherapy* (Vol. 32, Issue 9, pp. 645–646). Harper Collins Publishers. https://doi.org/10.1176/ps.32.9.645

Chapter 7

Conclusion

It is important for me to explain to the reader why this book is called *Decolonising Counselling and Psychotherapy – Depoliticised Pathways Towards Intersectional Practice*. There are a couple of reasons for this long, and perhaps slightly misleading, title. The first one is simply that Decolonising Therapy was already taking in a book by the brilliant Jennifer Mullan (2023). I say that with a hint of mirth in my writer's voice, and a sense of mischief that actually the easiest title for all of us would have been simply Decolonising Therapy, because the book then does what it says on the metaphorical tin.

The second, more serious angle is this; as lecturers in psychology, counselling and psychotherapy we are moral teachers. We have an inherent sense of what is right and wrong within us, that sits outside of the political and legal structures which define us. Morality is a core part of who we are. That we all access and embody that morality in diverse ways, is an incredible truth, and there are many of us for whom what is moral in one aspect is not moral in another. Hence, the need for said laws to regulate our professions. Separately though, the political sphere, plays on our morality, nay it informs so much of who we are. It tells us often what is right and what is wrong. It guides us to either adhere to a way of being or not to, to accept refugees or not, to fight against the woke mob or join their ranks, to believe in political correctness or to denigrate feminism, or whether we should use pronouns or reject them.

The politics of the global north very much pulls on our morality and yet when politics and morality are closely aligned, when there is a drive to do the 'right *political* thing,' both within the moral fabric of a people and also the political sphere in which they are embedded, then actually great things can be done, movements can take shape, change can occur. When the political sphere though moves towards its own ideology and strives for a truth in its own belief that the far right or far left should be the only moral centre of a way of being, what it can often do is stretch its population, its people, away from their own sense of morality towards something which is not truly theirs.

We see this an awful lot with the rise of populism (Kaltwasser Rovira et al., 2019). The movement so far to the political right across so many countries, this was often posited in its earliest days as a means of giving a voice to those who identified

DOI: 10.4324/9781032614342-7

with, say the Working Class, those who were Blue Collared and more often white. This co-option of a huge group of people who quite understandably felt they were not being seen and heard and respected by the political left, meant that they were a ready army for those of the right who were aiming for a politic of exclusion and nationalism.

Over the past few years though, what we have seen in this political shift to the right is that things have occurred, incidents have happened, riots have taken place, which have led those voters, those people who bought into said arguments, to start to question their own morality in the face of things which are going on around them (Duggan, 2014; Various, 2021a; Wilson, 2017). The true reality of the Brexit debate in the United Kingdom, a debate built on the winning of an election won by those who wanted to leave by such a narrow margin that there were questions as to whether it was truly representative of the population of the United Kingdom. This was an election built upon a number of semi-truths and a good few number of lies and fears, so that it was no surprise for many of us that many people have subsequently, when faced with the reality, rolled back their ideas and wished for a different outcome (Boffey, 2018).

Similar versions of this happen in the United States. The kidnapping of democracy by Donald J. Trump which led to questions being raised, law suits being advocated for, and riots occurring on 6 January 2021 on the Capitol Buildings of Washington, were symptomatic of the populus right's desire not for a democratic rite of passage and transition of power, but to maintain control over the world in which they have found themselves inhabiting (Various, 2021b). In that case, the number of lawsuits levelled against perpetrators and those who were guilty of, for example, the riots on 6 January 2021, and culminating in the indictments raised again former Trump, say an awful lot about how democracy's moral centre had been shifted so far to the right that it took a whilst for it to recover itself and to realign itself towards its centre. Should it remain there is not for me to say. Will it remain there is down for all of us to actually work out between us, but what is important is for us to be able to start to recognise that morality and the political are often closely aligned but that one can misuse the other to the extent that we are left questioning just who we have become in the wider world.

When George Floyd was murdered, the number of complaints about culture wars that I came across both within our profession and without, said an awful lot about not just the fear that many individuals, groups, universities and colleges had about exploring issues of difference and diversity, but also about their own morality when faced with the murder of a black father on American streets (Cammaerts, 2022; Digby, 1992; Heritage, 2022; Mills, 2003). This was compounded in some ways by a British government and others around the world who took issue with discussions around things such as white supremacy, patriarchy and capitalism. Seeing them as part of the woke agenda to indoctrinate children in ways and means that were not for them.

This though contrasted for myself, and for many others around me, with those organisations, colleges and universities, again within psychotherapy and without, who took it upon themselves to challenge the political narrative. There have been genuine motivations to bypass the ideas and systemically driven moralities already in place, seeing them as insufficient when working with the diverse range of peoples paying their fees to attend said universities. For me, this has been quite heartening to see, that the political in its own way has started to lose an element of control over its population because it had gone too far to the right and stretched the moral fibre of its people to breaking point (Samuels, 2004; Various, 2022, 2023).

The thing about Lockdowns and George Floyd and their symbolic meaning, was that actually people sat with themselves and worked out for themselves how they wanted the world to be. The #MeToo movement, the murder of Sarah Everard, other aspects in this sudden, interesting, moral change back to a way of being that had perhaps been lost in the rise of populism (Morton, 2021). I say perhaps, maybe I should say definitely lost, but I question myself because is morality, true morality, ever really lost? I do not really think that it is. In the recovery by so many individuals and groups, in the desire to do so much more and to be more for the other, there was a level of hope placed before students, practitioners, courses, clients and many others within our profession.

This is what I mean about de-politicising psychotherapy. It is a return to our moral centre, a desire to actually do the best for our clients across the board; with the board being an intersectional one. We are seeing, hearing from, witnessing, observing and empathising with difference in a way that we probably have not done in over a generation, if not more. In doing so we are the woke mob, we are politically correct, we are self-identifying as to who we are what we believe in, thereby taking back identity and morality from those who would misuse it as a form of control.

This book is another brick in that Pink Floyd wall of development and asks practitioners, lecturers and centres of counselling and psychotherapy training and research, to look at just where their own moral sense, their own identity, their own gender, sexuality, racial perspective, ability or any other part of their intersectional identity actually is. It asks them to strongly consider how this moral centre, when co-opted by the politics of blindness and compliance, has been used to contain, maintain and become a part of structural inequalities. The form of decolonisation that I am talking about here is not performative, it is coming, nay it is here, and it will keep on going, and it will do so for a number of reasons, some of which I have already laid out in this book.

In one of our earliest chapters, we looked at the idea of knowledge and who gets to control knowledge and form knowledge, and just what knowledge is. Exploring our knowledge base and how we make sense of the world has not ended, did not end with the likes of Freud, Winnicott, Rogers and Yalom. It is not just built around the ideas of four white men. There are so many other women theorists out there whose ideas add so much more colour to the perspectives we teach on our courses, and there are so many good activists and psychotherapists of difference, I will say it again of intersectional differences, who have good things, intelligent things, important things to say about who we are and how we work.

This was where the movement between the colonisation of concepts to the individuation of ideas, actually frees up our thinking and takes us back to a place of being curious, continually so, more so perhaps than before, about the range and breadth of human experience. In many ways, because our profession is, for example, as much embedded within capitalism as any other profession, the sheer number of theorists who will plant their flag in the sand for them to say that they are the one and they hold the best ideas about trauma, about working with violent clients or about working with rotted transference, therefore means that it is very hard for our profession to breathe. It is tough for us to hold any idea of not knowing, of the continued exploration that we all undergo in this profession as we develop and create other ideas.

So, this idea about the individuation of ideas means that we step back from definitively saying *this is it*. To echo this idea; this book is *not* it. This book opens a door and encourages people to start to think about decolonisation across its many forms. This book in many ways is also built upon or alongside other ideas of decolonisation (thank you Jennifer Mullan), ideas which have already come out around this topic area and plants them, nay slides them into the spaces left within psychotherapy and counselling where there is a desire to look at how we can make our work, our profession, our trainings and our ideas more diverse.

The next chapter builds on this. When it comes to our trainings, they have become very much of a muchness across the board. There are very few organisations who do much more than follow the prescribed route of training and understanding that was laid out by theorists many years ago and is reinforced by our governing bodies. Therefore, our trainings have always been exclusionary. The smallest of tweaks that any of us need to make just to bring in one or two more people of difference are barely considered, because they take us away from the original ways of working which, from their very inception, have been quite ableist. Our ways of understanding human behaviour when failing to factor in issues around difference and diversity, then mean that we actually end up pathologising a lot more women and persons of colour, or those who are neurodiverse, based around concepts that we believe are universal. For example, the failure to actually exploring where there are flaws, if not gaps in knowledge, that might help us to understand what it is like to be an autistic student on a training course in say Gestalt therapy.

Closer intersectional consideration as to how we recruit our students, the placement areas that we end up working within, the routes through training, all of these are ways forward for our courses for our profession and although these might seem like they are very complex, the fact that they do work in their own ways should be one of the driving factors in making these things happen. My catchphrase for all of this work is always going to be, *It's not just about decolonisation, it's not just about changing training books, it's far more nuanced than that.*

How we practice, where we practice, the ways in which we practice, was the stage after this. Before the Pandemic, so many of us sought out practice areas in major cities like London, Manchester or Edinburgh. We rented nice rooms, paid good money, bought into the cultural Middle Class systemic way of being a psychotherapist. We wanted to be seen in the best places, or we wanted to be able to meet the needs of our clients but did not quite know how to do so, given that there was actually a structural system built around practice which we were not really fully aware of, even if it caused us pain, discomfort and anxiety.

The sudden change in what we do and how we do it, which still needs to be better understood in the research that needs to come in around us, suggests that actually we have bought into wearing a coat which no longer fits us, but which we were not even aware was starting to burst at the seams, like Bruce Banner in the Incredible Hulk. This cultural sea change that we are walking through right now is no different for counselling and psychotherapy and therefore means that we have at our fingertips the ways in which we can redefine our practices so that they become more inclusive. Working online, therefore giving access to clients who perhaps are otherwise enabled, is an obvious example of this, but these things also mean that the techniques that we might use, the creative ways of working, need to be adapted, tweaked, changed or newly developed to fit in with the new parameters in which our profession is walking through.

The next part is always of course the therapist themselves, or ourselves, because I am one of you, I am one of the many. Constantly considering how my ideas perhaps marginalise, constantly looking at and reflecting on the deeper levels of internalised colonisation that I will have, of course have been a part of, is a massive part to recognising how I can work with this with my clients. In my exploratory piece in that particular chapter, I looked at the world of dreams to recognise that actually colonisation, as I have said, is not just about the external, it is not just about books, it is also about the internalisations. bell hooks considers this idea quite succinctly, seeing that when we actually start to discover and find what she called the small part within ourselves that uses the coloniser's tools. The part which uses its language, ways and means to manipulate us, to silence us, to push us back into the shadows, then actually start to rediscover our voice, our ideas, the fact that we are so intelligent, that we are so reasonable, that we do not have to settle and be grateful, that we then become more greatly empowered and individuated within ourselves.

And then, of course, finally there is the research. The ways in which we conduct research. Who are we as researchers? How, as our colonised identity led to us taking up a position about how we see the world and how we interact with the world, which is very much one of colonisation. Stepping outside of all of these structures not only brings with it challenges, but also brings with it those people who have not quite been seen, who have not quite experienced the wealth and breadth of counselling and psychotherapy. One of the most common complaints that I get as a man of colour and as a practitioner when clients of colour come to see me, is that they are often afraid that somebody who is white, for example, will not understand them, will not understand their world, or that their view of counselling and psychotherapy has always been that it is a white profession.

It is hugely encouraging that so many practitioners of difference are challenging this narrative. Where it is slightly more problematic is that they are doing so more often than not from the outskirts of our trainings and our profession, building silos, fortresses of solitude, whereby they can do the work they need to, and where the other might find, discover and feel safe with them. Chapter 2, and the movement of ideas and knowledge to the centre, speaks towards this and the more that these externalised, strong systems are encouraged to come more centrally, the more likely it is that our courses will then start to develop and grow even more so.

Lastly, I have a final wish for this book, and it is one that I have never thought about before with any of my books. My hope for this book is that not only does it bring change and that it encourages our profession to think about and look at the ways in which it can adapt to the increasing challenges of the new century, but that at some point in the next generation this book becomes obsolete. I want to see this book disappear. I want to see the ideas, not so much taken on by others, but built on by theorists of colour, theorists of different genders and sexualities, theorists of different abilities, ages, neurodiversity's, by theorists as the other. Maybe in my arrogance, I hope that they remember me and this book at some point, but should they not, then that is fine, and I wish them all well. My work will have been done and the structure that is counselling and psychotherapy will have continued being built by those who are far more intelligent, brilliant, spiritual and creative than I am.

References

Boffey, D. (2018, November). Empire 2.0: The fantasy that's fuelling Tory divisions on Brexit. *Guardian Online*, 1. www.theguardian.com/politics/2018/nov/08/empire-fantasy-fuelling-tory-divisions-on-brexit

Cammaerts, B. (2022). The abnormalisation of social justice: The 'anti-woke culture war' discourse in the UK. *Discourse and Society*. https://doi.org/10.1177/09579265221095407

Digby, T. O. M. F. (1992). *Political correctness and the fear of feminism*. The Humanist; Mar 1992; 52, 2; Art, Design & Architecture Collection, p. 7.

Duggan, E. (2014, January 8). Racist bullying: Far-right agenda on immigration "being taken into classrooms." *The Independent*, 1. www.independent.co.uk/news/education/education-news/racist-bullying-farright-agenda-on-immigration-being-taken-into-classrooms-9045148.html

Heritage, S. (2022, September). We are all losers in the 'woke v racist' Little Mermaid culture war. *Guardian Online*, 1. www.theguardian.com/film/2022/sep/15/little-mermaid-disney-trailer-culture-war-ariel-black-white

Kaltwasser Rovira, C., Taggart, P., Ocho Espejo, P., & Ostiguy, P. (2019). *The Oxford handbook of populism* (illustrate). OUP Oxford.

Mills, S. (2003). Caught between sexism, anti-sexism and "political correctness": Feminist women's negotiations with naming practices. *Discourse and Society*, *14*(1), 87–110. https://doi.org/10.1177/0957926503014001931

Morton, B. (2021). *Sarah Everard: How Wayne Couzens planned her murder*. BBC News Online. www.bbc.co.uk/news/uk-58746108

Mullan, J. (2023). *Decolonizing psychotherapy*. W. W. Norton and Company.

Samuels, A. (2004). Politics on the couch? Psychotherapy and society—Some possibilities and some limitations. *Psychoanalytic Dialogues*, *14*(6), 817–834. https://doi.org/10.1080/10481881409348809

Various. (2021a). *Has George Floyd changed Britain?* ITV. www.itv.com/presscentre/ep1week19/trevor-mcdonald-charlene-white-has-george-floyd-changed-britain#

Various. (2021b). *U.S. capitol riot.* The New York Times. www.nytimes.com/spotlight/us-capitol-riots-investigations

Various. (2022). *Queering psychotherapy* (J. C. Czyzselska (ed.)). Karnac Books Ltd.

Various. (2023). *Therapists challenging racism and oppression* (N. Zahid & R. Cooke (eds.)). PCCS Books Ltd.

Wilson, J. (2017). *I was in Charlottesville. Trump was wrong about violence on the left.* The Guardian.   www.theguardian.com/us-news/2017/aug/16/charlottesville-violence-right-left-trump

Index

For Product Safety Concerns and Information please contact our EU
representative GPSR@taylorandfrancis.com
Taylor & Francis Verlag GmbH, Kaufingerstraße 24, 80331 München, Germany